Table of Contents

Preface

In this, the 6th publication of his exciting series of books, Swami Ram Charran presents the deep secrets behind the rituals that claim to be a worshipping of an evil God that requires sometimes Human lives as well as Animal lives in exchange for blessings of material gains and a selfish greediness for control & power of other people's life. Here in a world of human lust for sexual satisfaction, lewd sexual indulgences are performed with the excuse that there is a God who approves all this taking of life in exchange for blessings, or that some powerful evil force exists that needs to be tranquilized by the offer of animal life so that peace can come on Earth and its people. An absurd excuse for killing lustfully without conscience and violating the rule that that word that is called GOD can only mean that it's a divine force that GOD GIVES LIFE , GOD DOES NOT TAKE LIFE......If there was such God the world would cease to exist and everybody would be sacrificing each other for want of material blessing. THANK GOD that such a destructive law does not exist in nature and that there are good powerful forces in nature itself that intervenes when such an unnatural law starts to take root in the universe: In the Bhagwat Geeta, a great epic in Hinduism it is stated that the voice of the universe speaks thusly...

Yada Yada Hi Dharmasya
Glani Bhavatu Bhavata
Sambhava Yuge Yuge...

Meaning: As soon as the universe is in danger and about to be destroyed, I shall take form as man to come and save the world from age to age ......

In this book you will be able to understand why people suffer such things as rapes, incest, murder, starvation, wars and family extinction. You will find out the karma of all these and how man creates his own evil in his life and how its handed down the family line. The effects on family sufferings are linked to such sacrificial worships of the Hindu deity known as Kal Bhairo, the Muslim ritual known as Qurabani, the worship of demons in Tantric Worship, the sacrifice of chickens in Voodooism, the bath of Rabbits blood in Santeria worship and so on. You will finally have the true knowledge behind the cause of your children's sufferings as a result of evil acts by family ancestors. You will know why the Kennedy's family line was destroyed or why complete family members are destroyed in such mishaps as accidents, fires, drowning and mafia type shootings and so on...

THERE IS ONLY ONE LAW OF THE UNIVERSE:
No Person Has The Right To Take Life Or Determine When Another Organism Should Cease To Exist.

The Heendu Learning Center

The Heendu Learning Center, also known as JYOTISH ASHRAM, was first established in 1990 by Swami Ram Charran for the purpose of bringing back ancient Vedic Scientific knowledge that had been lost in history. Originally, the Heendu Learning Center was affiliated with the *Hindu Society of America Temple of South Florida.* The temple was originally established by the joint of efforts of Pundit S. Doobay, a Hindu Priest, and Swami Ram Charran, who contributed more than $70,000 towards the building of this temple.

As of 1993, the *Heendu Learning Center* separated from the Hindu Society of America and formed its affiliation with *Amar Jyoti Mandir (Temple) Of South Florida*. Since 1993 Swami Ram Charran and the Heendu Learning Center have assisted over 30,000 people. His contribution towards the return of ancient knowledge back to Hinduism has resulted in the changing and improvement of many people's lives.

The Heendu Learning Center publishes many books and periodicals; the general concentration is on Vedic Astrology, ritual science and scientific analysis of universal forces. Research is in continuous process and results are published in an annual magazine called, *THE PATRA*. The Heendu Learning Center has combined its efforts as a member of the *American Federation of*

Astrologers to provide easy and simple understanding of the exact sciences of Vedic Astrology.

Swami Ram Charran had promoted this Vedic knowledge through many seminars, lectures, television, radio interviews, yagans, astrological conventions, and many other types of media. His videotapes, cassettes and books are all distributed through the Heendu Learning Center.

The intense work carried on by the Ashram Center in the promotion of knowledge survives on donations provided by the members and the management group. Donations are received from the *Heendu Learning Center Inc.* for the management of the religious and spiritual services provided. The Ashram also promotes the teaching of Vedic Astrology, Learning of Hindu Music, Courses on the Vedas and Puranas, the science of Vedic Rituals and Pujas and much more information on the Vedic Sciences. All questions, subscriptions, memberships and comments will be welcomed.

The Heendu Learning Center is located in Miami, Florida. This location is considered the headquarters consisting of the Temple, the retail store, the office, and e-stores. The head of the Learning Center is Swami Ram Charran, his son (Leukas), and two daughters (Leuana & Luresa) assist in the running of the Center, his wife (Seeta) manages the Puja and Ritual Services Department. The Center can be monitored or reached by going to the website, www.swamiram.com.

Swami Ram Charran travels frequently to different locations. The following information can be useful to contact Swami Ram Charran and find out when he is travelling to a location near you:

Website: http://www.swamiram.com *
E-mail: swamicharan@yahoo.com

Introduction

The Devil Made Me Do It…..

Is usually the excuse of many when they have taken the life of another or they have done wrong against God and nature…

Buying a chicken at the public is not the same as killing a chicken in the name of some "God". First of all you have to remember that GOD IN ITS TRUE FORM WILL NOT ACCEPT THE TAKING OF ANOTHER LIFE…in violation of the Ten Commandments …rather a TRUE GOD IS ONE THAT WILL GIVE NEW LIFE CONSTANTLY TO THE UNIVERSE.

The person who buys the chicken at the public grocery store or at the butcher will incur some, but little karmic retribution whereas when the soul of the chicken to be sacrificed is directed by prayer type words the meat eaten has now taken on a negative path and thus begins to affect the doer or sacrificer in a negative way….

Sacrificing a life in a ritual form is totally different from raising a chicken or animal for food consumption.

A belief in *magic* as a means of influencing the world seems to have been common in all cultures. Some of these beliefs crossed over into nascent *religions*, influencing rites and religious celebrations. Over time, religiously-based supernatural events ("*miracles*") acquired their own flavor, separating themselves from standard magic. Some modern religions such as Neopaganism embrace connections to magic, while others retain only echoes.

Unlike other ("nature-based") magic, religiously based magic almost always involves requesting the intervention of a deity or deities to enact the desired effect. It is up to the good pleasure of the contacted deity whether to grant the request or not; the supplicant is, individually, powerless (though some might claim a personal divine gift, such as speaking in tongues increases the possibility that the request will be fulfilled.

Acknowledgements & Message from the Author

A Challenge was made by Swami Ram Charran to all the Brahmin Pundits in India, North America and The Caribbean to reveal where in the Vedic scriptures that it is fully approved to worship any form of God by killing and offering chickens, Goats, Pigs, Rum and Cigarettes as offerings to benefit one self with divine powers and happiness. This challenge was also supported by Vishnu Sookar, President of the Durga Temple Toronto Canada, Pundit Krishna at the Krishna Bazaar Store in Brooklyn and Pundit Rama Maharaj in Miami. So far NO ONE has been able to present this proof. My meeting once with Pundit Mahendra Doobay, who has a Kal Bhairo Statue with a Dog in the center of his Temple Altar, became bitter when I challenged him to present evidence of this "so called "form of worship. In the presence of Pundit Krishna, Mr. Doobay claimed that "Kal Bhairo" is the brother of "Goddess Durga" and insisted that it is written in the "Devi Bhagwatam". When asked where in the Scripture of this book it can be found, he refused to provide this proof, his words were "Find it yourself! With this type of answer, I bowed humbly and walked away. This is the kind of ignorance that is among our Hindu leaders that have brought Hinduism to a Pagan level. Instead of being admired as the greatest science that has all the power to make mankind find peace and prosperity, Outsiders who have very little knowledge of true Hinduism, now think that our great religion is just a cult like any other cult where lives are sacrificed for gaining divine benefits from a God who is greedy for cigarettes, rum and meat.

How did I find out about "Kal-Bhairo"? Not from the scriptures! As you will see in this book, it was through experience. By helping people to stop their worship of the devil in the form of Kal Bhairo, I was able to solve their problems in life. Many women, who could not have children, fell sick or experienced sexual encounters with spirits, are now leading happy and prosperous lives when I removed the Kal-Bhairo worship from their lives. That's how I discovered that Kal- Bhairo worship is not good. Further research showed that families who worshipped with sacrifice etc. faced extinction and usually the generation comes to end by not having any more male children. Such is the law of the universe.

I would like to thank Vishnu Sookar for refusing to place the Statue of Kal Bhairo in the Devi Temple in Canada, based on our challenge. As of this day my challenge to find out who really is Kal Bhairo has not been answered. There is not evidence of Kal-Bhairo worship by rum etc in our scriptures. I also want to thank Swami Balgopal ji, Pundit Harry Balgobin, Pundit Doobay from Trinidad, My Guru, Gurumayi Chivalasanda and many others from Nepal in supporting my position on this.

About the Author

THE MISSION & THE MAN BEHIND IT
Physicist Swami Ram Charran

Sri Swami Ram is a true Jyotish. He has utilized his combined academic background in Quantum Mechanics and Computer Technology to perfect the knowledge of Jyotish, obtained from the ancient Vedic scriptures. He developed a sophisticated mathematical software application that allows him to pin-point specific incidents in a person's life and narrows those incidents down to specific times of occurrence.

For example, in Chapter 8, it is explained that Swami-ji was able to tell not only that Paul was physically abused but he was also able to tell the exact period of time that he was subjected to such abuse. Further, Swami-ji was able to tell the mother with great accuracy the type of life that Paul was living in the gay community. He predicted that death would occur in the family if the couple remained married. Swami-ji identified that Paul was suffering from the effects of Reverse Kundalini, a situation triggered by the initial traumatic incidence of sexual abuse when he was nine years old.

For the sake of simplicity and to protect client privilege and confidentiality, Swami-ji uses a Numbering

System. He determined that Paul was a Number 7. He also determined that the girl whom Paul had married is a Number 2. Thus when Paul and his wife unite, they become a Number 9(7 + 2 = 9) which signifies Death in the near future. In fact at the time of writing, Paul has already made two attempts to commit suicide. Please note that a prominent Pundit Astrologer in New York City had incorrectly advised the family that the proposed marriage between Paul and the girl would be a good match. At the consultation, Swami-ji told the family that the match was a deadly one and that any knowledgeable pundit should have known that.

My dear devotees, this commentary is made in the most respectful way with only one aim in mind. And that aim is to unequivocally state that the various forms of commercial Astrology that is being practiced by Pundits put people's lives at risk. The single-most important recommendation that I can make in this paper is for each householder to gain an understanding of the difference between Astrology and Jyotish. Only then will the practicing Pundits be forced to upgrade their knowledge and reduce the risk about the predictions that they make on peoples lives. Through the Jyotish readings, Swami-ji found that if Paul had consummated the marriage and was continuing to have frequent sexual intercourse with his wife after she arrived in New York, the family would have faced untold disasters, including the possibility of Death. In fact, Swami-ji asserted that if Paul had made a third attempt at suicide, the chances are that he would have been successful.

Chapter 1
Encounter with the Devil

The Effects of Worshipping Dead Spirits
(Bhairo Baba)

[Based on a personal interview with a 70-year old gentleman who lost his first wife to the Hindu Dark forces (Kal Bhairo).]

Lallu lowered his head and spoke very quietly at first. It was as if he was whispering to himself. I forced myself to drown out the external sounds of passing vehicles on nearby Finch Avenue and hung on desperately to his every word.

"Wa me go tell you son," he whispered. "It is so hard. Every time I remember how she died, I grieve. I used to get very angry at first but as the years go by, I became less angry and more saddened." I sat quietly on a chair facing him under a temporary tarpaulin tent in the back-yard of a town house in Scarborough, Canada. The Janeu had just finished and a 12-year old lad received his right or passage into manhood. Most of the other invited guests were either eating of chatting in small groups. In the midst of many, Lallu and I seemed

1

removed. We were caught up in our own world of an experience long past. He was re-living those events past and I was documenting the experience.

"I was very young," he began. "I was 20 and she was just 16 when we got married. People used to get married very young in those days you know. In a few years, we had five children: three girls and two boys. I owned a Toyota Crown and used to drive hire car [taxi service] between Georgetown and Air Base [Timehri Airport, Guyana]. Times were tough you know. I had to work really long hours to support my wife and dependent children. I was never a really a religious person but I attended religious functions. Like most people in Guyana, I had Hindu, Moslem and Christian friends; so I would attend religious services, weddings, burials and so on. I guess I prayed a little in my own way and over the years, I had learned quite a few of the sacred Vedic mantras from some of the Brahman pundits.

We had a small house in Grove Village on the East Bank [Demerara, Guyana]. My wife and I had a good relationship. She looked after the house and cared for the children, you know. Like most people, teeth and tongue does bite sometimes, [Referring to occasional quarrels between husband and wife] but nothing major. All in all we were a poor but happy family. One day, I returned home to see my wife sitting on the front steps. She looked sort of spaced out you know. I said 'hello' to her but she just stared at me. Her eyes bulged and she looked me up and down. Her face was dark with a really, really mean look. It was as if at any moment she would just lash out at me. I tried to think back if we had a quarrel that day to make her so angry but nothing came to mind. I looked around and saw that all the children were OK. I went into the house and saw that everything was in order. She had cleaned the house and cooked food. She had bathed the younger children and changed their clothes. So nothing seemed out of the ordinary. I went and bathed my skin and changed my clothes. Then I asked my oldest daughter what happened to her mom. My daughter said that she was like that all day. She said that mom seemed to be in a trance. But she also seemed like she was vexed [angry] or something. So the children avoided her all day.

Again, I tried to talk with her. I asked, 'Wa happen Baby?' But I received no response, only a cold blank stare. Her eyes run up and down my body as if she was sizing me up or something. I eat some dinner and put the children to bed. Baby never moved from the steps although darkness stepped in. I told her let's go to bed and tried to hold her hand. She knocked my hand off with some force and got up and walked to bed. I asked her if she wanted to go to the doctor. No response. I hoped that after she slept that things will be better. No such luck. The behavior continued for several days and I really began to get worried. I talked to some of my friends and they suggested that 'something hold her'. [That she may be possessed by a spirit or the devil]. They suggested that I take her to see a Pundit [Hindu priest] to open book [check her Patra].

To cut a long story short, I took her to the village pundit and he was baffled. He said that she has a 'Gra' and that we have to do a special Puja. A few of my friends suggested that I take her to see Nuru who was a spiritual healer on the East Coast. So one afternoon I took her up there and begged Nuru to help her. By this time almost a week had gone by and Baby hadn't spoken a word. She was still in a trance-like state and always looked at me with that blank threatening glare. Nuru chanted some mantras and sprinkled her with some water. He offered her an agarbathi [incense stick] and asked her who she was. In a gruff male voice, Baby answered that she was 'Bhairo Baba'. When Nuru asked her what she wanted, she said that I have to do a Puja. The male voice in her called out a list of ingredients, flags, rum, and cigarettes and included a fowl-cock, a pig and a goat which had to be sacrificed. I said, 'but Baba, I don't have any money. Where will I get the money to buy all the things you want? I have 5 children and I have to struggle every day to put food on the table.'

'Don't worry,' the voice said. 'You will be able to have everything and must perform the Puja in 3 months'. We took our leave of Nuru and returned home. I begged Baba to leave my wife alone and he said, 'Go now. She will be all right.'

Soon, as I sit under this shade, I swear that the next thing I tell you will surprise the hell out of you. As soon as I turned out to work the following morning, I got a full load of passengers in Georgetown and as soon as I dropped them off at Air Base, the car was full again. All day it was like that. This never happened before. The next day, the same thing happened. I was not getting time to stop to eat even. This continued for several weeks. In less that 2 months I had more than enough money to buy all the things for the Puja and decided why wait. So I consulted with an old man on the East Coast who did this kind of Puja. His name was Suma. On the Sunday as arranged, I delivered all the things to Suma. He called up Bhairo Baba into my wife again and began to conduct the Puja rituals. Son, I don't know nothing about these types of Puja. Anyways, the animals were killed and hung upside down and about 18 flags, all color, were jukked [planted on bamboo poles] into the earth. I was tired and just wanted to go home. I begged Bhairo Baba that I have done what he wanted and that he must now leave my wife alone. I told Suma that I want no part of the meat or anything and left to return home.

Eh-eh. I see like Baby sometime-ish. At one time, I think that she feel good and at other times she seem like she gone back into her trance-like state. At night when we are in bed and I put me hand around her, she boxed [pushed violently] my hand away and shouted at me in a male voice to leave her alone. Well you know. I am a young man and all so I pushed to have sex. After all, she was my wife. But the more I pushed, the more violent she became. I began to get really mad. I want to jump on him and beat the shit out of him because I was really strong in those days you know. But I thought that I will hurt Baby really bad because it would be her body that would get the blows from me.

The next day, I wiped out a space in the house and put Baby to sit. I used a mantra to call up Bhairo Baba in her. He came up and I asked who he was. He said, 'Bhairo Baba.' I said 'What do you want?' He asked for rum and cigarettes. Now, son, I must tell you that Baby never smoked a cigarette in her life before and yet she was smoking and inhaling that cigarette like a seasoned smoker. She had a sort of satisfied smile on her face and she stared at me up and down. I asked him to leave my wife alone. I told him that I had done what he wanted. He said that he was not satisfied with the Puja. He said that the Puja was not done the way he wanted it. I said that I do not know anything about such Pujas and that is why I went and found a man [Suma] who knew about such things. He said that I have to do another Puja. I said that will be hard. I asked if there was anything else that will satisfy him. He said he will be pleased if I planted the 18 colored flags in my front yard. I said that I will do it if he will leave my wife alone. He did not answer and Baby became herself again for a short time.

Son, I planted the flags but Baby was never the same again. Every time I tried to make love to her at night, she pushed my hand away very violently and shouted at me in a male voice to leave her alone. Being a young man, I pushed and pushed for sex but she became really strong and would beat me up. Many nights I lay next to her and would hear her moaning and turning a twisting as if she was having sex with someone who I was not able to see. Next morning she will be tired and worn out. This went on for weeks and for months. One of my boy-child died. Later on, one of my girl children died. I could not take in any more and I left her. Today, my two remaining girl children are suffering untold punishment. My only other son is a drunkard and turned out to be a luun-ghera [someone who drinks rum and does not care for work family or upliftment in life]. Son, the grief is still in my heart for Baby. She was possessed by that devil until he finally sucked her dry and sucked the life from her body. I left and came away to Canada. A few years later, I was told by friends that Baby had died. I said a prayer for her soul and hoped at last that she finally found peace."

Lallu lowered his head and said nothing for a while. I remained quiet and continued to look at his pained face.

- "If there is one thing you learned from all this, what would that be?" I asked.

-. "Don't mess with the devil."

- "How do you mean?"

-. "Well Swami, people want quick fixes in life. They want money and luxuries. They do the Rum Puja and Kal Bhairo gives them what they ask for. But the debt they incur by accepting that riches can never be repaid. The devil will start small to entrap you. First he will ask for one fowl-cock to be sacrificed. Later it will be a pig or a goat. If you miss a Puja, he becomes nasty and takes one of your children. And he loves women. He loves to possess the female members of the family and in the end, the happiness and well-being of that family is destroyed. So what is the use of the wealth which you beg him for in the first place?"

I had no answer for Lallu. I could see his pain although so many years had passed. I sensed that although he tried to reconstruct his life and re-marry someone else as his life's partner that scarcely a day would go by when he does not think about Baby. Scarcely a day goes by when he does not imagine the sufferings of his daughters. Scarcely a day goes by when he does not think about his one remaining son and perhaps wonder if there is any hope for him.

I did not have the courage to ask but the question was on my mind. "Did Lallu himself invite Kal Bhairo into his life through a Puja in order to get a better life for his wife and children? How come all of a sudden his wife Baby became possessed?" Maybe it is her past Karma. Maybe it is the sins from her parents or ancestors who used to perform the Kal Bhairo Puja. But I guess I will never know.

Chapter 2
Who Is the Devil? The Hindu View

Who Is Kal Bhairo The Dark Looking
Deity Worshiped By Hindus?

K al Bhairo has its origins in the ancient Vedic scriptures. In the fight to take control of the universe, a tug-of-war ensued between the Devtas [divine forces] and Rakshas [evil forces] in the story of the churning of the ocean of milk. **To visualize the churning motion, think of the old fashioned way of churning butter using the ookrie [mortar] and moosar [pestle].** Lord Vishnu is the dominant God in this story

and oversees the entire operation by providing two extensions of his own form. In one form, he is the cosmic turtle resting in the depths of the milky ocean [the ookrie] and mountain Mehru is the pestle [moosar] which rests on his back. In his other form, he becomes Vasuki, the cosmic serpent whose middle is wrapped around the churning stick. The Devtas took hold of one end of Vasuki and the Rakshas took hold of the other end. As the tug-of-war began, the entire ocean churned. At first, all the poisons arose and were squirted out of the depths of the ocean, then Goddess Laxmi emerged and finally the elixir of immortality [amrita] was flushed out.

Lord Vishnu, adopting the form of the beautiful Mohini, began to share the amrita with the Devtas. One of the Rakshas disguised himself as a Devta and received some of the amrita. The imposter was quickly recognized by the Sun and the Moon who immediately told Lord Vishnu. Before the Raksha could drink the amrita, Lord Vishnu used his chakra weapon and cut the Raksha in half. But the Raksha had already swallowed the first few drops of the amrita and technically attained the higher status of a Devta. The one half of the Raksha's body was flung to the North and became known as RAHU [the North Node] and the other half became known as KETU [the South Node]. This is why in the NAV-GRAHA PUJA; we continue to worship both Rahu and Ketu as two of the nine planets which influence our lives.

Rahu is like the drunken vagabond of the family of Devtas who we continue to acknowledge during our puja ritual. But we do not want to invoke his influence into our lives. In other words, we do not want to do a puja directly to Rahu. He has the power to grant our requests but the price which we will have to pay is too high. Yet some pundits continue to do exactly this, while others unknowingly invoke Rahu into the lives of many by performing the Durga Puja incorrectly.

It is Rahu who has become known as Kal Bhairo in the West Indies and is depicted as the dark deity in Hinduism. He has a demon-like face with red eyes. His female counterpart is referred to as Katari. Worship of

Kal Bhairo is performed because of material greed. In order to satisfy some material desire, usually to acquire wealth, a live sacrifice of an animal is made and rum and cigarettes are offered to this deity. While some differences may exist in the performance of the worship, the desire and the outcomes are substantially the same.

In the Indian Province of Madhya Pradesh, devotees built a temple dedicated to the dark Deity **Bhairav** to whose idol, liquor is offered. African slaves who inhabited the British colonies in the West Indies brought Kal Bhairo from Africa as a **voodoo deity** with a black dog. In Guyana Kal Bhairo is also known as **Landmaster** and in Trinidad, he is called **Dee**. In the Muslim religion, the equivalent of the dark Deity is **Qurbani;** in Christianity, he is called **Satan;** in the Spanish community, he is known as **Santa Rina**. Amongst West Indians, Kal Bhairo worship takes place in the form of a **rum puja**, in which a chicken, goat or pig is sacrificed, rum and cigarettes are offered and a **black flag** is raised. Material wealth is usually asked for by the persons performing the puja and documented cases show that Kal Bhairo often grants their wishes. Pleasant and inviting as all this may sound however, worship of this dark deity is not without its problems and consequences, for any debt which is incurred must be repaid.

Once the sacrifice is made for the first time, no matter how many generations ago, Kal Bhairo demands continuance and current generation families who do not continue the tradition and who may not even know that their parents or grand-parents practiced Kal Bhairo worship feel the negative effects in their lives. **One may rightly ask why I should bear the consequences of the actions of my parents or fore-parents.** Let us examine the scenario of borrowed money. Your parents borrowed a loan from a bank and built the house in which you grew up. You enjoyed the fruits from that debt and when your parents die, the unpaid debt falls to you, the children. All unpaid debt is transferred through the future generations.

Each life form on earth was given a certain value. When your grandfather killed the chickens, goats or pigs, they terminated that life before its time. That soul did not get to complete its karma in its present form and now must wait in purgatory until it can be reborn again. In other words, the spirit of that animal becomes very angry and as more animals are killed over the years, the number of angry spirits increase and the debt grows. When a person dies an untimely death, that person's soul was not prepared for death and this soul may get lost and wander around in the astral dimension looking for a body to take re-birth. Similarly, when an animal is killed in ritual sacrifice, that defenseless animal has died an untimely death. The spirit of the animal is angry at the person who ended its life before its time. This angry spirit, in its effort to continue its karmic life on earth, has to possess a human body to continue the rest of the time it was supposed to live in the first place. The person most likely to be possessed by such an angry spirit is either the person who has taken the life of that animal, or all the people who have participated in the eating of the meat of the sacrificed animal. The possession of the person's body can vary in intensity dependent upon the person's karmic background, how religious the person was prior to the Kal Bhairo worship and what kind of foods they eat.

Sometimes, persons with good intent unknowingly attract Kal Bhairo into their lives due to a catastrophic **mistake** made by some **pundits** during a **Durga Puja** ritual. Mother Durga, the consort of Lord Shiva represents the procreative forces and family and devotees worship this Deity to receive her blessings. During the Puja ritual, nine plates of prasad offerings are

11

made to worship the nine forms of Mother Durga. Some of the less knowledgeable pundits offer the tenth plate to Kal Bhairo instead of to Lord Shiva. Now remember that Mother Durga is married to Lord Shiva and the symbolism of the tenth plate offering in the puja ritual is to recognize that union. **Therefore, how can a pundit be correct in offering that tenth plate to Kal Bhairo instead of to Lord Shiva?** The devotee and their family, thinking all is well, continue their lives only to find problems and hardships begin to infest their lives and often, mysterious occurrences begin to manifest themselves such as the appearance of worms or black bugs in the house. Family members begin to have bad dreams; tempers flare and quarrels and fights happen frequently; health problems surface; job problems occur; a fire may destroy the house and other financial distress result.

What are the Consequences of Debts to Kal Bhairo?

In the ancient Puranic texts, it is stated that during the first 35 days of a child's life after birth, one Deity will visit the child's body each day. When a child is born with a heavy load of karmic debt, however, the evil spirits prevent the visits of the Deities and they inhabit the child's body instead. In a recent case handled by Swami-Ji, a mother told him that when each of her children was being born, they will choke almost to the point of dying. Her priest always told her that she had to make an animal sacrifice to save the child and she did. This was a case where Kal Bhairo wanted to be repaid for past debts and so he choked the child to scare the parents who then killed an animal to satiate his thirst for blood. The parents made a choice for their innocent child who now incurred more bad karmas. As these children grew they began to encounter all types of problems and disaster after disaster forced the mother to seek the help of Swami-Ji.

You May Very Well Ask, Does Everyone Who Kills Animals for Food or In Sacrificial Rituals Incur a Load of Karmic Debt?

As stated before, Kal Bhairo usually grants the person their material wishes for wealth for a period of time but takes one important thing away - the person's true happiness. **What is a Hindu's ultimate happiness?** It is their children and their daily well-being. Usually the presence of Kal Bhairo in your life is indicated by any of the following:

- Kal Bhairo will usually take away a person's child through miscarriages, abortions or death at a young age. It is almost guaranteed that the first child or the youngest child will go in this way.
- The womb of women becomes twisted and they have severe back and neck pains. Therefore their enjoyment of love making and pleasurable sex life is taken away.
- Kal Bhairo sometimes takes the form of dead relatives and come in the night and makes love to females in the home. One sign of this is unexplained bruises on the body noticeable especially in the mornings.
- People who own animals may see that one or more of these animals die suddenly for no apparent reason. E.g.: a healthy milking cow will suddenly fall over and die for no explainable reason.

The circumstances will appear to be so natural that people generally miss the relationship between the DEATH of their child or animal and the DEBT owing to the dark Deity Kal Bhairo

How Can the Effect of Kal Bhairo Be Removed and Cured?

To remove the effects of Kal Bhairo, a householder must perform a **Durga Puja**. The purpose of this puja is to ask Mother Durga to accept them as her own children and so Lord Shiva becomes their new father. Through this puja, the person is granted re-birth with the new mother as Mother Durga and the new father as Lord Shiva. With these new parents, the sins of that person's earth-parents and grand-parents are no longer attached to them. This rebirth cleanses the householder from past bad karmas.

To break the curse from the entire family, all members must contribute equally to the monetary costs of performing the puja and the dakshina to the preceptor. Each family member must contribute an equal amount of money from their **own earnings**. Sometimes the evil is so attached to one family member that he will resist all attempts to believe that anything is wrong and will refuse to contribute his share or to participate in the puja. In such a case, if the other family members are willing to help and protect him, they must put the amount on behalf of that person and must add **10% more** to the total cost. In this way, all the family members come under the protection of the GOD-PARENTS. If someone does not participate, that person will continue to suffer.

Once the Durga Puja is complete, the family will begin to notice changes in their lives. As the positive change cycle begins the family must continue to attach themselves to God through the worship of Lord Shiva. The following should be done:

- A Lord **Shiva Puja** should be performed each year
- Family members should chant the **mantras** provided by the holy person

- The family should set up an altar in the homes and bathe the **Shivling** when they kneel to say their prayers.

Devotees of Lord Shiva will find that after they return from Kal Bhairo, they eventually will develop high psychic ability, their 3rd eye will open and they will have visions of Lord Shiva and other Devtas.

Swami-Ji noticed that people born under the **Deity Laxmi** are able to fight off the debts of bad karmas and break the curse, usually on their own. Others are not so successful and must seek help from Mother Durga and Lord Shiva.

Symptoms of Persons Possessed by Kal Bhairo

Generally, a person who worships Kal Bhairo will have the following symptoms:

- Their body will darken in color
- Their eyes will have dark rings around them
- Their eyes may become red or pink
- Their body will vibrate during prayers
- They will experience pain in the knees
- Women will have uterus problems
- The person will experience back pains, neck pains and headaches
- The person will have a lot of blockages in life - no job, broken marriage
- Women may experience sexual contact with evil spirits
- If religious mantras are being recited, the person may get up and dance
- The person may become addicted to tobacco and alcohol
- The person is always dressed in black clothes and is attracted to the color black

How Does Kal Bhairo Come Into Your Life?

- From debts owed by parents or grandparents
- By eating food from a Kal Bhairo sacrifice
- By eating prasad at a Kal Bhairo or Katari Puja
- By eating food from a death ritual
- By eating food from someone who is possessed by Kal Bhairo
- By having sexual contact with a person possessed by Kal Bhairo
- By eating red meat such as duck, beef or goat
- By sleeping in a North-South position
- By performing a Durga Puja and offering the 10th prasad plate to Kal Bhairo

Can I Correct the Effects of Kal Bhairo and Reduce or Eliminate My Karmic Debts?

YES, YES, and YES. This can definitely be done. To prevent the effects of Kal Bhairo in your life, do avoid the causes as outlined above. In the unavoidable cases where the debt and bad karmas originated from parents, fore-parents or in cases where Kal Bhairo was attracted into your life because your pundit did not perform the Durga Puja ritual correctly, consult a holy person who is knowledgeable in the Vedic scriptures.

There is help in overcoming the negative forces of Kal Bhairo. But like the story of the [Churning of the Ocean] the first things that will be eliminated will be the poisons. This will manifest itself in DOUBT, in NEGATIVE THOUGHTS and once a little progress is made, the person will have a STRONG DESIRE TO GO BACK TO OLD WAYS AND BAD HABITS.

Once you are willing to face your own fears, Swami-Ji will help you change your life from misery to one of true happiness.

Chapter 3
Who Is the Devil – The Christian View

S atan was created by God as one of his archangels. The interpretation of his name is protector of the Dead souls. All of the archangels or spirits who were in eternity with Him were privileged to witness the creation of Satan, Michael and Gabriel as archangels and also the great host of angels both good and bad. They are of various ranks and endowments bestowed upon

them were well organized. From the inception they were created as whole beings but after a period of probation the majority of them (2/3) of the angels fell from their state of innocence into committing the first act of sin through the presence of evil. Both Michael and Gabriel along with the 1/3 of the angels remained with God in eternity as sinless supernatural beings.

From an archangel, Satan became Lucifer who is also famously known as the devil. Other meanings of Satan are as follow: enemy or adversary, the chief of the fallen angels, the grand adversary of God and Man, hostile to everything good, the devil, accuser of the brethren, Beelzebub, deceiver of the whole world, the great dragon, the antichrist, the beast, the false prophet, the evil one, the father of lies, the god of this world, the god of this evil age, the old serpent, the prince of power of the air, the tempter, the ruler of a powerful kingdom standing in opposition to God. Also the principle title name devil means slander, the archenemy of both god and man.

There is a very old scripture which says how Satan (Hindu *Rawana*) originated but for certain he was not created as an evil being. Because of the presence of evil, he yields to that influence of becoming a rebel and takes the initiative to over throw almighty God from His position of God to become as the most High God, while in a state of Holiness, he apparently led the other angels into rebellion with him. He is a being of superhuman power and wisdom, but not omnipotent or omniscience. He tries to frustrate God's plans and purpose for human beings. His principle method of attack is by temptation and his power is limited so he can go only as far as God permits. On Judgment Day he will face the wrath of God by being cast into hell to remain there forever.

In the book of Ezekiel 28:12-19 there is a vivid explanation of Satan (Yamraj) the son-of-the-morning. It describes him before he ever became the devil/Satan as full of wisdom and perfect in his beauty. He was decked in every precious stone as his apparel or covering. He was perfect in all his ways from the day he was created until iniquity was found in him. He was very wealthy with his possessions. His heart lifted up in vanity because of his beauty and so he abused his God given wisdom to corrupt his mind to become like the highest God. In the book of Isaiah 14:12-20 is the episode of how God humbled Bhairava by casting him out of his kingdom. The Scripture says that as he ascended above the heights of the clouds with 2/3 of God's angels to battle against the Almighty God to dethrone Him but he was instantly cast out by falling from heaven lightning to Earth. From that time on he became the devil/Satan, the prince of this world and the god of this evil world (a false god/demigod) and a strong opposition to God. As was already mentioned, the first sin was committed in heaven because the devil wanted to become like God but failed in his endeavor. Now that he was cast down to earth with the fallen angels (they are presently referred to as demons or evil spirits being invisible and can take possession of people), he is presently and is continuing to be in opposing to disrupt all of God's plans and in desperate effort become like the most High God to be worshipped by all of mankind. For instance, when God created man and placed Adam and Eve in the Garden of Eden to live and have full dominion over all of God's creation.

The devil/Satan intervened and took possession of the serpent, a beast which was very close and resembled a human being. The scripture describes the serpent as having hands and feet and with the gift of speech until the devil spoke through his lips. The serpent was tempted and sexually aroused and she reproduced the vagabond, Cain, a direct offspring of the devil. Soon after the curse God in His wisdom deformed the serpent into a lower classification of the animal kingdoms, a reptile, by removing all its limbs and changing his bone structure so that this sex act cannot be repeated again, and the reproduction through the hybridization of both man and beast cannot continue. Regardless, man has already become hybrid through Cain marrying his half sister who is Adam and Eve's daughter and they in turn brought forth hybrid children. Eventually this process continued on as the sons of God (i.e. Adam and Eve's children and their children children's children) reproduced through the daughters of men (i.e. Cain's children and their children's children). Through marriage the human race through hybridization has continued to be contaminated until this day. Just to mention, the scientists of yesteryear were all baffled and most of them today are still being misled to believe that man was evolved from the ape and cannot fathom of hybridization act caused by both man and the serpent mingling their seeds. God in His wisdom has destroyed that missing link by changing the bone structure of the serpent with the curse. The vital evidence has been destroyed by God Himself which today is hid from the wise and the prudent and even intellectual theologians, who would condemn and contradict such theory and biblical truth. This is a very deep revelation for an unbeliever to see and accept but is revealed to babes and sucklings. The devil probably was taking a good look when God was creating man and so successfully tampered by injecting himself into the human race through hybridization causing the reproduction of the many races of the world. Foremost, mankind has now been plunged into death and sin. Man is now born in sin by sex and shaped by iniquity, but thanks to God He sent His only Begotten Son. He was born of the Virgin Mary but was conceived by the Holy Ghost and not by sexual intercourse as it were with all of mankind. The devil is still present in the world and has work to do, to steal, kill and to destroy as many souls as he can conquer to take to hell with him when his time should have come to go to that lost eternity. But as was mentioned before he seems to have under his control the majority of the world's population under his jurisdiction, maybe over 90%, while God on the other hand, is coming for his faithful few, His chosen bride, which He will take away in rapture. The devil is still on the loose on his final leg of his mission manifesting himself as the antichrist, the false prophet, and the beast spoken of in the book of Revelation.

In closing, take serious note that Jesus Christ is the son of the true God who created the world and all living things including mankind while Satan the son-of-the-morning is the "god" of this evil age who is famously known as the devil which means the archenemy of God and of man and also as Satan which means enemy and adversary. Both of them are being worshipped by all of mankind. The Bible declares in the book of St. Luke 16:13 that "No man can serve two masters: for either he will hate the one and love the other; or else he will hold on to the one, and despise the other. Ye cannot serve God and "mammon (riches or money)." In other words, you are either worshipping Jesus Christ as God or Satan (Kal Bhairo) as the God of this evil age. And just to give a little hint which can be shocking news for the Christian world that more than 90% of the world's population are worshipping Satan (Kal Bhairo) at this moment as their God and almost all have rejected Jesus Christ as God except for a faithful few who are indeed worshipping Him according to the Word of God in Spirit and in Truth and are considered to be His Chosen Ones-His Eternal Sons and Daughters.

Clearly the Christian view is that a person can choose which path they want to follow...there are only one of two...GOOD or EVIL. It's up to the individual to choose.

The Devil Meets Jesus Christ
Temptation to Leave Godly Path

Vs. 7-8 - Satan unleashes his second sortie against Job afflicted Job with a terrible disease. From the various descriptions of Job's condition in the book (Job 2:8; 7:4-5; 13:14; 13:28; 16:16; 16:8; 17:1; 19:20; 19:26; 30:17; 30:30), it has been strongly suggested that this was not "boils" as the Authorized Version renders it, but rather a case of Black Leprosy. The disease produces swelling in the limbs, itching, flaking of the skin, a change in color of the skin and intense pain. Those who have it are described as appearing like Elephants or Lions; hence another name for the disease is Elephantiasis or Leontiasis. We know that this disease changed Job's physical appearance because his friends were not able to recognize him (Job 2:12). Not a single part of Job's body was unaffected by this disease. The text says that he was infected from the soles of his feet to the crown of his head. Not a single part of him could find rest from this disease (Job 3:26; 30:17).

Job then took a piece of broken pottery (also acting as an instrument for scratching), to scrape away the epidermal remnants of the diseased and infected skin. Job 7:5 describes the condition as a continual cycle of the skins decay, hardening, and then breaking out once again. Sitting in ashes was a common method of mourning whether for others or for one's self (see 2 Samuel 13:9; Ezekiel 27:30; Jonah 3:6).

Vs. 9-10 - Job's wife enters the picture and does a little work for Satan. Instead of offering comforts to her husband as a good wife would do, she questions whether he ought to remain faithful and suggest that he simply "curse God and die" instead of enduring through such grief. This, of course, was exactly what Satan wanted Job to do (1:11) and we learn that even unwitting people are often tools of Satan's evil.

Her question was in regard to Job's integrity, particularly, the statement that Job had made in 1:21, "blessed be the name of the Lord." Evidently Job's wife doesn't believe that after this second round of affliction that Job need hold fast to such a statement. Her conclusion was that Job should simply curse God and then die. Some have suggested that Job's wife's words were uttered in a fit of despair herself having recently lost her children as well as all that her husband had to provide for her comforts. While that was the case, such a loss never justifies blasphemy against God. Job, knowing this, was wise. Job's wife on the other hand was foolish and so Job charges her as being such. Herein lies one of the great lessons of the book of Job, namely, that regardless what comes our way in life, God is always holy, righteous, and good and never merits curse from His creation but always

The Temptation of Jesus

Jesus, full of the Holy Spirit, returned from the Jordan and was led by the Spirit into the desert, where for forty days he fasted. In Mathew 4 the devil tempts him repeatedly and it is related this way:

> **4:1** *Then Jesus was led by the Spirit into the wilderness to be tempted by the devil.* **2** *After he fasted forty days and forty nights he was famished.* **3** *The tempter (devil) came and said to him, "If you are the Son of God, command these stones to become bread."* **4** *But he answered, "It is written,* **'Man does not live by bread alone, but by every word** *(mantra)* **that comes from the mouth of God.'** **5** *Then the devil took him to the holy city, had him stand on the highest point of the temple,* **6** *and said to him, "If you are the Son of God, throw yourself down. For it is written,* **'He will command his angels concerning you'** *and* **'with their hands they will lift you up, so that you will not strike your foot against a stone.'"** **7** *Jesus said to him, "Once again it is written:* **'You are not to put the Lord your God to the test.'"** **8** *Again, the devil took him to a very high mountain, and showed him all the kingdoms of the world and their grandeur.* **9** *And he said to him, "I will give you all these things if you throw yourself to the ground and*

worship me." **10** *Then Jesus said to him, "Go away, Satan! For it is written: '***You are to worship the Lord your God and serve*** only* ***him.****'"* **11** *Then the devil left him, and angels came and began ministering to his needs.*

Kal Bhairo Meets Jesus Christ

It is well known that in Guyana and Trinidad that "Kal Bhairo", also known as "Dee Baba" is worshipped for the purpose of increasing wealth and success in business. The other forms of "Kal Bhairo" in both of these countries are known as "Land Master" or "Sanganee Baba" or "Bush Master" or simply "Master". These so called gods are worshipped with alcohol, cigarettes, cheese, and sacrificed animals. The souls of these animals once released become spirits with unfinished karmas. However, after "Kal Bhairo" is worshipped, this so called deity will promote great financial profits for the worshipper. As a result, you will find that many people who worship "Kal Bhairo" tend to acquire a lot of material wealth. But before we proceed lets take a look at the conversation between Lord Jesus Christ and Satan (Kal Bhairo).

If you compare a "Kal Bhairo" picture and a "Kal Bhairo" worshipper to an alcoholic and to Lucifer (Satan), they all have some common qualities. All of them have red eyes, dark skin, and a thirst for alcohol and meat. In the Holy Bible, it is documented that Satan met Christ and proceeded to tempt Him at least three times.

In the first temptation of Christ, Satan took Christ to a high mountain and showed him the whole world and its material wealth and said to Christ, **"bow before me and all of this on earth will be yours".**

Christ replied, *"Man does not live by bread (wealth) only but by every word that proceeded out of the mouth (mantra)"*.

It is clear from this conversation that "Kal Bhairo" (Satan) approached Christ and asked Him to do his worship or PUJA. The fact that Christ did not worship Satan supports the fact that "Kal Bhairo", the representation of evil or negative forces, should not be worshipped. The consequences of Devil worship are severe. As written in the Holy Bible, CHRIST DIED FOR OUR SINS BY BEING THE SACRIFICIAL LAMB OF GOD. Christ knew that the children are the ones who will suffer as a result of the parents wrong actions. The sacrifice of animals to perform "Kal Bhairo" worship is wrong and thus will result in suffering. Through the worship, you receive material wealth. But once you receive, you must repay. That repayment is in your suffering which results in loss of Peace of Mind.

What Is Your Peace Of Mind?

A person enjoys peace of mind when they are healthy, when they enjoy a happy marriage life and when their children are respectful, obedient and pursue knowledge and lifelong learning. When you accept wealth from Satan or "Kal Bhairo" what is he going to take from you in exchange?

He will take YOUR PEACE OF MIND. What is your ultimate peace? Your children who are most dear to you, your spouse who is your support, and your health, all of which are essential for happy living. Why would any parent want to bring this kind of karma on their children? Is the greed for wealth worthy of the price of the debt resulting from a willingness to sell your peace of mind to the devil "Kal Bhairo"?

Chapter 4
Who Is the Devil – The Muslim View

The Muslims call it a GIN, GINN, JINN or a Guide. This is the result of Qurbani or what we call "Sacrifice for God". The Radical Muslims follow this path of worship even though "THE KORAN" does not approve of it. The true Allah of God never preached about Qurbani in the Holy Books. In fact "The Koran" speaks out against the drinking or use of alcohol and smoking, or intoxicating drugs by a true Muslim. It does not support sacrifice of animals for Allah in any way and never places women below the feet of men. Mohammed was so radical in ways that he even went against his own philosophy of the Holy Word.

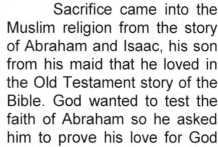

Sacrifice came into the Muslim religion from the story of Abraham and Isaac, his son from his maid that he loved in the Old Testament story of the Bible. God wanted to test the faith of Abraham so he asked him to prove his love for God by sacrificing his only son, Isaac to show his belief. Abraham decided to do so, but before he can kill Isaac with a knife, an angel of the Lord held his hand and stopped the sacrifice. Isaac's life was saved by the faith Abraham had in his God. However a man's word must be carried out once it is uttered, for as Christ said Man must live by his words. A promise is a promise and so to fulfill the promise Abraham caught a Lamb and sacrificed it instead.

The Muslims interpreted this to mean that Allah or God is happy when they give a life to him and so the sacrifice of lambs was encouraged. A closer look at this will reveal that the law of Karma governed the actions of Abraham. **God never wants life...in fact God gives life**.... Because Abraham had already promised the life of his son as an act of proving his faith, he had to replace that promise by following the instructions of the angel to kill the lamb instead: "A life for a life". However the radical Muslim who is not educated in the philosophy of the Koran, will interpret this the wrong way, that is , that by killing an animal they will save themselves...NOT TRUE!!!. The first part of the law of **"Action is Equal to Reaction"** has not been acted upon; therefore the action of killing the lamb becomes the first part of the Newtonian Law. In that case the reaction is the death of a Human life or many lives in exchange for that sacrifice. It is the same thing that happens in Voodooism, Kal-Bhairo Puja, Satanic sacrifices, Santeria and the Jewish sacrifice of Chickens for Passover.

Jesus Christ understood this and clearly dictated to the people that he came to save them from their sins, and that he is the "Lamb of God" that sacrificed himself for the sake of all who believed him. Clearly Christ understood the ramifications of sacrificing animals to God. He had hoped that by his crucifixion people would stop performing this sinful act in the eyes of God. It is also strange that Muslims adopted one part of the Bible as their own but ignored the other parts that preach against 'Qurbani". In today's world many of the Muslim priests ignore the rules of the Koran and encourage the drinking of alcohol and smoking of cigarettes. These young "MAGIS" of today are nothing compared to the "Old Wise Magi's" in the Old days. They do not have the knowledge of the scriptures as the old "Fakirs" did. The fakirs had tremendous knowledge of the laws of nature.

Ginn, the Spirit of the Hammam

According to Islamic lore, the Ginn, a spirit who dwells in the water of springs and in the darkness of caves finds the damp darkness of the hammam ideal. And, what does one do when one encounters the Ginn? Etiquette is provided in the Figh (Islamic Jurisprudence). One should speak the Balmala, which is an invocation that means *"in the name of Allah"* The Ginn should leave after hearing these words; but, if he doesn't, one is urged to postpone one's visit; otherwise the Ginn might slap the visitor in the face with a noise, which will either render the visitor's voice useless or dislocate his jaw.

Of course, not all Ginns were malicious or even mischievous. If you were to ask a tellak about his particular hammam spirit, there is a chance that he might nonchalantly introduce you to the Ginn: "This is our Ginn who shows himself frequently and recites poetry as well."

In some areas, the devil was reputed to use the hammam as his house. If one was not interested in meeting the devil, one would not bathe between the last two prayers of the day. That was the time when the devil and friends enjoyed their baths. If you found yourself in the hammam during the devil's turn, you must open the encounter with an Adan (a recital from a religious text). That should send the devil running and, according to lore, farting away.

Often baths were protected from unfriendly spirits by placing an apotropaic mark on the door. Moslems and Christians of Cairo were known to paint crosses on the doors

Jinn

By Alan G. Hefner

In Arabian and Muslim folklore jinns are ugly and evil demons having supernatural powers which they can bestow on persons having powers to call them up. In the Western world they are called genies.

Legend has it that <u>King Solomon</u> possessed a ring, probably a diamond, with which he called up jinns to help his armies in battle. The concept that this king employed the help of jinns may have originated from 1 Kings 6:7,

> *"And the house, when it was in building, was built of stone made ready before it was brought there, so there was neither hammer nor axe nor hand tool of iron heard in the house, while it was in building."*

In Islam, jinns are fiery spirits (Qur'an 15:27) particularly associated with the desert. While they are disruptive of human life, they are considered worthy of being saved. A person dying in a state of great sin may be changed into a jinni in the period of a barzakh, separation or barrier.

The highest of the jinns is <u>Iblis</u>, formerly called <u>Azazel</u>, the prince of darkness, or the Devil. The jinns were thought by some to be spirits that are lower than angels because they are made of fire and are not immortal. They can take on human and animal shapes to influence men to do good or evil. They are quick to punish those indebted to them who do not follow their many rules.

In the "*Arabian Nights*" jinns or genies came from Aladdin's Lamp. There are several myths concerning the home of the jinns. According to Persian mythology some of them live in a place called Jinnistan. Others say jinns live with other supernatural beings in the Kaf, mystical emerald mountains surrounding the earth

Ibn Abdul Barr said, "The jinn, according to the scholars of the language, are of different types:

1. If one is mentioning the jinn purely of themselves, they are called *jinni*.*
2. If one is mentioning the jinn that live among mankind, they are called *aamar* whose plural is *amaar*.
3. If one is mentioning the ones that antagonize the young, they are called *arwaah*.
4. If one is mentioning the evil ones that antagonize humans they are called *shaitan* for the singular [and *shayateen* for plural].
5. If they cause even more harm and become strong, they are called *afreet*."**

In conclusion, there is no reason for sacrificing life to God...whether he is Allah, or Jesus, or Abrahim, it is still wrong to take life. Besides, sacrificing the life of an animal is only second to cannibalism, an uncivilized part of history in the world when men ate men. **Men did not realize it was wrong to eat each other until one day they themselves were about to be cooked by others...then consciousness was born.**

Chapter 5
The Voodoo View

Origins of Voodoo

Voodoo is a derivative of the world's oldest known religions which have been around in Africa since the beginning of human civilization. Some conservative estimates these civilizations and religions to be over ten thousand years old. This then identify Voodoo as probably the best example of African syncretism in the Americas. Although its essential wisdom originated in different parts of Africa long before the Europeans started the slave trade, the structure of Voodoo, as we know it today, was born in Haiti during the European colonization of Hispaniola. Ironically, it was the enforced immigration of enslaved Africans from different ethnic groups that provided the circumstances for the development of Voodoo. European colonists thought that by desolating the ethnic groups, these could not come together as a community. However, in the misery of slavery, the transplanted Africans found in their faith a common thread.

They began to invoke not only their own Gods, but to practice rites other than their own. In this process, they comingled and modified rituals of various ethnic groups. The result of such fusion was that the different religious groups integrated their beliefs, thereby creating a new religion: Voodoo. The word "voodoo" comes from the West African word "vodun," meaning spirit. This Afro-Caribbean religion mixed practices from many African ethnics groups such as the Fon, the Nago, the Ibos, Dahomeans, Congos, Senegalese, Haussars, Caplaous, Mondungues, Mandinge, Angolese, Libyans, Ethiopians, and the Malgaches.

The Essence of Voodoo

Within the Voodoo society, there are no accidents. Practitioners believe that nothing and no event has a life of its own. That is why "vous deux", you two, you too. The universe is all one. Each thing affects something else. Scientists know that. Nature knows it. Many spiritualists agree that we are not separate; we all serve as parts of One. So, in essence, what you do unto another, you do unto you, because you ARE the other. Voo doo: View you. We are mirrors of each others souls. God is manifest through the spirits of ancestors who can bring good or harm and must be honored in ceremonies. There is a sacred cycle between the living and the dead. Believers ask for their misery to end. Rituals include prayers, drumming, singing, dancing, and animal sacrifice.

The serpent figures heavily in the Voodoo faith. The word Voodoo has been translated as "the snake under whose auspices gather all who share the faith". The high priest and/or priestess of the faith (often called Papa or Maman) are the vehicles for the expression of the serpent's power. The supreme deity is Bon Dieu. There are hundreds of spirits called Loa who control nature, health, wealth and happiness of mortals. The Loa form a pantheon of deities that include Damballah, Ezili, Ogu, Agwe, Legba and others. During Voodoo ceremonies these Loa can possess the bodies of the ceremony participants. Loa appear by "possessing" the faithful, who in turn become the Loa, relaying advice, warnings and desires. Voodoo is an animist faith. That is, objects and natural phenomena are believed to possess holy significance, to possess a soul. Thus the Loa Agwe is the divine presence behind the hurricane.

Music and dance are key elements to Voodoo ceremonies. Ceremonies were often termed by whites "Night Dancing" or "Voodoo Dancing". This dancing is not simply a prelude to sexual frenzy, as it has often been portrayed. The dance is an expression of spirituality, of connection with divinity and the spirit world.

Voodoo is a practical religion, playing an important role in the family and the community. One's ancestors, for instance, are believed to be a part of the world of the spirits, of the Loas, and this is one way that Voodoo serves to root its participants in their own history and tradition. Another practical aspect of Voodoo ceremonies is that participants often come before the priest or priestess to seek advice, spiritual guidance, or help with their problems. The priest or priestess then, through divine aid, offer help such as healing through the use of herbs or medicines (using knowledge that has been passed down within the religion itself), or healing through faith itself as is common in other religions. Voodoo teaches a respect for the natural world.

Unfortunately, the public's perception of voodoo rites and rituals seems often to point to the evil or malicious side of things. There are healing spells, nature spells, love spells, purification spells, and joyous celebration spells. Spirits may be invoked to bring harmony and peace, birth and rebirth, increased abundance of luck, material happiness, and renewed health. The fact is, for those who believe it, voodoo is powerful. It is also empowering to the person who practices it.

Voodoo and Its Fight to Survive

Despite Voodoo's noble status as one of the world's oldest religions, it has been typically characterized as barbaric, primitive, sexually licentious practice based on superstition and spectacle. Much of this image however, is due to a concerted effort by Europeans, who have a massive fear of anything African, to suppress and distort a legitimate and unique religion that flourished among their enslaved Africans. When slavers brought these peoples across the ocean to the Americas, the African's brought their religion with them. However, since slavery included stripping the slaves of their language, culture, and heritage, this religion had to take some different forms. It had to be practiced in secret, since in some places it was punishable by death, and it had to adapt to the loss of their African languages. In order to survive, Voodoo also adopted many elements of Christianity. When the French who were the colonizers of Haiti, realized that the religion of the Africans was a threat to the colonial system, they prohibited all African religion practices and severely punished the practitioners of Voodoo with imprisonment, lashings and hangings. This religious struggle continued for three centuries, but none of the punishments could extinguish the faith of the Africans. This process of acculturation helped Voodoo to grow under harsh cultural conditions in many areas of the Americas.

Voodoo survives as a legitimate religion in a number of areas of the world, Brazil where it is called "Candomblé" and the English speaking Caribbean where it is called "Obeah". The Ewe people of southern Togo and southeastern Ghana -- two countries in West Africa -- are devout believers. In most of the United States however, white slavers were successful in stripping slaves of their Voodoo traditions and beliefs. Thus Voodoo is, for most African Americans, yet another part of their heritage that they can only try to re-discover.

The Power of Voodoo

The strength that the Africans in Haiti gained from their religion was so strong and powerful, that they were able to survive the cruel persecution of the French rulers against Voodoo. It was in the midst of this struggle that the revolution was conspired. The Voodoo priests consulted their oracle and learned how the political battle would have to be fought in order for them to be victorious. The revolution exploded in 1791 with a Petro ritual and continued until 1804 when the Haitians finally won independence. Today the system of Voodoo reflects its history. We can see the African ethnic mixture in the names of different rites and in the pantheon of Gods or Loas, which is composed of deities from all parts of Africa.

Vodun Beliefs

Vodun or Vodoo, like Christianity, is a religion of many traditions. Each group follows a different spiritual path and worships a slightly different pantheon of spirits, called **Loa**. The word means "mystery" in the Yoruba language.

Yoruba traditional belief included a chief God **Olorun**, who is remote and unknowable. He authorized a lesser God **Obatala** to create the earth and all life forms. A battle between the two Gods led to Obatala's temporary banishment.

There are hundreds of minor spirits. Those which originated from Dahomey are called **Rada**; those who were added later are often deceased leaders in the new world and are called **Petro**. Some of these are

- Agwe: spirit of the sea
- Aida Wedo: rainbow spirit
- Ayza: protector
- Baka: an evil spirit who takes the form of an animal
- Baron Samedi: guardian of the grave
- Dambala (or Damballah-wedo): serpent spirit
- Erinle: spirit of the forests

- Ezili (or Erzulie): female spirit of love
- Mawu Lisa: spirit of creation
- Ogou Balanjo: spirit of healing
- Ogun (or Ogu Bodagris): spirit of war
- Osun: spirit of healing streams
- Sango (or Shango): spirit of storms
- Yemanja: female spirit of waters
- Zaka (or Oko): spirit of agriculture

There are a number of points of similarity between Roman Catholicism and Vodun:

- Both believe in a supreme being.
- The Loa resemble Christian Saints, in that they were once people who led exceptional lives, and are usually given a single responsibility or special attribute.
- Both believe in an afterlife.
- Both have, as the centerpiece of some of their ceremonies, a ritual sacrifice and consumption of flesh and blood.
- Both believe in the existence of invisible evil spirits or demons.
- Followers of Vodun believe that each person has a **mettet** (master of the head) which corresponds to a Christian's patron saint.

Followers of Vodun believe that each person has a soul which is composed of two parts: a **gros bon ange** or "big guardian angel", and a **ti bon ange** or "little guardian angel". The latter leaves the body during sleep and when the person is possessed by a Loa during a ritual. There is a concern that the ti bon ange can be damaged or captured by evil sorcery while it is free of the body.

Vodun Rituals

The purpose of rituals is to make contact with a spirit, to gain their favor by offering them animal sacrifices and gifts, to obtain help in the form of more abundant food, higher standard of living, and improved health. Human and Loa depend upon each other; humans provide food and other materials; the Loa provide health, protection from evil spirits and good fortune. Rituals are held to celebrate lucky events, to attempt to escape a run of bad fortune, to celebrate a seasonal day of celebration associated with a Loa, for healing, at birth, marriage and death.

Vodun priests can be male (**houngan** or hungan), or female (**mambo**). A Vodun temple is called a **hounfour** (or humfort). At its center is a **poteau-mitan** a pole where the God and spirits communicate with the people. An altar will be elaborately decorated with candles, pictures of Christian saints, symbolic items related to the Loa, etc. Rituals consist of some of the following components:

- A Feast before the Main Ceremony
- Creation of a Veve, a pattern of flour or cornmeal on the floor which is unique to the Loa for whom the ritual is to be conducted
- Shaking a Rattle and Beating Drums which have been cleansed and purified
- Chanting
- Dancing by the houngan and/or mambo and the hounsis (students studying

Vodun). The dancing will typically build in intensity until one of the dancers (usually a hounsis) becomes possessed by a Loa and falls. His or her ti bon ange has left their body and the spirit has taken control. The possessed dancer will behave as the Loa and is treated with respect and ceremony by the others present.

- Animal Sacrifice; this may be a goat, sheep, chicken, or dog. They are usually humanely killed by slitting their throat; blood is collected in a vessel. The possessed dancer may drink some of the blood. The hunger of the Loa is then believed to be satisfied. The animal is usually cooked and eaten. Animal sacrifice is a method of consecrating food for consumption by followers of Vodun, their gods and ancestors.

Chapter 6
The Spanish View: Santeria

When African slaves were imported to America, they were taught Christianity, but some people continued to hold their traditional beliefs. The result was a blending of traditional West African beliefs with Christianity. Today, many Afro-American folk religions continue to be practiced in the Caribbean, particularly among the poor and less educated people. They include Voodoo in Haiti, Santeria in Cuba, Shango in Trinidad, and Kuminia or Pocomania in Jamaica.

The Afro-American folk religions emphasize magical practices designed to bring good luck to their devotees or harm to their enemies. Ceremonies often include the ritual sacrifice of animals. The religions worship the spirits of the dead, but the spirits are given the names of Christian saints. This blending of beliefs allowed the Africans to retain their native faith while appearing to convert to Christianity.

The folk religions also provide an additional function, particularly in the remote sections of Haiti. Many practitioners of the religions are able to use tropical plants to relieve pain and cure illnesses. This is the only medical care available to some people.

Many people of the Caribbean profess to be Christians, but feel comfortable with the rituals of the folk religions. In 1998, Pope John Paul II visited Cuba, where he urged Catholics to reject the practice of Santeria. In addition to the Caribbean, the folk religions are also practiced in American cities with large Caribbean populations. They include New Orleans, Miami, New York City, and Los Angeles.

Santeria also known as "La Regla de Lukumi," is an Afro-Caribbean religious tradition derived from traditional beliefs of the Yoruba people of Nigeria. The Santeria/Yoruba tradition is comprised of a hierarchical structure according to priesthood level and authority. Orisha "ile" or temples are usually governed by Orisha Priests known as Babalorishas, "father of orisha", or Iyalorishas, "mothers of orisha", and serve as the junior Ile or second in the hierarchical religious structure. The Babalorishas and Iyalorishas are referred to as *"Santeros(as)"* and if they function as diviners of the Orishas they can be considered Oriates. The highest level of achievement for males is to become a priest of Ifa (ee-fah). Ifa Priests receive Orunmila who is the Orisha of Prophecy, Wisdom and all Knowledge. Ifa Priests are known by their titles such as "Babalawo" or "Father Who Knows the Secrets". Ifa Ile or Temples of Ifa serve as the senior to all Orisha Ile in the Traditional Orisha-Ifa / Santería Community. The Sacred Oracle of Ika-Fun or Ika Ofun serves as confirmation

What is Santeria and What Does It Have To Do With Fidel and Cuba?

Santeria, (Santería in Spanish) is a set of related religious systems that fuse Catholic beliefs with traditional Yoruba beliefs. In the Yoruba language, Lukumí means "friends" and also applies to descendants of Yorùbá slaves in Cuba, their music and dance, and the cubanized dialect of the Yorùbá language.

Santeria (also known as, Way of the Saints), a derisive term applied by the Spanish to mock followers seeming over devotion to the saints and their perceived neglect of God. The slaves' Christian masters did not allow them to practice their various West African religions. The slaves found a way around this by masking the Ifa's Orishas as Christian saints while maintaining their original identities. Often this combining is called by Euro-centric anthropologist and other social scientist as syncretism. A term that is being used less and less as Afro-centric scholars have pointed out that all religions are syncretic, i.e. the Judeo-Christian root of European religiosity. Nevertheless, the masters thought their slaves had become "good Christians" and were praising the saints, when in actuality they were continuing their traditional practices.

What are the Deities, Beliefs and Ceremonies of the Santeria Religion and Why Do They Have Live Chickens in Their Religious Shops? (I am not sure of the spelling but it is common among Caribbean immigrants in New York)

Best Answer - Chosen by Voters
The Afro-American folk religions emphasize magical practices designed to bring good luck to their devotees or harm to their enemies. Ceremonies often include the ritual sacrifice of animals. The religions worship the spirits of the dead, but the spirits given the names of Christian saints. This blending of beliefs allowed the Africans to retain their native faith while appearing to convert to Christianity.

The folk religions also provide an additional function, particularly in the remote sections of Haiti. Many practitioners of the religions are able to use tropical plants to relieve pain and cure illnesses. This is the only medical care available to some people.

Many people of the Caribbean profess to be Christians, but feel comfortable with the rituals of the folk religions. In 1998, Pope John Paul II visited Cuba, where he urged Catholics to reject the practice of Santeria. In addition to the Caribbean, the folk religions are also practiced in American cities with large Caribbean populations. They include New Orleans, Miami, New York City, and Los Angeles.

Chapter 7
The Letters Speak For Themselves

*Here is some of the research and letters
received by Swami Ram regarding this
subject. You may judge for your self.*

Letter #1 from Devotee - Shoma

Namaste! My name is Shoma. I am married with 2
children. I recently visited a Kali temple with my mother in
law, and the experience was very troubling. After the
distribution of prasad, they called upon the devils while
playing loud drums upon 3 men. I went to Durga. He told
me to make 7 malas to offer to Kal Bhairo Baba for 7
weeks after I explained my personal problem. I guess I
just want to know if this is just a one time thing, if I would
eventually have to do the sacrifices puja and stuff in the
future. It is not something I grew up with doing and really
don't want to get too committed. Please help

Letter #2 from Devotee – The Kali Church in Guyana

Date of Birth: 6th April 1971.
Dear Swami,
Please help me! I communicated with you before. Please email me I am constantly being violated by evil spirits for many years now. I read your articles and I found the reasons for it. My ancestral lineage was involved in animal sacrifice and some other relatives. I personally have been affected now. On Sunday 13 Feb, 2005 I visited the Eccles Durga Mandir - I was told that I have to do 9 weeks devotions to Mother Durga (big mother), and every Sunday I would have to plead to Suruj, Ganesh, Hanuman, Ganga, Kathri Matha, Sangani, Kali Matha, Bhiro Babba and Agori Baba to open up by way. I have been dreaming of some of these deities. Presently I am not well. I am looking for a good pundit to help me. Presently I am not able to find anyone to help me. What should I do? Mother Durga who came up in a spirit and to me to do these worship asked that I start Sunday coming. Could you help me or refer me to another pundit in Guyana. His telephone # and name would be helpful to me.

Reply from Swami Ram for Letters # 1 and 2

I am glad you wrote me, BE CAREFUL, THIS IS NOT A ONE TIME THING, and KALBHAIRO IS NOT GOD.....I am surprised that you do not know that Shiva , Durga, Laxmi are all the Gods together with them you do not get the problems you have now. Avoid going to the Kali church...god does not take, or require rum, cigarette and sacrifice of life. God gives life.....if you would like to stop your problems of back pain, headaches, bad dreams and blockages you need to do a cleaning and a puja to lord

Shiva in a regular temple not a kali temple....call me if you need more info 305 *** ****...leave a message I will call you back....also go to my website www.swamiram.com and look up evil spirits ...you will find plenty of information about your problem and Kal Bhairo.....
Blessings
Swami Ram

Letter #3

Dear Swami,
Thanks for the advice. I knew you would have told me that.

Firstly, over six months ago, I met a gentleman by the name of Lennox through an interfaith ministry, who studied in India and claim to have some knowledge in spiritual healing. He is a Hindu and would often counsel people who need spiritual help. I spoke to him about my experiences in life and the spiritual attacks that I have endured over time and the many rituals that were done in our generation and previous generations. He said that he knew a very knowledgeable Hindu priest who can help me. I asked him, if these people were dealing with Bhairo and Katari, he said no. He said that this place is a Mandir and no sacrifice and evil is practised [sic], and it's a placed where people go for healing often. He made arrangement for me to go on Sunday (13 Feb), and said that I must fast for 3 days, which I agree. I arrive there at 8:45am. Before I enter the Mandir, I saw a sign read "**No leather is allowed", 'You must fast for 3 day before entering the Mandir**." (I was shocked). Anyhow, we proceed to the back and waited. There were 2 buildings. From questioning, he said that one building is where people who worship lower deity go and the other those who worship higher deity. I sat there for two hours and observed people going in and taking rum and fruits and agarbathi and lighting the deities. I could not see the name of the deities. But people were busy in both building. I questioned one young man and he told me that they do not do evil, that these were like Clinics that heal people and hundreds of people were healed. He invited me in one of the buildings and showed me the statue of Jesus.

When the general service was about to start at 11:00 am, we all went in and sat on the ground facing the many deities (this was the front building - the one they refer to as those with the higher deity). There were about 130 persons there. The service began simply as regular prayers but to my amazement the drum began to beat while the pundits reading the mantra to the various deity and people dressed in yellow and red across there wait in line and began to swing their head in a frightening manner and dancing (it was scary). This went on until two women began to dance with a cane and a Neem plant in their hand. The woman was outside the building and people were going before her.

I was called outside by Lennox saying that I have to go for my treatment, at the door the man told me to pay G$200 (Guyana dollar) which I did. I told Lennox I was scared and another man heard me and said not to be scared. However, I went before a woman (claim to be Mother Durga) and she was shaking and looks terrifying with a cane and a Neem plant in her hand.

She told me that I have had many problems, can't sleep in the night, trouble upon trouble and that I am not able to marry and have children, people have been taking my money, iniquity was done to me and that I have been looking for help all over the place and have not being finding any. She said I come to the right place and that she can help me and that I must do nine weeks fast and for nine Sundays I must come to the Mandir and make devotion to Suruj, Ganesh, Hanuman, Ganga, Katari Matha, Sangani, Kali Matha, Bhairo Baba and Agori Baba. Further, she stresses after the nine weeks when I am healed that I must do her Puja or else she would punish me terribly and I must start this Sunday coming that is Sunday (Feb 20). She asked her helper with her to write it down on a paper and give it to me. Further, she said that any wishes I have I must write in on a parchment paper and put it in a black cloth. (I did not understand this). However, she said I must come back and do the 9 week puja. Then she took the Neem leaf and water and fans it around me and tells me to go. When I came out I sat waiting for the priest to read my Patra. However, he said he heard that I am a Christian. He asked if I had a bible, I said yes and I took it out and showed him. He told me to make the sign of the cross 3 times and open it. It was opened at Isaiah 30:19 and he read it. He said that is what I am going through. After he was finished I left with Lennox. In the bus he asked me if I had ever seen anything like this. I do not answer; however, I came off the bus told him it was my first experience. I even told him about what I have read on the internet (swamiram.com) and it relations to the practice of this Mandir. He told me that their practice is not evil since many people have been healed and it is the only help available to most people with my condition. It was a goose bump experience for me.

Hope to hear from you Swami. I spoke with the Guru at the Ghandi Youth Organisation [sic] and made a 1:30 appointment for tomorrow.

Name withheld for protection

Reply from Swami Ram

Hi Ms Devotee, I am sorry that you are going thru this experience....It all started with your Parents and Grandparents, and the subsequent sexual abuse you received at your early child hood from family members...In going to the Kali church....you have received additional curses and more negative karmas from there...so instead of helping you they actually made it worse....The people who are claiming to have Mother Durga in them must me questioned firstly about their own lives...If they are that powerful to bring Gods in their body then how come they themselves have many problems in their lives...Lots of these people who are shaking and trembling during possessions (by so called Godly sprits) have HEALTH PROBLEMS, FINANCIAL, FAMILY and MARRIAGE PROBLEMS OF THEIR OWN....HOW CO-ME THE GODS DO NOT HELP THEM? ANYWAY...CAN A DROWNING MAN HELP A DROWNING MAN? MAN IS ALREADY AN IMAGE OF GOD AS GENESIS STATED...God made you in his own image. All you have to do is remember that, Miss P. When our body is violated...it is because evil has taken over it and then we cannot experience the good things in life which are godly in nature...One of god's greatest gift is Love, Marriage, and Birth; when we do not have this the world cannot continue thus God will cease to exist....If the Gods allow people to worship the devil (such as Kal Bhairo, Kateri , Sangani etc) then the world will be in trouble so you will notice that ALL THOSE KALI CHURCH DEVOTEES HAVE PROBLEMS WITH CHILDREN OR ARE BEING DENIED CHILDREN BECAUSE GOD WILL NOT ALLOW THEIR GENERATION TO CONTINUE IN THIS WORLD.....God does not want to encourage evil worship...PEOPLE WHO ARE GODLY WILL HAVE A

FAMILY AND WILL PROGRESS THE WORLD...Which side should you be on?..

Anyway here is what you should do to get out of this matter, so that you can be happily married, rich and have a family that will progress the world.....

DO NOT ANTTEND ANY TEMPLES PRESENTLY UNTIL AFTER THE FASTING PERIOD IS OVER....DO NOT PERFORM ANYMORE RITUALS GIVEN TO YOU BY THE KALI PRIESTS

YOU DO NOT NEED TO BECOME A HINDU FOR THIS AS CHRIST IS TRULY THE SON OF GOD AND YOU CAN BELIEVE IN HIM AND STILL REMOVE ALL THE EVIL YOURSELF BY PRAYING EVERY NIGHT REPEATING THE 27TH PSALM, THE 128TH PSALM AND THE 102TH PSALM.

YOU need to be a vegetarian for at least 6 months...NO FISH, NO MEAT, and NO EGGS. This will detoxify your body so that whatever was given to you for eating by your ancestors as well as the church etc can be eliminated...

YOU NEED TO PLACE A SOLID PROTECTION AROUND YOUR SELF...USING A SPECIAL BATH...Bathe every evening with a special mixture of 3 limes, a pack of crushed camphor, A tablespoon of Rose water and an oz of Florida Water (sells at Satro store in GT)..All mixed in a gallon of water...do not wash it off just wipe yourself dry with a towel....this must be done for a period of 15 days before you start sleeping better....

YOU NEED TO DRINK THE FOLLOWING MIXTURE EVERYDAY FOR CLEANSING THE BODY OF EVIL: Mix one teaspoon of Nutmeg and nine cloves with head in a glass of milk and drink this every morning after reading the 27th psalm

Please start doing this from now and when I come there I will do the rest for you....Ask the priest at Gandhi

youth to do a Shiva puja for you as that is what I recommend.....
Swami Ram sends his blessings

Letter #4

Dear Swami,
Swami, I am not accepting your recommendations that Kal Bhairo is the devil. I think that he is god and I pray to him. You wrong, you do not know what you talking about. Baba Bhairo is good to me and gives me what I ask after sacrifice.

Reply from Swami Ram

Hi Resh, Jai Seeta Ram! I am sorry to see that you think this is a fight...but this is really a discussion hopefully between two intelligent people...why are you making it a fight?...you seem to be showing Kal Bhairo qualities already....Gods do not fight, they debate peacefully. However a debate like what you are asking will be unfair as you have NO knowledge of my side of the story....The only way you can qualify to have such a debate is for you to experience both sides like how I have done as shown in my books....I RECOMMEND that you stop all meat, fish and eggs for 45 days, chant OM NAMA SHIVAYA for 108 times throw away all your Black clothes(including underwear etc), sleep east-west and eat only Vegetarian foods during that time....at the end of that tell me if you did better in your Money and Prosperity...(Make sure you are fair) then let me know if you are ready for a debate.....(Make sure you bathe with some lime and camphor the first 9 days) ..
I will look forward to hear from you......

PLEASE NOTE: Your debate has already started as I will be printing your questions and my answer in the 2006 Patra books which will give everyone an opportunity to hear your views. You have my blessings and love
Swami Ram

Letter #5

Dear Swami,
I don't know where you come telling me that Kal Bhairava is no good. In India they worship her in the temples. I don't like you telling me that my god is evil.

Reply from Swami Ram

Ram Ram,
Who are you?...you are a person who does not recognize that kali is really Durga and that when we speak of worshipping kali...we are really worshipping her as Durga which includes kali as one of the forms of Durga...in her mother form she is Durga..in her destructive form she is kali...i am sorry to know that you do not know the full story....when lord Shiva had to play dead so as to stop her from destroying the Devtas too....mother kali was created by the gods to destroy at that time one of which include the demons such as Kal Bhairo (not Kal Bhairava)....the kali temples in India do not sacrifice life to god...instead they worship kali as Durga to appease her....you are completely misguided...so don't come again...come to my side of the gods.....please answer me a question...are you happily married with a family and loving husband, a big house an expensive car and lots of prosperity?...if not you are on the wrong side of the universe.....
Blessings, Swami Ram

Letter #6 – Experiences of a Devotee

Subject: Experiences
Date: Thu, 1 Apr 2004
Dear Swami
Ram Ram
Here is some of my experiences during Naurata/Ram Naumi.
> Day 1
> I played your tape, I could hear the words echoing in my head, at about 2-3 a.m I woke up to go to the bathroom and my soul was repeating the mantra, at some point in the morning Lord Krishna appear on the right side just above my eye brow as a baby.
> Day 2
>May day started out the similar way with the mantra. I could not remember everything but it was very beautiful and amazing, Lord Krishna appear when he was about 20 yrs, than appear in the form of Lord Vishnu on the right side above my eyebrow but more to left side by my nose, the sky was mild blue, somewhat like a baby blue in color, at this time many of the God's and Goddess appear. Then a massive explosion of tornado fire came out of my head, soon> after that electricity current like lightening appear in waves vertically over my forehead Latchman woke me up stating that I making noises.......
> Day 3
> During meditation someone like a Guru/Spiritual master appear, descending from above and sit before me and kept his presents above my head. I could feel his presents, I know what he look like.... I have not kept a record of everything so I am unable to tell u at what point Lord Buddah/Guru Nanak appear, but on Ram Naumi day meditation - Jesus Christ appear, he was paving the way for me widely, it was like a "V", the point where the

two strokes meet Jesus Christ was there, I was at the wide point and he was opening the way for me, on both side there was massive amount of people, they look like Jesus Christ Disciples from the way there were dress.......I did not stay too long in mediation, because I know I need guidance....Nevertheless, on this day my deepest darkest secrets was reveal before me, where I had to faced reality and find solutions......... What does blue perl mean from your tape? In the> Science of the Internal Universe how do u remove negative forces that possess as positive forces? I do have many questions, and yes we do have to meet. Latchman Told me that u will be in Canada ending of April.
> May God shower his divine blessing upon u for spreading his words and teaching and helping the people.
> God's Blessing
> Shelia

Letter # 7

A devotee sent letter about bad experiences with Hindu Priest

Reply from Swami Ram

Swami Ram
Date: Sun, 27 Jun 2004 21:40:07 -0700 (PDT)
From: "Swami Ram" <swamicharan@yahoo.com>
Subject: Re: Hindu Priests from Guyana

Hi Carmen Blessings,
I agree that some of the Pundits from Guyana are rich, and I am sure its because they have become bandits in their own time when earning that money, however by

55

comparing to India, its very different ...In India presently People hardly pray and attend temples...Only outsiders and tourists go to temples in India.....The Guyanese pundits must be credited fairly for spreading Hinduism rapidly in the USA, whether its by their Ego, their greediness or their own selfish habits...Guyanese people are the only people to have preserved the Vedic Customs and Culture in the West since India fell to the British. Today that inheritance has paid off and if the pundits from Guyana are enjoying the fruits of that legacy then so be it...As a devotee you have the choice of choosing the Pundits that are not Bandits and let the Bad pundits pay for their own Karma....
May God Bless You
Swami Ram Charran

Letter# 8 from Devotee

----- Original Message ----
From: Devotee
To: Swami Ram <swamicharan@yahoo.com>
Sent: Friday, November 17, 2006 9:03:03 AM
Subject: RE: namaste

I also noticed you have a section where you look up your birthday and it tells you the God/Goddess you are associated with, although the trend seems to just be repeating the same ones in the same order throughout the year. I always thought that these things were calculated based upon a different calendar system, and not the "English" or the one we are used to in Canada?

My next question comes after reading your biography and learning that you are indeed Guyanese. I found your pages on Kal Bhairo quite interesting and was wondering

what your view of Mother Kateri is? I know the "Indian" people call her something else along the lines of Barucha Ma and she is associated with the hijras in India; although for us Guyanese people who is Mother Kateri really?
Hope you can help.
Samantha

Reply from Swami Ram

Hi Samantha, the Hindi calendar is different, Kateri known as KOTERI in the Vedas is known as demon goddess that eats human flesh and is considered a devourer of men's sexual energy
Blessings
Swami Ram

Letter # 9
----- Original Message ----
From: Devotee
To: swamicharan@yahoo.com
Sent: Monday, November 27, 2006 12:21:00 AM
Subject: Madreveeran/Munishparam Puja

Swami ji Nmaskaram,
My forefathers have performed the above puja with sacrifice of roosters and rum/gin. Would appreciate on how we can find more details about what they were doing is correct or not. I am south Indian person living in Fiji.

Devotee
Employee Relations Manager
Human Resources Department
Shangri-la's Fijian Resort, Fiji Islands

Reply from Swami Ram

JAI SHRI KRISHNA, This puja is still considered to be a puja to the evil demons...and not godly...known as a Kal Bhairo puja, this must be stopped or else it will destroy everyone in the family eventually....to stop this follow all instructions for lord Shiva puja and stop all meat eating and alcohol drinking...avoid the color black
Swami Ram sends blessings

Letter #10

----- Original Message ----
From: Naiee P <naiee.p@tam-trinidad.com>
Sent: Thursday, October 4, 2007 12:25:30 PM
Subject: bhairo

Good day sir,
I have read your articles on Bhairo Baba, I go to a Kali temple and Bhairo Baba saved my life. You have many negative articles about him, but you don't know of people whose lives and the lives of their children have been saved by him and Kali Maa. I just wanted to ask you to talk to some people who have gotten positive help, reformed alcoholics, people's whose marriages have been saved. And I have never done sacrifice as I am Brahmin. Spirits interfere with peoples lives and others use I black magic and sometimes the only one who can help is the one you slander. You say Bhairo is not connected to Lord Shiva but my connection to Lord Shiva has grown stronger since praying to Bhairo and Bhairo Baba told me to offer Havan to lord Shiva. This is just my experience and my opinion but he des not sound like the monster you make him out to be.
Om Namah Shivay
Sita Ram

Reply from Swami Ram

Hi Naiee, I appreciate your good concern about all that I say about Bhairo, but there is confusion among Hindus between Shiva and Bhairo AND Shiva and KAL BHAIRAVA, who is a true, form of Shiva that guards the burial grounds.

I did not come up with these conclusions of Bhairo by myself, it's because of the people that came to see me that created my analysis of this whole thing about Bhairo. After seeing over 30, 000 people and after having practical experiences with their lives,.... by making them recognize that sacrifices were not a good way to pray to god and making them leave the Kal Bhairo temple , their lives were changed around 180 degrees.

I personally have no solid opinion on Bhairo, even though I never knew about him until I started helping people with their problems. As a staunch Shiva devotee, I have found that Kal Bhairo in some countries is not the Kal Bhairo you are talking about...This Bhairo they worship requires the Killing of Goats, Chicken, Fowl cocks, drinking of rum, Vibrating you body and saying that you are God, smoking of cigarettes, and becoming possessed like a lunatic. I do not call this godly worship at all, neither should you. None of our true Hindu Gods shake or vibrate...Shiva is still immovable as ever..when in meditation...... People have two paths to follow, GOOD or BAD...you can choose which one you wish to follow.....Such will be your life....meanwhile, I will continue to fight against ADARMA...which is the duty of all Hindus..to eradicate unhappiness, using knowledge to kill ignorance...this is required of every brahmin....Thru my help the very same people who could not have children now have children...thousands have been helped this way by me....Marriages that were on the verge of destruction have been rescued by me...Many who could not be healed by Doctors have been helped by me.....ALL by making them pray the proper way to the devtas.........the facts speak for themselves.....

May Lord Shiva give you the blessing to help many people with knowledge to pray the right way...
Jai Seeta Ram
Swami Ram

Letter #11 from Devotee

On Thu, Nov 26, 2009 at 4:02 AM, danny wrote:
Seeta Ram Swamiji,

I am very glad you have sent me the bath and special oil packages, I wanted to start the oil treatment but I am taking a medication presently for high cholesterol which contains fish oil, should I start the special treatment or should I stop taking the medication. I am going to start the bath from 11/29/09 and would like to start the oil treatment as well; I hope to get a response before I go about doing something wrong.

My wife has already completed the bath cycle, now she is going to start the 35 days of the mantras chanting.

Also I would like you to advise us on our son's situation, as we had discussed how to get him out of prison as soon as possible, as I had explained in my last email they are being held in deportation custody, what can I do, Since February I have followed the pundits in my area and did many pujas, when I came across your website I feel very strongly there is hope.

Please help us Swamiji.

Reply from Swami Ram

Hi Danny, Jai seeta ram
If your son's situation was that important then you should not have waited so long to start your fast...If you are hungry, would you not cook that day?...it's the same, why did you keep God's work waiting...then how can God help you quickly..I was waiting to hear from you since I sent the materials and instructions and mantras a month ago. I am very disappointed that you took so long to start the mantras and the fast.

When a man is in trouble he should waste no time in doing his prayers. The oil and any herbal stuff are like eating Bajee or dholl (spinach and split peas) it has no effect on your medication. Herbal cures have no side effects. You should be able to stop the medication when you start the natural cures I gave you. Medications are drugs that do not help you to cure anything...they just control it.

Being that you are in a bad house; the spirits have suceeded in changing your mind about starting your prayers...which I did warn you about on the phone when we spoke...Even though I warned you it still happened. The sprits in your home control your mind by creating fear. The fact that you were afraid to start godly and holy prayers means that the spirits are very much in control of your life which is why you are suffering these problems.

YOU NEED TO START IMMEDIATELY...if you wish to make your problems go away. Make sure you read the instructions properly. All meat eating needs to cease in the home and all black clothes need to be removed if you want your children to be blessed with happiness. As long as your wife does not start the prayers, your son will not get the blessings. Let me know how she felt after the powder bath. Call the Ashram on

Monday if you have any questions and speak to Marta if you wish to do so

Blessings,
Swami Ram

Letter #12 from Devotee

From: chetram narain <cnarain12@gmail.com>
To: swamicharan@yahoo.com
Sent: Tue, November 30, 2010 9:33:04 PM
Subject: Greetings Swamiji

Pranam Swami
I have been reading your book; I understand all you're saying. My guru also speak the same also, he spend some of his life in teaching those that animal life should not be taken also. Keep up the great work; I will be joining you later on to speak the truth about dharma.

Thank you very much

Letter #13 from Devotee

Hello Swami Ram,
I've been away for a while. I can't believe about the people in Guyana who were Beheaded, I truly understand now the danger of Kateri/ Kal Bhairo worship. I recently went to a kali mat temple (run by Guyanese people) and I made sure to only make my offering to Durga, Kali, Lakshmi and Saraswaty Mata (not the Kateri ma murti). I also noticed many bottles of rum when I was leaving, it made me very uncomfortable. In regards to my problem, I don't know if you're still in Toronto. Something in my soul tells me that my problem is a result of Karma, is there any way you can give me a karma burning

mantra or Kundalini mantra I can start doing jaap with? I think that Durga Ma is daily giving me the strength to deal with this, but she is also telling me that this will be a personal battle. I don't plan to turn to anybody else but you regarding this.

Thank You

Reply from Swami Ram

Durga Miracle in Guyana- It's really a Warning!!

I have received a lot of Emails on this so here is what I think. Certain questions have to be asked first and then answered. Why that specific Mandir? Why also only the kali Church in Port Mourant, Guyana?...Why only those mandirs where Kali is worshipped with animal sacrifice?...Why only where the priests there perform Kal-Bhairo worship with Rum and cigarettes?...Why has it not happened in regular Mandirs where animal sacrifices are not performed?...The fact that Saraswaty is crying can only be a warning to the members of such temples and to all of impending danger ahead!!!.

We all have to wait and see whether the devotees who received the TIKA from Mother Durga got some great blessings in their life. Drawing on the experience in the past what has happened to places like New Orleans, Haiti, Pakistan, Iraq, Iran, Indonesia and Fiji where sacrifices are performed a lot; the result has been: Earthquakes, Tsunamis, and hurricanes that have destroyed these places severely. I can only say that as we come to the end of Kaliyug in 2012 these warnings which include the drinking of milk by Ganesh and others during Pitri Paksh (only) are telling us that we should prepare for possible destruction to those people and places where they are praying to Demons as God by offering life of animals in exchange for blessings (which are temporary in nature).

The Miracle Of Durga Is Not A Miracle But A Warning!!!

The Miracle of Durga is not a miracle, but a warning for Guyana, Suriname, Trinidad and others. As you may closely observe, the Saraswaty Murti was crying, and the Sindoor is falling from the eyes of the Murti of Durga. Not only that the Sindoor is falling from the eyes wherever Kal–Bhairo and Kateri pujas are performed which included not only the Kali churches in Williamsburg and Lusignan, Corentyne, etc., but also some of the private homes of devotees of the Kali Temples. **IT'S THE CRYING OF ALL THE MOTHERS**. Why is it that the sindoors are not happening this way in regular temples and the other murtis (male) are not giving out the sindoors or the tears? Does that mean that all other pundit temples are not holy?

Remember as I always said in the past that, the 21st century is the century of the female. Not only that, the beginning of the end of Kaliyuga is about to happen in 2012. The Goddesses are sad as many people are going to face destruction because of the fact that they have been offering sacrificed animals' lives to Mother...**Mother Does Not Accept Death...Mother Gives Life!!..Only Lord Yamraj Accepts Death**...The fact that this is happening in Guyana only and possibly later in Suriname, indicates that those countries are about to face some disasters in about one year. Remember I predicted the Guyana Flood that happened in 2006, on channel 6 with CN Sharma on his show, even *though it had not happened in one-hundred (100) years. These signs that we are seeing, forecast that Guyana will be facing more disasters in another year from now which is 2012.*

For many years Swami Ram has been talking about the wrong way some priests have been performing Hinduism in Guyana, Suriname and Trinidad. Pt Rudra Sharma of the Radha Krishna Mandir is one of the Pundits who claimed that Kal-Bhairo is a God and challenged Swami Ram on a Channel 6 debate, but did not show up for the debate when Swami Ram got there. The debate never took place. Another debate took place in the Devi Mandir in Canada where Swami Ram was consulted by Vishnu Sookar, President of the temple, as to whether a Kal–Bhairo Murti should be installed in the Temple. Swami Ram asked Vishnu Sookar to find out from reputed priests and Swamis located in India, Trinidad, Guyana and England as well as the USA and no one could come up with a proper answer about the validity of Kal-Bhairo worship. Many of the pundits confused the form of Lord Shiva called Kal-Bhairava with this rum drinking and cigarette smoking deity called Kal-Bhairo. After extensive research Mr. Sookar, still the president declined the installation of the Kal-Bhairo Murti in Canada's Devi Mandir and concluded that they do not need any deity who drinks Rum, smokes cigarette and accepted dead animals as its offering. It is sad to know that our uneducated pundits are still carrying this tradition of ancient devil worship brought to Guyana by the early Dutch settlers and African tribal slaves connected to Voodoo and Santeria, etc. These Kali temples are totally misguiding and are looked upon by Modern Spiritualist in the west as Black magic practices. As True Hindus we should all try to eliminate this type of worship which is similar to Qurbani etc. **Hinduism is a religion and**

science of non-violence against all life including those of animals.

If you need proof of what Swami Ram is saying, look at what happen to Haiti, Iran, Iraq, Indonesia, Islamabad, Israel (where Christ was sacrificed), New Orleans (Voodoo). The Earthquakes, the Tsunamis, The hurricanes and the floods and the wars are only happening where sacrifices have been made to the so-called deities referred to as Gods.

Notice also that when Zarkawi was chopping off people's heads on TV the earthquake came to Islamabad, Pakistan; and the Tsunami came before in Indonesia killing many Muslims. If this is not a message from God and the universe then what is?

What PT Rudra Sharma and other pundits need to realize is that there is still time to correct the problems we Hindus face in this new century and take this warning from Durga as a signal that he should encourage the pundits in Guyana to cease all sacrificial ceremonies and promote **Hindu Dharma** *as the true science of religion that promotes continuity of the universe. I knew his father, Pt. Gowkaran Sharma, and I met his Mother and they both admired my effort to get Hinduism recognized as a True Scientific religion of the world. I hope that he will help me also in this effort.*

Namashkaar! (I see the god in you)

Letter #14 from Devotee

rayj950@aol.com

Very good Swami, I think this is so true what you're saying, I second you on this. I also hope that the Pundits out there will support you on your good work, and help to make this world a better place.

Jai seeta ram,
Raymon

Letter #15 from Devotee

Anjanie Badhwa

Very true. Nice to see the word: Namashkaar. That's how we greeted people back home - usually hands clasp and a little bow. But it was translated as "I bow to the divine in you."

Letter #16 from Devotee

On Sun, Oct 24, 2010 at 11:57 AM, Sita Prosoud> wrote:

Dear Swamiji
Sita Ram and trust you are in the best of health with Bhagwan's grace.
It is indeed a blessing to receive your e-mail on the recent development in Guyana. My mind is just

wavering. Once again thank you - I think you should come to Guyana and do a Satsangh.

Do have a blessed day, Sita

Reply from Swami Ram

To: <u>Sita Prosoud</u>
Sent: Sunday, October 24, 2010 1:31 PM
Subject: Re: [Swami Ram's Official Site] DURGA MIRACLE IN GUYANA- its really a warning!!

Hi Sita
JAI SEETA RAM
I am planning to be there in November if all goes well...
Swami Ram sends blessings

Letter #17 from Devotee

--- On **Wed, 5/28/08, sadia song < >** wrote:
From: sadia song < >
Subject: Drinking Problem with my Husband
To: <u>heendu@yahoo.com</u>, <u>swamiram@yahoo.com</u>
Date: Wednesday, May 28, 2008, 1:55 PM

Dear Swami Ram,

I recently watched your show while you were in Guyana a few days ago. Until that day I thought all hope was lost for me. So I am contacting you with hope that my letter will reach you and that I can finally solve the problems I am having with my husband which seems to have gotten worst over the last two weeks.

You see I met him in 1997 Youghist Singh born on 21st March 1979. He was much younger then, we met at a night spot and have been together until now. Not to say that it was all smooth sailing we did have problems along the way. And I must say a lot has also changed for us too and not for the better but let me begin now with how it all started.

We dated on and off for about a year after we met then I migrated to the US. I stayed there for another year then moved back to Guyana due to his consistent begging me to come back to Guyana to live with him. I did the first few months were ok then the changes began, which I overlook now since he was young I thought he was not ready to settle down.

During our period of living together we moved into his parents first home that they lived in, and we were never happy there (Mon Re Pos). You see his parent (dad) normally does a Durga work every 3 years. The Jhandi went well but the sacrifice work (killing of the goat) was done on the Monday and caused a lot of problems, first we fought, then his dad got angry with the mother and beat her up really bad. This is how they lived most of the time when they were together in the same house I was told. His mom had to go out for him and began to do the Landmaster work (rum, bread & cheese, cigarettes, two white candles) she said this was to calm him down when he drank. Now my husband which is her son, he drank a lot, stayed out a lot, had a lot of women friends, we fought most of the time, hardly spoke to each other after the work they did. Eventually we separated I went my way he went back home where his parents lived. We still continued to see each other on and off and we eventually ended up back together now at his home we are still together now but with more problems. His drinking has caused him to become very sickly, he two weeks ago had a seizure from a fall he had. From that day his drinking has increased, he lost a lot of weight he is almost skin and bone now; he falls down a lot and hits his head. He even messes himself at times in his drunken state. I feel so sorry for him I have tried everything I can to make him stop, tablets to help stop alcoholism, doctors to help, and recently to a pundit which he agreed to while he was drunk but I can never get him to commit to any long term help since he goes back to his old habits only days after seeking help. I went to a woman for help, heard she was really good but the bathe is going to be expensive since he does not work I cannot afford it at the moment I am the only working person in the home. I also want to know I am doing the right thing and not waste what little money I have. He also once told me he went to someone who told him he needed to bathe but he never went back, he even visited someone in Suriname. I tried to tell his mom what we should do but they do not support me since no action was ever taken. I also queried about if they are involved in Kal Bhairo work since the woman whom I went to asked me "who does Kal Bhairo work" and since I had no idea I told her I don't know. But what I do know is when his parents lived with us his mom normally does this full moon work and since she moved out I continued it. However since the year began I stopped it on and off since I no longer want to continue it and I do not fully understand what I am doing. The last time I did it was in our back yard before the moon rose.

Now after I saw your show on TV I visited your website and I read all about Kal Bhairo now I am really scared. I am kindly seeking your advise on how I can help my husband to get better also and myself. We do not need riches all I need is for us to work be happy and healthy. Why I included myself is because at times I feel I am having sex in my sleep which happens a lot, I also cannot stand sleeping with my husband sometimes which is strange because I do love him a lot. I pray to god, I pray at the altar in my home and it's always the same desire for my husband to get better and stop drinking he is so young to have his life snuffed out which makes me sad. So please Swami-ji help us.

Reply from Swami Ram
From: Swami Ramcharran <heendu@yahoo.com>
To: sadia song
Cc: swamicharan@yahoo.com
Sent: Thu, May 29, 2008 3:45:09 PM
Subject: Re: Drinking Problem with my Husband

Hi, Jai Seeta ram

I am very happy that you watched the show in Guyana I hope it was very helpful to you in many ways. Please go to the website www.swamiram.com and look up your birthday where it says "check you yearly forecast". You will be able to put in your birth date and know how the year 2008 is for you now. You will also be able to read about your Ishta Devta predictions. Please also do not hesitate to join our free membership. Joe Satro will be able to help you also by providing you with my books and Patras about your life.

If you need a personal reading, I will be coming back to Guyana in November of 2008, to promote your **Personal Ishta Devta Handbook For 2009**, *which tells you about your life using your exact birthday. You can call Joseph Satro in Guyana to set up a meeting with me, when I come. His phone number is on the web site. If you are in Trinidad, you need to contact Howard Sawh to set up a meeting in Trinidad around the same time. Howard's number is 1 868 712 5343*

I will check the information you have submitted to me and in a few days will reply you. Make sure I have the correct name as it is on your passport or id and your correct date of birth and time.

Please remember if you are eating red meat such as Duck and Goat, Beef or Pork, your life can never be corrected and your predictions will not be good. So if you want your life to change you have to give up those meats. Chicken & fish are not so bad. You should also fast for a period of 45 days and avoid the color Black completely in your life forever. That means all clothes including underwear and Bra, etc. Black shoes are ok. Be sure to read about DEE PUJA and KAL BHAIRO PUJA on the website. These are wrong prayers and can affect your life very badly with bad luck. If your parents are doing these then definitely you will have marriage and love problems.

You can order any books about your life from Heendu Learning Center. You can also send you donations directly from our website. Your donations are appreciated as it will help with my trips to Guyana and elsewhere to spread this wonderful science.

With blessings, great love and respect I welcome you to VEDIC SCIENCE OF LIFECODES
Swami Ram Charran

Letter #18 from Devotee

From: sadia song
Subject: Re: Drinking Problem with my Husband
To: heendu@yahoo.com
Date: Friday, September 10, 2010, 4:33 PM

Dear Swami Ram,

It has been a while since I have sent this email in regards to my husband. Just to let you know he died on 22nd June, 2010.
I just would like to know if and when you would next be in Guyana I still have some unanswered questions regarding his death.
I need advise if you have any.

Thank you,

Chapter 8
Confusion between God and Devil

Reverse Energy in the Chakras or Kundalini

I n Hindu mythology Lord Vishnu, our Hindu God or the Cosmic Universe, rests on the thousand hooded snake or serpent energy called Sheshnaag. This is called Serpent Energy because all energy travels in a wave like form and so the wavelike motion is comparable to the movement of a snake. The Bible states that God created Man in His own image. Thus all elements contained in the Universe are also contained in the Human Body. The foundation of the universe in Hinduism known is known as the Sheshnaag or Kundalini Energy and the human Sheshnaag is represented by the skull and backbone that provides support to our universe - our human body.

The skull represents the head of the Serpent, the spine represents the body of the Serpent and the tailbone represents the tail of the serpent energy. In the human body, the tailbone of the spinal column comes to rest in the area of the Muladhara Chakra in which resides the sleeping serpent energy called the Kundalini. In a scientific sense, this Kundalini can be imagined as a dormant ball of nuclear energy that is kept safely housed in a protective casement of lead and heavy water. If that protective casing should break suddenly as it is done in an atomic bomb, it will release a massive explosion of nuclear energy and cause untold destruction such as the one the world experienced at Hiroshima or at the Chernobyl nuclear facility in Russia. (Similarly, if this Kundalini energy is aroused suddenly in the human body without proper guidance from a Holy Guru, it can cause untold destruction in the human body system and lead to insanity, loss of sexuality, depression, homosexuality and more.

Normal Kundalini awakening occurs as a person reaches adolescence, and then peaks at age twenty-one. This serpent coiled at the base of the spine is comparable to a coiled spring slowly unwinding its energy until the age of 21 is reached. Between birth and age 14, if the unwinding of this energy is interfered with through abuse or molestation, then this will be considered a sudden or rude awakening of the Kundalini.

One of the most dangerous aspects of the sudden awakening of this Kundalini energy is called the Reverse Kundalini. In this state, the head of the serpent switches place with its tail and causes a severe disruption within the human body systems. The person with a Reverse Kundalini usually acts outside the norms of society and are quite often labeled as 'crazy'.

This article will discuss the causes of Reverse Kundalini, illustrate the practical life impacts of Reverse Kundalini and describe ways to manage and eventually correct the severe trauma caused by Reverse Kundalini.

Case History

In September 2003, a worried mother came to seek the help of Sri Swami Ram at the New York location of the

Heendu Learning Center. She explained that her son Paul is refusing to consummate the marriage with his new wife Maya, and that this was causing severe tension and embarrassment in the family. As Swami-ji dug deeper into the case, he found out that when the boy was born, he was on the verge of death. A Pujarie (priest) advised that if the parents performed a ritual to Kal Bhairo, the child could be saved. In their ignorance about Kal Bhairo and the devastating effects that any association with this Devil can have on a family, the parents agreed and they sacrificed the life of a pig in order to save the child. The child did not die but when he grew up to be about nine years old, Rick, a friend of the father began to sexually abuse the young lad. This abuse continued until the young man fled to the United States.

Paul started a new life in New York City but his sexual drive became so intense that he had no choice but to find a partner to relieve himself. Usually he will masturbate himself more than five times per day because of this intense desire for sex. He sought out anyone who was willing to have sex with him. Since it was very difficult to approach women at that young age, he sought out male friends who had similar desires. He became very active in his sexual life with other boys from his old community and later also, in the Gay community in New York.

In 2002, the parents used their influence to force the young man to go to Guyana and marry a girl in an arranged ceremony. Paul went along with his parents' wishes. While there, his sexual urges got the better of him and he had sex with his new bride. He returned to the United States and filed the proper immigration papers to bring his new wife to live with him in New York. However, while his wife papers were in the process and she was waiting in Guyana, he soon returned to his old way of life in the Gay community in New York. When he learnt that his new bride became pregnant as a result of his sexual liaison with her, Paul insisted that she must secure an abortion before she immigrated to the United States. She bent to his wishes and aborted the fetus. In 2003, she joined Paul in New York and in the five months that they were living together, he did not touch her in a loving or sexual way. The girl complained to her mother-in-law who ended up at the Heendu Learning Center to obtain a Jyotish reading from Swami-ji that would detail the future of Paul's life and his marriage.

The Kal Bhairo Effect on Paul

The spirit of the pig that was sacrificed when Paul was born became very angry because it was sold to the Devil called Kal Bhairo in exchange for Paul's life. The vengeance of that spirit against Paul was severe and as he grew, the angry spirit sought revenge. With guidance from Kal Bhairo, that angry spirit continuously influenced the subtle mind of the friend of Paul's father who was a trusted family member with unlimited access to the growing child. With the angry spirit as guide, the predator soon embarked on his mission of destruction against the defenseless body of young Paul.

In ordinary loving sexual encounters, the energy splits into two segments in the region of the Muladhara Chakra and is slowly released. When there is a vicious sexual attack however, during which the Devilish perpetrator's sole aim is to carry out its vengeance and punish its victim, the cumulative energy in the region of the Muladhara Chakra does not get an opportunity to be released slowly but simply explodes. In extreme cases, this causes the Kundalini of the victim to open and release its own energy in a mighty implosion. The Kundalini energy turns inside-out as it shoots up the narrow passage of the Sushumna carrying the energy-tail of the snake towards the energy-head and bringing the head to where the tail used to be.

Now the energy-snake or human Sheshnaag is turned upside down. The mouth of the snake is at the region of the Muladhara Chakra. It is a scientific fact that a real snake will hiss, snap and bite its prey viciously. So too in this way, we are able to imagine the sexual impulses of someone with a Reverse Kundalini. Their sexual appetite becomes voracious. When they do have sex with others, they tend to be rough and can become vicious at times. This was the effect that the reversal of the Kundalini had on Paul.

But why did the angry spirit of the pig become attracted to Rick, the friend of Paul's father? The simple answer is because Rick had some bhandana (bondage ties) with Kal Bhairo. In all likelihood, he was a devotee of the Dark Force who performed animal sacrifices to propitiate the Devil. He was in a good position to access the growing child and would be able to act when the time was right.

Why Paul and Maya got married to each other? Again because of some bhandana that existed between them. In this case, unlike the case with Rick, Swami-ji had access to Maya and thus was able to determine that her parents used to perform Katari sacrifices. These are sacrifices to Kal Bhairo in his form as the demon called Katari. God tends to bring Kal Bhairo descendants together so that they can destroy each other and so the worship of the devil will not be propagated. Most families who practice Kal Bhairo sacrifices eventually face extinction.

How to Correct the Reverse Kundalini

A Reverse Kundalini can be returned to normal but this can be done only by a holy person who is highly advanced in the Vedic philosophy. Quite often it is a lengthy process that begins with an education of what has actually happened to the individual. Medical science simply labels such individuals as crazy and treats them with various forms of medication that helps to keep them in a state of quiet stupor. However, a highly transcended Guru is able to initiate the process of correction by first helping the individual understand what is really happening to them then begin the normalization process by first performing a Shiva Vraat. Once this is done, a Guru-Disciple relationship begins between the Holy person and the subject and through the positive influence of the sacred energies from the Guru, the subject will slowly begin to heal and return to a normal life style.

Chapter 9
Should Prayers Be Performed To Evil Spirits Such As Kal Bhairo, Satan, Gins And Others?

The one resounding question that I hear people ask Swami-Ji over and over again is, "Why are there so many problems in my life?" They then go on to relate their various illnesses, problems with spouses, problems with children, problems with finances and numerous other life challenges that they may be facing at the time. Although Swami-Ji sees thousands of different people every year, he has found that there is always a pattern or trend to the nature of the suffering. And this is because the causal factors almost always are linked to the circumstances during conception, pregnancy and birth; unrighteous ways of living; effects of bhutas (ghosts) in the home; quality and types of meals that people eat; involvement with pujas for Dee or Kal Bhairo.

The sacred Hindu text - The Bhagavad Gita - states that when dharma [righteousness] gives way to adharma [unrighteousness], Bhagwan as Cosmic Consciousness will embody Himself and take birth to rescue the planet. Bhagwan, God, Cosmic Consciousness or whatever name we choose to call the Creator, Preserver and Destroyer of the universe represent the positive forces in our lives in this material existence.

Bhagavad Gita Ch 4. V.7
Yadaa-Yadaa Hi Dharmasya//Glaanir Bhavati Bharata Abhyutthaanam Adharmasya//Tadaa Tmaanam Srjaamy Aham.

Transliteration: Whenever there is decay of dharma and rise of adharma, then I embody Myself, 0 Bharata. In this verse, the Lord [Rrsna] is saying to His devotee [Arjuna] that when dharma which is conducive to man's growth and progress gives way to adharma which prevents man's evolution, then the Cosmic Intelligence will embody itself in human form. [E.g.: Lord Vishnu embodied Himself in human form as Sri Rama]. There is so much violence and human suffering in the world. Everyday the media exploits this to its fullest and the constant bombardment has had a profound negative impact on my mind to the extent that a few years ago I decided to stop watching television or reading the newspapers. In this way I was able to calm the mind through meditation and practiced mindfulness in order to cope with my life in the everyday world. Like I, millions of people across the globe are finding inner peace through the practices of yoga and meditation. Perhaps this burgeoning practice of yoga and meditation at the grassroots level is one of the corrective forms that Bhagwan has chosen to combat adharma and influence dharma in the world?

Pious Hindus, who follow the dharmic path, adore, meditate upon and propitiate the positive energies of Hindu Deities by performing the 16 upacaras as detailed in the Rag Veda [RV10.90]. Such devotees receive the blessings of the Gods and their lives become fulfilled in many positive ways so that they enjoy good health,

81

prosperity and true happiness that almost everyone seeks.

The opposite or negative forces exist in the universe as well. By twisting certain of the sacred propitiatory rites and rituals, a sacred precept can become a practitioner of sorcery or devil worship and honor the negative forces. One of the forms of devil worship is the performance of Dee or Kal Bhairo rituals. Once this is done to the satisfaction of the negative force or devil, the person will usually get their requests granted. Quite often this reward is in the form of material riches. Material riches could take the form of destructive money or positive money for the benefit of others. Laxmi is the bestower of positive wealth which will help the world to progress whereas the devil will produce negative wealth which will affect the health and progress of the family units. We already know that the opposite of Maha Laxmi is Kala Laxmi - destructive wealth. So people begin to believe that they are doing the right thing. But think about it for a moment. When honoring the negative force, a person has to do things backwards. For instance, the practice has to:

- be done in a lonely place
- be performed at night
- involve the sacrifice of live animals
- Worshippers must face south - the region of Yamraj- Lord of the dead.
- the mantra verses must be spelled backwards
- sometimes the ritual is performed to hurt others because of covetousness or greed
- the 'priests' who carry out such practices always seem to be unhappy
- the people who 'worship' in this negative way seem to sneak round and hide from God fearing people

- their features appear darker and ugly

How can practices with such backward performance be a correct or good practice? Yes, it does give material riches. But this will last only for a limited period of time. Then more sacrifices must be performed or else many things begin to go wrong with the person's life and the new-found wealth may soon begin to disappear. In the meantime, while to all outward appearances the person seems to be happy and prosperous, their personal lives get turned inside out. For instance:

- the husband may become impotent
- he may begin to drink or smoke a lot
- he may get severe back pain
- the womb of the wife may become twisted
- she may suffer with severe belly pain
- she may suffer with back pain as well
- children may begin to go astray and drop out of school
- they may turn to alcohol, cigarettes, promiscuous sex, drugs or other vices
- the family begins to spend more and more money on health care
- spend more to perform more sacrifices and rituals
- spend on lawyers to help them with various court matters which begin to surface from nowhere

So where are the real rewards of receiving riches by performing sacrificial rituals to the negative forces such as Dee or Kal Bhairo? Where are the benefits of doing a Land Master Puja or Rum Puja? Where are the benefits of sacrificing the innocent life of that chicken, goat or pig to feed the devil? How can any amount of money compensate for the pain, hurt and sorrow for becoming involved in the forces of darkness? And do you really think this is the end to your sufferings? Let us see what happens to some of the female members in the family:

- unable to sleep well at night
- menstrual period may be frequently late
- suffer severe cramps and pains during menstruation
- see whitish or creamish streaks amidst the menstrual blood
- may feel very sexually excited during the night
- do not want to have physical relations with husband or husband is not able to perform
- may dream of having sexual intercourse
- may 'feel' that someone or something is having intercourse with them during the night
- are always tired after waking up in the mornings
- unexplainable black and blue marks on their legs or inner thighs

Is this degree of suffering really worth the material riches? Is it worth the karmic suffering you ordain upon your children, grand-children and great-grandchildren down the road? What is the answer? Stop the CAUSE for the problems. Stop performing sacrificial rituals. If you never knowingly conducted such a ritual, find out if your parents or grand-parents performed them. Find out if your priest knowingly or un-knowingly invited the dark forces into your life by giving the tenth plate to Kal Bhairo during your Durga Puja. The rightful husband of Durga is Shiva and he should be the one to get the tenth plate. Please note that there are no known facts to confirm that Durga has a brother called Kal Bhairo. Swami-Ji or any other holy person with true knowledge of the ancient scriptures will be able to help you. Begin to propitiate the positive energies in the universe [Gods]. Although your rewards may appear to be realized more slowly, you and your progeny will reap the benefits of good health, prosperity and true happiness in this material life. You will be able to live in that comfortable home; you will be able to drive that expensive car; you will see your children become educated; you will enjoy good health and prosperity.

Why Is Hanuman Puja So Important On Saturdays?

Let us look at Hindu Mythology and The Story of the Hanuman Puja to see how happiness and prosperity can be invited into our lives. Those of us who are older will remember that Guyana was at one time referred to as the 'Bread Basket of the Caribbean'. When we look back to that time we see some very revealing trends. The pundits were from the older generation who knew the ancient scriptures and were able to conduct the puja rituals in the proper way to please the Gods. One such puja - the Hanuman Puja - commonly referred to as JHANDI - was conducted regularly on Saturdays all across the coastline of that happy and prosperous nation. Let us examine the reason that the Hanuman Puja grants Happiness and Prosperity when conducted on a Saturday.

The story begins with Narad Muni who is the astrologer of the Gods in Hindu mythology. In this capacity he has to remain a Bramhcharya - one who has taken the vow of celibacy. One day he saw a beautiful girl and fell in love with her. Now a Bramhcharya is not supposed to get married but he was so madly in love that he decided to forget his vows of celibacy. So he went to Lord Vishnu and Lord Shiva and told them of his great love. A swayamvara (a celebration where young people meet to choose their marriage partners) was arranged and the young men all lined up to see which one of them will be selected to be the husband of the beautiful damsel. Through divine intervention, Vishnu and Shiva arranged it so that when the girl looked at Narad, she will

85

perceive his face as that of a monkey. In the meanwhile, Vishnu stood in the lineup along with the other young men and happened to be the one who was chosen. After He was garlanded by the pretty damsel, Vishnu and Shiva were laughing at the joke they played on Narad. Just about the same time, Narad happened to see his reflection in a pool of water. He became very angry and cursed Lord Vishnu that someone will steal his wife. He then cursed Shiva that He will only be able to help Lord Vishnu in the form of a monkey. Later when the world was under threat of destruction by the Rakshas under the powerful leadership of Ravana, Lord Vishnu incarnated Himself as Lord Rama to save the world from destruction. His wife accompanied Him in material form as the beautiful Mother Sita. Because of Narad's curse, Ravana stole Sita and Lord Shiva had to incarnate himself as the monkey- faced Hanuman to save Mother Sita from Lanka. As Hanuman was making his way into Lanka to rescue Sita, he saw Shane Devta [the planet Saturn] tied up by Ravana and lying face down. Now Shane is the one who takes note of how people manage their prosperity. When people abuse their wealth, show-off, and are 'briga' or boastful, Shane will look at them and give them a Shane Gra. Once this happens, their money will begin to disappear and the family will begin to suffer for a period of seven-and-a-half years. So when Shane recognized Hanuman and begged to be released from the bondage of the powerful Ravana, Hanuman replied, "Once I release you and you look at me, I will get your Gra." Shani promised, "No. Anyone who performs your Puja on my day [Saturday] will not be affected by me." So Hanuman released Shane and his promise came into being.

Hindus, who knew the ancient scriptures and the mysticism in the meanings behind the stories, knew the proper rituals to perform in order to achieve success in this material life. As the older pundits died, a lot of the knowledge disappeared with them. Not many modem pundits had time to research the scriptures and quite a few got caught up in the dark side of the rituals because of covetousness, greed and get-rich-quick desires of their followers. The more that such dark practices were followed, the more people began to follow them. The more such practices became common, the more they became 'truth' in the minds of the people. The dark practices thus became a vicious circle of devil worship for the gain of wealth which may result in more suffering and more worship and sacrifices to ease the suffering. The second and third generations begin to suffer because of the sinful actions of the parents. Where will all this end? What should we do to end this cycle of dark practices in the Hindu communities of Guyana the Caribbean?

To quote an expression which is featured in the writings of Sugita Gempaku who was instrumental in bringing an understanding of the internal body parts to ancient Dutch medicine: memboku or aratameru. Translated into English, the meaning becomes: changing one's outlook. We have to change our outlook. We have to change the way we 'see' things in our practice and malpractice of Hindu rituals within the Guyana and Caribbean communities at home and abroad. And we have to do this from the perspective of knowledge.

Paulo Freire, a prominent Brazilian writer and educator, reiterates in his writings that knowledge is the path to liberation and freedom. He describes liberating education as dialectic, involving both action and reflection while not privileging either. In our society, it is very unlikely that an uneducated, unskilled, poor villager or inner-city dweller will ever be in a position to get the attention of community leaders, authority figures, politicians or religious practitioners. To get such attention and to cause change, the voice must come not from a position of subservience but from a position of dominance. Such firmness of foundation has to emerge thorough knowledge and confidence fostered through an understanding of the inner self and an understanding of the Hindu scriptures. We want to encourage those who have acquired the knowledge to become teachers, mentors and role models for others like themselves. Thus when a practicing pundit performs a wrong or demonic ritual which invites Dee or Kal Bhairo into your life, you as the yagman or worshipper will know to educate the 'pundit'. This will have a ripple effect in the world of the punditam who will now be forced to become educated in practicing the rituals to worship God and cease and desist from inadvertently or intentionally practicing sorcery or devil worship. Through the correct knowledge, our Guyanese and Caribbean 'family' will be able to get rid the effects of Dee and Kal Bhairo - the spirit - from their lives.

Chapter 10
Confusion among Hindus between Kal Bhairo and Kal Bhairava (A Form of Shiva)

T urn left at the next intersection," Swami-ji said. I guided the car into the left-hand turn lane. I waited calmly until the oncoming traffic was clear before making the left turn from Biscayne Blvd. onto NE 28 Street. This was Miami on a warm April afternoon. I did not know what to expect for this was my very first visit to what Swami-ji often affectionately refers to as the 'Miami Ashram'. From our discussions over the past year, I had formed a mental impression of the Ashram but never shared my vision with anyone. Within seconds of making the left turn, I set eyes on the glistening waters of Biscayne Bay. A short right hand turn brought us unto the Ashram grounds and I parked diagonally in a spot close to the entrance of the rear gate. I allowed the building and the perimeter of the property to merge with my peripheral vision of the waters of the Bay. I felt an immense urge to leap out and dance, for I was very happy. The location for the Jyotish Ashram and Hindu Learning Center was ideal. There is no doubt in my mind that this was all made possible through the divine intervention of the Devtas. Swami-ji knew of my inner joy but in his typical style, I was only permitted minimal time

89

to bask in the bliss of the moment. There was still much to be done.

"We have to clarify the difference between Kala Bhairava and Kal Bhairo," he stated as he began to exit the vehicle. "I have been receiving a number of e-mails since our articles on Kal Bhairo were posted on the website. The jest of the e-mails tells me that there is some confusion in people's minds about the difference between the two."

I remained silent. I knew what would be coming next and I never want to distract Swami-ji from his thoughts.

"It is not strange that the name of the evil spirit known as Kal Bhairo bears a close resemblance to the spelling of Kala Bhairava. You see, Kala Bhairava is one of the forms of Lord Shiva. In this form, Shiva the Lord of Time is the guardian of the burial grounds and crematorium sites. He guards the perimeter of these locations for one principal reason. "

Although I wanted to ask a question at this point, I did not want to interrupt the thoughts of my mentor. He continued, "He guards the perimeter of the burial grounds and crematorium sites in order to protect the living from the dead. The spirits of the dead are kept within the perimeter of the cemetery so that they are not able to harm the innocent living people as they go about their daily lives. But there are certain people who like to play with spirits. They know how to capture the spirits and make them work. And of course spirits are miserable disembodied beings. They long for some action. They love to poke fun at the living and will do so at the bidding of their masters. But I keep warning you that you must never attempt to play with spirits. They can destroy you very quickly."

"Are you saying that the people who like to capture these evil spirits refer to them as Kal Bhairo in order to give others the impression that they are dealing with a form of Lord Shiva called Kala Bhairava?" I interrupted.

"Exactly," my mentor replied as he clapped his hands in glee. "People are very protective of their little area of expertise. They are very devious and will stop at nothing to make money. They want the physical senses to enjoy all the material things and so they don't care if they fool innocent people into believing that they are invoking Lord Shiva when in fact they are invoking the devil. They will never tell the people about the severe consequences of dealing with evil spirits. And people simply go along with the pujaris or what I call the Princes of the Dark, because they believe that they are dealing with Lord Shiva in the form of Kala Bhairava."

"If we take off the letter 'a' from the end of 'Kala' we get 'Kal'. And if we replace the 'ava' from 'Bhairava' with the letter 'o', we get 'Bhairo'. Quite an ingenuous plan on the part of the swindlers who want to make money from innocent people," I surmised.

"Some of these people are not so innocent. They are plain greedy. Someone with knowledge of the dark side tells them that they can get rich. And what do these people do? They agree to do anything. They do not ask if it is dangerous or not. All they think about is the money. People love riches. They think that riches bring happiness. But once they get sucked in, there is very little they can do in order to get themselves out. Every year the pujaris tell them that they have to perform rituals."

"But the pujaris do not tell them that the rituals are performed to pacify the desires of the evil spirits I bet," I countered.

"Can you find an honest thief?" my mentor asked. Without waiting for my response, he continued, "You see, when Lord Shiva guards the perimeter of the burial grounds, the spirits must get His permission before they can leave. And spirits can get leave from 12.00 midnight.

But under the strict rules imposed by the Lord of Time, they must return before the time of Brahma Muhurta. This is the early morning period just before dawn when the living beings start to come awake. The reason for this curfew or restriction to the hours of the dark is to avoid any commingling with the living beings and the spirits of the dead."

"That is why parents warn the youths who like to stay out late that they must make sure that they are in the house before 12.00 midnight?" I asked.

"Children and young people have no right to be outdoors at such late hours. However, because of the modern world that we live in, people have to be out of the house at all hours. But the trick is that when they come in, they must enter the house backwards. This shows any spirit that is following the person that they are not allowed to enter that house. I know," he continued," you want to know how disembodied spirits can harm living people."

It was almost as if he could read my mind at times. So I humbly nodded and allowed my mentor to continue.

"We are all spirits residing in a shell. This shell is our human body. Because of our five senses of sight, hearing, touch, smell and taste we are able to perceive the environment around us. We are able to perform actions. Some of those actions require the strength of bones and muscle. If we want to push this glass across the table-top for instance, we have to first think about the action. Only after the thought that we are able to extend our hand, tense the right muscles and give the glass a good push so that it moves across the table like this." My guru demonstrated with the glass that he was holding and slid the glass across the table before he continued.

"Remember that I first had to think about the action before I could perform it. Now when the body dies, the spirit-soul continues to live on in accordance with the karmas performed during its lifetime in the human form.

People who performed righteous actions will achieve Moksha immediately. People who perform both good and bad actions will first have to suffer for a period in hell for their bad actions before transcending into the heavenly realm. The others who commit mainly bad actions are stuck in limbo land. So they are guarded by Lord Shiva as they suffer for their wrongs. Do you really think that if the spirit-soul in the human form thought bad things and did bad actions when it was alive in the human body that it will automatically change when it loses the body in death?" I knew that this was a rhetorical question so I did not even attempt to answer.

"Of course not," he continued. "The vibrations of the disembodied spirit-soul will continue to be bad. The spirit will want to continue to perform bad actions. If it was accustomed to be mean and hurtful to others during its lifetime, it will continue that way as a disembodied spirit after death. It can hurt others in just the same ways. You must remember that as I demonstrated with the glass, the thought of pushing the object precedes the action. In this same way, the disembodied spirit is able to move objects with its vibrations similar to thought waves."

"This is why people hear doors slamming or objects moving around the house when an evil spirit inhabits that location" I offered.

"Exactly!, but in addition to throwing things around the house or opening and slamming doors shut to scare people, the influence of the disembodied evil spirits can be more subtle. They play with the minds of the living. I don't care whether you believe me or not. I am just telling you. Evil spirits residing in a home play with the minds of the inhabitants of that home. This is why you will notice a lot of family conflicts in homes where an evil spirits reside. There are also a lot of money problems. You remember the situation with Kamal? He worked very hard and over the ten years that they lived in that house, he brought in over a million dollars. He lived a frugal lifestyle and yet what did he have to show for it: nothing. All his money piddled away in unexplainable ways. The spirit will influence the mind of his wife into believing that she wants the kitchen renovated. This costs tens of thousands. Then they get robbed by the trades' people. Then the plumbing in the house will break. Then a fire will start for some unexplainable reason. Then the family car breaks down over and over again, and on and on. And when he called me in, how many spirits did we find in the location?"

"Two," I answered.

"One was the previous owner who was attached to the property. The other was planted on the premises because of jealousy for Kamal and his family. You see, Kamal worked hard and was doing well at his job. He was promoted over many other people who thought that they should have been the ones to be promoted. So one of his colleagues found a pujari who does rituals to the Dark Forces and they planted an evil spirit to destroy Kamal's life."

"How can they find such a spirit?" I queried.

"Very easy, once you know what to do. Evil spirits exist anywhere where a burial or cremation takes place outside of a designated area. For example many people bury a dead baby in their backyard because they believe that there is no need for such a young infant to have a formal burial or cremation. Some people may bury their parent in the farm where they spent all their lives. Other spirits may exist for more bizarre reasons. You may remember the old folk stories about the Dutchman syndrome in many parts of Guyana. The Dutch used to bury their money in earthenware containers called Dutch bottles. To protect the money, they will sacrifice the life of a poor laborer and order the spirit to guard the money."

"That is why we were warned as youths never to touch a Dutch bottle if we ever find one in the farm areas," I recalled.

"The pujari has the knowledge to locate such a spirit," Swami-ji continued. "Alternatively, the pujari may go to a burial ground or to a crematorium site between 12.00 midnight and 4.00 am and perform a ritual to attract a particular spirit. Then he will instruct the spirit on his assigned duties before releasing the spirit on the premises of the family to be harmed. Remember that the spirit is under the constraint of the pujari and cannot escape. Once planted, it will be locked in within the perimeter of the household. Now you may ask what's in it for the spirit. The pujari may allow it to inhale aromatic scents. Spirits are disembodied and eat through scent. In addition, the spirit gets a chance to get away from all the other competing spirits held within the boundaries of the crematorium. The spirit gets a free reign to play its destructive tricks on the members of a household. This play with the minds of the householders is for the benefit and enjoyment of the captured spirit. In the end, the pujari gets paid handsomely. The person who hired the pujari gets his revenge. The spirit gets to play. And the household is destroyed with a series of events that causes untold suffering and sorrows."

"So when people perform sacrificial rituals to Kal Bhairo, Dee, Landmaster and so on they are really dealing with the Devil?" I asked as a form of confirmation.

"Think about it in this way," my mentor replied. "God created the universe and all living beings that populate it. Why would God require one of its living beings to sacrifice the life of another living being? Why would God require a man to sacrifice the life of a goat or chicken? God created them both. He gave life to both according to their respective karmas. If God is the creator of all, why would he require a life to be sacrificed? How can He be pleased by a 'gift' of something that is already His creation?"

I really had no answer.

Swami-ji continued. "By taking a life before its time, the spirit of that animal becomes entangled in bondage. That spirit is angry because it was sacrificed to the Devil. And so you can see how angry spirits infest areas where Kal Bhairo rituals are performed."

Swami-ji looked across the Bay and was lost in thought. I knew that my lesson for the day had ended and I slowly opened the gate and entered the Ashram to reflect on my learning. It is plain commonsense. Why would people continue to sacrifice animals? How can they continue to think that a God that created all must be prayed to by bringing an innocent animal to a violent and untimely death? Can they not see that only the Devil will require dead flesh and blood? Can they not fathom that they are conned into Devil worship anytime someone suggests that a ritual has to be performed by sacrificing a life? And how can some people really think that Kala Bhairava, guardian of the crematorium who protects the living from the dead can be the same as Devil known as Kal Bhairo that causes untold suffering to the lives of so many? I began to understand the almost insurmountable task that my Guru-dev has accepted from the Gods – the task to educate and to heal the suffering from the effects of Kal Bhairo.

Can the Guru Mantra Ease your Suffering and Change your Life?

The path of the Guru is sacred. From his deep understanding of the Vedas, Swami Ram Charran of the Heendu Learning Center and Jyotish Ashram has revived this path to help you rejuvenate yourself through the sacred Mantra. With the knowledge imparted to you by Swami-ji and the pursuit of your own effort and practice, you will be able to ease your suffering and build a life of good health, happiness and prosperity.

People from all walks of life come to the Ashram to find relief from their pain and suffering. Often times they say that they feel disconnected from life; that something is missing from their lives; that their focus and drive to achieve has diminished; that there is no real grounding in their lives. What they are saying is that they want to feel 'plugged in' again. They want to feel a sense of connection. This is all about 'meaning' in people's lives. Out of this sense of meaning, comes a sense of purpose and usefulness - a sense of belonging to something larger than the Self. But how does someone become connected? How do they begin to enjoy the happiness of a blissful life? How do they become free from the yoke of their miseries? The answer lies in the simplicity and understanding of the Guru Mantra (given by the Divine Teacher and found in the Scriptures):

Gurubrahma Guruvisnur // Gurudevo
Maheshvarah
Gurureva Parabrahma // Tasmai Srigurave Namah

The syllable 'gu' means the darkness of ignorance and the syllable 'ru' represents the light of knowledge. The spiritual teacher or guru is symbolized as our creator, our preserver and the destroyer in the Guru Mantra above.

A guru enables a suffering person to take control of his or her own live and transform it to a life of happiness and prosperity. One of the ways that this can be done is through a specific Mantra given by the Guru. A mantra is really sound. Through our knowledge of the physical sciences, we know that sound causes vibrations to take place. Constant repetition of the Mantra causes vibration to take place in the individual cells and organs within the human body. Over time, the mantra causes noticeable changes to take place. Suffering ceases and the person develops a renewed outlook about life, and starts to feel connected again as more and more positive events begin to happen in life. But what is the right Mantra for you?

A mantra from a book is simply written words on a page. Through the Science of the Vedic scriptures, the Guru will first bring the mantra to life and give it force. He will then instruct you on its use. He will tell you how and when to repeat it. Repetition does not take anything away from your every-day life. You may repeat it aloud or you may repeat it silently. You can repeat it while showering, while traveling to work, while working, while cooking, while performing chores, while preparing for sleep. It becomes like a tune of your favorite song. You begin to enjoy it. And the more you repeat it, the more you will notice pleasant changes in your life. You begin to look back on your life of suffering and misery and wonder where it went. You will find that you become revitalized. Your new life will be filled with happiness and joy. You will begin to feel connected with your family again; you will begin to feel connected with your temple and your community; you will even enjoy your work better because you will begin to see people in a more positive light. Through this one small act on your part, you will be able to leave behind a life of suffering and misery and build one of joy and prosperity.

Swami Ram Charran un-shrouds the mystery of the Vedic teachings and helps us to understand them in scientific and practical ways. He understands the sense of dis-connection that people feel when they come to him for help. But more importantly, he knows what to do in order to help them to become re-connected once again. To explain the workings and effectiveness of the Mantra, Swami-ji tells us that our human body is really a combination of four sheaths - sort of like the sheaths of an onion that encases the core at its center. The four sheaths are:

1. Physical body - this is the body that we see in our state of physical awareness.
2. Astral body - this is the one that exist in the dream state.
3. Causal body - this is the one that exist in the state of deep sleep.
4. Supra causal body - this is the one that exist in the form of pure light.

The sound vibrations of the Mantra slowly penetrate the body sheaths and continued repetition with firm determination, dedication and devotion, cause the vibrations to eventually reach the very source of our 'I-ness' or our Inner-Self. At this core, our being exist in the form of pure light and the light of our individual being merges with the universal light or Cosmic Consciousness to give us a sense of completeness and wholesomeness. Once this connection of the light from our innermost sheath is made with the universal light of the Cosmic Consciousness, we become 'plugged-in' again and our suffering dissipates and our happiness begins. All this is happening at a very deep level and we are not even aware of it. The only thing that we become aware of is that our outlook or 'view' of life changes. We become aware that more and more happy events take place and that the sorrowful ones that had pestered our lives for so long become lesser and lesser. At the ultimate point when the mantra vibrations cause our inner light to connect with the universal light, we become very grounded and like a baby, we see joys in places that others are not able to discern. Swami Ram Charran can help your experience this joyous state of living and of life.

Quiz

It is said that in the beginning there was only Space, then, came the Light. And in this Lighted Space, there was a small vibration that caused wave-like movement to take place. And then this movement took place in a certain direction. It is also said that the Hindu Gods are the representation of physical aspects in the universe.

(a): What are the names of the Hindu Gods that represent Space and Light?

(b): What was the sound that caused the first vibration?

E-mail your responses to: Swamicharan@yahoo.com

100

Chapter 11
The Devil Made Me Do It.

T he Devil made me do it." This is a thought often expressed by young and old alike when they speak or act in some non-conventional manner. A person may act 'out of character' for some unknown or unexplainable reason. Upon realizing the stupidity or thoughtlessness of their words or actions, they simply blurt out, "The Devil made me do it." This has come to be accepted in our society as a form of apology. The truth is however, that the Devil, negative energies, evil spirits or whatever other name we choose to give this phenomenon in the world of paranormal studies, do create subtle interference patterns in the human mind that causes someone to behave in a manner outside their regular norm. In places such as Guyana and some islands of the West Indies, this evil spirit is popularly known as Kal Bhairo. The cult of Kal Bhairo worshippers flourish mainly as a hidden or underground activity. It thrives on the five deadly sins of Kama (Lust), Khroda (Anger), Lobha (Greed), Moha (Desire) and Ahankar (Pride).

We are living in the age of materiality where man exercises an often unquenchable thirst for material possessions. They develop an insatiable desire to acquire more and rarely do they give due consideration as to whether they need it or not. The mere idea that they 'have' more than others seem to be the key in their unending quest to fulfil those material desires. It is this quest for quick material wealth that drives man from the path of Dharma (righteousness) to Adharma (unrighteousness). The cult of Kal Bhairo has reached the stage of Adharma. My Guru-dev, Sri Swami Ram of the Jyotish Ashram and Hindu Learning Center has been working ceaselessly for more than 14 years to heal people from the effects of Kal Bhairo. During the healing process, he teaches them the proper corrective actions that they can take to remove themselves from the unending cycle of animal sacrifices to the Devil. This article provides the results of Swami-ji's findings in his study of 96 people over a two-year period.

Methodology

The 96 participants were selected at random and represent approximately 5% of the population that came to seek help from Swami-ji over the two year period April 01, 2001 to March 31, 2003. Although the sample was drawn mainly from an Indo-Guyanese and Indo-Caribbean population, it included members from other nationalities including a fair representation among Latin Americans. The sample was drawn predominantly from the inner-city population of 1st and 2nd generation immigrants within the cosmopolitan centers of Miami, New York, St. Paul and Toronto. The number of females in the sample outnumbered males in a ratio of approximately 3 to 1. The family histories were traced back as far as possible depending on memory of the oldest living member within each family group.

Results

Our previous articles on Kal Bhairo Chapters 1, 2, 3, 4, and 5 establish the existence of Kal Bhairo, state how Kal Bhairo is attracted into someone's life, show the effects and noticeable symptoms, discusses the cure and finally, make a clear distinction between the Devil called Kal Bhairo and the form of Lord Shiva known as Kala Bhairava. The purpose of this current article is to reflect on the findings of a two-year study of Kal Bhairo that shows the multi-generational impact of this Evil Force on a Khul or family lineage. The results have revealed the following:

There is a significant pattern of suffering and death among the 6th and 9th children in families that have practised Kal Bhairo sacrifices. That among the more serious worshippers of this Dark Force, there is a vehement resistance to accept that killing of animals as a form of sacrifice has negative consequences to the sacrificers over the long term.

The effects of suffering and death as a result of Kal Bhairo can be lessened or stopped altogether. Stopping the effects of Kal Bhairo and preventing the effects from being passed on to future generations is a tough task. Success can only be achieved with the help from Swami-ji combined with the efforts from the suffering family members.

Discussion of Results

In most circumstances, Kal Bhairo is invited into a family when animal sacrifices are offered to the Evil Force in exchange for material wealth. Somewhere along the family lineage, some lustful, angry, greedy, desirous or proud person wanted something really bad. In all possibility, that person came into contact with a pujarie who was operating on the Dark Side and they cut a deal of sorts. If the idea was to satisfy their lust for a woman, then the sacrificial offering would be made and the woman would come under the magic spell of the man who requested help from Kal Bhairo. If the idea was anger, then the person at whom the anger was aimed would come to harm. If the idea was greed as it most often is, wealth and material possessions would accrue to the person who offered the sacrifice. In each case however, the sacrificer comes under the shadow of the Devil. To all intents and purposes, he appears to have no recourse. Once he is sucked in by the first ritualistic animal sacrifice, he will gain whatever it was that he had bargained for - but only for a short time. Within about 10 months or so, he will begin to see signs of trouble and either through a dream, vision or some form of intuition which may appear as rational thought, he will begin to think that he has some kind of 'work' to do. 'Work' used in this sense means a ritualistic sacrifice. Close to the 1-year anniversary, he will find himself doing another sacrifice to appease the Devil and thereafter, the ritual becomes an annual routine. As soon as he delays, all kinds of trouble and misfortune will befall him as harsh reminders. Once this original sacrificer dies, or becomes too old to continue, the annual routine falls upon one of the off springs.

Swami-ji has found that often times, the original sacrificer dies without informing anyone that this ritual must continue. On the other hand the off springs thought (unwittingly so!) that the requirement died along with the original sacrificer. In still other situations, he found that as the generations become more westernized, the off springs refuse to participate in such bizarre rituals, especially since they do not know what they are doing or why they have to do it. This is where the real problems begin. Immense suffering ensues to end finally in death under miserable circumstances. But Swami-ji has found that there is a definite order or trend to the pattern of deaths.

In large families, he found that the brunt of the suffering and eventual death will fall to the 6th and 9th children. Once the first child dies, the child immediately after will move into that vacant spot. For instance, if the 6th child dies, then the 7th child will move into the vacant 6th space and begins to suffer. In multi-generational families where all the great-grand parents and grand-parents have died, the living parents will take the place as #1 and #2. Thus if there are 5 children, the father will be #1, the mother #2, the first child is #3 and so on. The last child in this family becomes #7. Therefore, the suffering will fall upon the 4th child in the order of birth because he has taken the #6 position in this particular family. Swami-ji has found a few exceptions to the order of suffering and death in the sample but this may be due to the fact that he has had to rely on the memory of the oldest living member of the family. Often times, there is a reluctance to talk about such sensitive and such painful memories. In other circumstances, there may simply be errors in recollection among the family member. In the main, however, we can conclude that Swami-ji's findings indicate a definite order to the suffering and eventual death of the 6th and 9th positions in the families who suffer from the Kal Bhairo effects.

Wrong Forms of Worship

Please Do Not Confuse Kal-Bhairo with Kal-Bhairava

Kala Bhairava is a Sanskrit form of Lord Shiva that guards the burial ground so that the souls of the dead ancestors are preserved Kala Bhairava is of only one form

Kal Bhairo is a Sanskrit name for condemned souls of sacrificed animals who haunt human bodies and rob religious people of their goods karmas by misguiding them and draining their energies.....

Kal Bhairo takes the forms of many evil spirits and forms that are mostly flesh eating demons........it can also pretend to be a dead relative......
Katari is a female form of Kal Bhairo and is interpreted in the Vedas as a flesh eating demon.....

When a person is of a godly nature, their body is steady in prayer.....
When a person's body is shaking or vibrating or rocking back and forth in prayer that is not godly in nature......

Chapter 12
The Scientific Procedure of a Puja or Hindu Ritual

*A step by step process of changing the
Destiny or Future of one's Life*

Every time we create an action in the universe the whole universe rearranges itself to match that action. In this universe each one of us is an essential element that can create change for all, for example...

If a person dies the whole world history is rearranged to match that event. If a child is born, again, the whole world is rearranged to match the birth of this child. He or she could be the next president, prime minister, or doctor, etc., that will help change thousands of lives. Whenever someone gets married the universe must rearrange itself to receive the children of this marriage who will in turn change the future history of the world. So as you can see, an extension of Newton's law of "ACTION AND REACTION ARE EQUAL" would be "A SMALL ACTION IS NECESSARY FOR THE CREATION OF A LARGE UNIVERSAL REACTION."

The Ancient Hindu Scientists or Rishis were fully aware of the laws of action versus Universal Reaction and so with this knowledge, they implemented the scientific methods that were necessary to create controlled reactions in the universe. Thusly, there is a necessity of rituals.

If whenever we create an action, it affects the universe then why not create controlled actions that will generate the reactions that will bring prosperity and happiness for all, thus assuring our own happiness?

In performing Pujas, or Hindu Rituals, the methods were developed as follows:

1. Create a simulated version of the universe in the home and then perform specific actions that will create for us a journey throughout the universe, creating changes as we traverse it.
2. Prepare our body and soul to become the creator of specific actions that will affect the universe, such as purification, inner cleansing, and so on, so that our soul and mind becomes a 'launched space ship,' so to speak.
3. Ask Lord Ganesh (Remover of Obstacles) to remove all hindrances or spiritual blocks to this journey into the universe by taking off our spiritual vices such as our qualities of lust anger, greediness, ego, etc.
4. Ask Gowrie Mata (Mother of the universe) for permission to enter into the universe so that we can create our reactions, for without a mother, no one can come into this world, nor can any Gods be born in the universe without a woman. It is only though the woman that all reality comes into the universe, and so the female energy's permission is greatly needed.

5. Ask Mother Earth (Pritivi Mata) for permission to leave the earth so that we can proceed into the universe, make our request from the specific karmic forces or deity and then return back to earth.

6. Cross the Seven Oceans, or Seven Atmospheres of the Earth (Kalash, Ganga, Varuna, Devta Puja) so that we can get to the outer universe where Lakshmi (the Moon and the Sun) is located. The seven oceans match equally the seven layers of clouds or atmospheres around the earth and this must be crossed before our spiritual space ship can enter the universe.

7. Now that you have reached the Moon and the Sun you may now perform Lakshmi Puja and ask the Goddess of Prosperity to bring some success and happiness into your life, thus creating some changes in the world that will match your request. With the light of Lakshmi, we also must be granted enlightenment from Saraswaty, and solidity from Durga.

8. Having been granted wealth and prosperity, now you will have to request daily control of your life from the movements of the Nine Planets (The Nav Graha Devtas). So Nav Graha Puja is performed to each Graha requesting that you receive positive rays of life from each one of them, making sure that you understand that some of these Grahas are enemies to each other, and the PUJA is performed with proper knowledge.

9. Having received permission from Mother Earth, removed the obstacles by Ganesh, obtained permission from Gowrie, crossed the Seven Oceans, requested the blessings of Lakshmi for more light, and visited each planet in the Solar System, we are now ready to ascend to...

a. Mount Kalash (after Pluto) to perform complete puja and request to Lord Shiva or the Goddess Durga for fulfillment of our desires to change the world and rearrange the universe to suit our purpose. Lord Shiva is known as the Lord of Time and Durga, the Goddess of Procreation of the World.

b. *You may stop here for Lord Shiva and do Havan to compete Puja or if you have decided to do a Durga Puja, then the subsequent steps will be followed...*

c. After going to Lord Shiva, Lord Brahma made the request for Lord Shiva to get married.

Using all Puja Samagree in a Pan leaf, these steps are done for Durga Puja

1. Inviting the 1st female half Lord Shiva – Sati, also known as Brahma Charini.

2. Inviting the 2nd female half of Lord Shiva - Parvati, also known as SHALPUTRI.

3. Inviting the 3rd female half of Lord Shiva - Gowrie, also known as CHANGRAGANTA.

4. Inviting the 4th female half of Lord Shiva - Rudrani, also known as KUSHMANDI.

5. Inviting the 5th female half of Lord Shiva - Ratty, also known as SKANDAMATA.

6. Inviting the 6th female half of Lord Shiva - Kali, also known as KATYANI.

7. Inviting the 7th female half of Lord Shiva - Rohini, also known as GANGA.
8. Inviting the 8th female half of Lord Shiva - Shakti, also known as MAHAGAURI.
9. Inviting the 9th female half of Lord Shiva - Indrani, also known as SIDDIDATRI.
10. Bringing al the 9 forms into the form of Nav-Durga
11. Ritual to the procreative energy of the universe called Durga
12. Marrying Durga to Lord Shiva
13. Releasing of the egg - Cutting of the nutmeg
14. Protecting & growing of the egg - Hirany Garbha
15. Breaking of the egg - Birth from the mother
16. Cutting of the banana flower - A symbol of the creation for children
17. Blessing the child with worldly prosperity
18. Marrying Durga to Lord Shiva
19. Ritual to install the flag of the Deity
20. Contemplation on Nav-Durga - The Slokas
21. Havan or Fire Ritual to conclude puja
22. Closing Prayers before Artie

As you can see, the Hindus do not do Magic in their rituals; in fact, they are very scientific in their methods for changing the Universe. If a proper and knowledgeable person does the Puja as stated, then the Puja is sure to become successful.

If Lakshmi Puja is performed before Ganesh Puja, then the process is upside down. If Nav-Graha Puja is performed first, then the process is backward. Every Puja must follow a set procedure; there can only be one way to go into the universe.

The following page indicates how a puja should be done scientifically.

A Map of the Puja Procedure

THE CORRECT PROCEDURE OF A HINDU RITUAL

GANGA PUJA   GANESH PUJA

HANUMAN PUJA   KOOLA PUJA

DURGA PUJA   SATANARAYAN PUJA

LORD SHIVA

NAVGRAHA PUJA

LAXMI PUJA

KALASH PUJA

GANESH PUJA

GOWRI PUJA

MOTHER EARTH POOJA

113

Chapter 13
What Is The True Science Behind Hindu Worship?
Things That You Were Never Told...

As we said this is the election of certain events at a suitable time when all the forces of nature are in harmony. Each moment has got its potency and as CARL JUNG said "whatever is born or done this moment of time has the qualities of this moment of time." Cosmic radiation pouring at the moment on earth from outer space and coming from various stars and planets act on our brain cells which take up the cosmic radiation and transform them into electric impulses. These impulses set in motion our thoughts, words and deeds, and also the course of our action. Muhurta therefore gives valuable directions by following which the person will be enabled to remove, neutralize, counteract, or overcome the evils indicated by any malefic position of the planets in a chart. Thus muhurta helps one to minimize or modify the full extent of the evils of our past karmas.

To determine the correct muhurta a birth chart should be completed and a gochar chart for the time in question should also be done. The house positions of the planets are to be considered as given and an appropriate time followed. Tithi days and numbers are given in the

CALENDAR OF LUNAR DAYS at the back of this book. The Stars are also given.

The Kinds of Worship

"WORSHIP is of three kinds: those that are performed daily, that are offered on particular occasions, and that are made for the attainment of special aims." (Rudra-yamala Tantra [614])

The daily rituals as well as the rituals ordained for certain days of the year should be performed by everyone. They are man's religious duties, his participation in the cosmic life and its cycles.

"A man must have a chosen deity, but he must also honor the family deity, the village deity, the village guardian angel, the village genie (naga), on the prescribed occasions." (Vijayananda Tripathi, "Devata tattva," Sanmarga, III, 1942)

On the other hand, worship performed to obtain the realization of a desire has no compelling character and is done only by those who feel the need for it. Yet if we use worship as the instrument of gain, whether spiritual or material, it is essential to know which kind of divinity we should propitiate and through which procedure. The divinity worshipped and the techniques of worship are different if the aim of worship is to achieve a particular result, obtain a particular quality, and reach a particular stage of worldly or spiritual accomplishment. When the saint prays to obtain liberation, the thief to succeed in his enterprise, the soldier to kill his enemy, although each may address his prayer to the same divine name, the

115

divinity which may acknowledge it is in fact a different state of being, a different god.

When we invoke an abstraction in the hope of saving our life or winning a war, our prayer is wrongly addressed because an abstraction can have nothing to do with the forms and interests of the manifest world. It cannot answer prayers, much less favor worshippers. Only the minor deities, the subtle beings who are part of the inner life of things, can co-operate with man in such matters, and it is these deities which should be approached through the proper ritual channels. A forest deity, however, will have no power to help man in spheres of abstract realization.

> *"Man becomes what he worships. His desire is the essential form of his becoming."* Krishna, the embodiment of love, says in the Bhagavadgita (9.25 [615]):

> *"Those who worship the gods become gods; those who worship Ancestors become Ancestors, those who worship the elements master the elements, and those who worship me gain me."*

Those who worship Yamraj become Death-like; those who worship the Devil become like the Devil and so lives like one...

In the West, and in some places in India, people have been misguided by many false priests who encourage them to worship the lower spirits, or ghosts, who may have been people who were accidentally killed or willfully sacrificed by others, and for which this lost soul never found freedom to go to the heavens. Such souls require someone to worship them before they can be freed, so they appear in people's dreams assuming the appearance of Swamis, Pundits, and Devtas and courage them to do wrongful worship.

By the time the person realizes that he has sold his mind to the devil, it is usually too late and the spirit would already have attained some freedom to heaven. Incidentally, after one year, because he or she had tricked the human person, the soul is in misery again, and continues to look for more human prey to trick for another year of Moksha.

Inauspicious or Incorrect Rituals: Obeah or Black Magic Prayers

If prayers to Kal Bhairo are practiced then the history of the family, the town the village and the country is changed.....

PLEASE NOTE that the area of all the countries where sacrifice of animals are done is very tense

The following Pujas or Rituals should not be done by anyone who seeks happiness and peace. Doing any of these pujas will result in family misery, abortions, miscarriages, financial downfall, blockages, sickness, separations, accidents, love problems, imprisonments, and more...

None of these are found in the Vedic Texts of Hindus as something to be worshipped.

Sanganee Puja
Sometimes referred to as Sea-Master or Bush-Master; involves sacrifice and sometimes falsely referred to as the planet Saturn.

Kal-Bhairo Puja
Very popular in the West, involves sacrifice of goats, pigs, or lambs. In Muslim, it is the same as Qurbani; In Trinidad, it is known as Dee.

Dee Puja
It involves the giving of rum, cigarettes, cheese and crackers, etc.

Landmaster Puja
Usually, when a person was killed and buried in the land, without proper prayers and pujas, he or she becomes the spirit of the land. There is only one Landmaster and that is Dharti Maa or Mother Earth.

Katari Puja
Usually involves the killing of a specially grown chicken or fowl, whose meat is similar to duck meat. This ritual is also similar to Voodoo.

Kali Maya Puja (Sacrificial)
The real Kali Puja is really Durga Puja, but it does not involve sacrifice of animals. When sacrifice is done in Kali's name, it destroys the female generation of that person and can make the family extinct. There is no direct Puja to Kali in her destructive form.

In the Bhagavad Purana there is a list given of the deities who are to be worshipped for particular aims.

- "He who wishes for the illumination of knowledge should worship the Immensity (Brahman).
- "He who wishes for the pleasures of the senses should worship Might (Indra), the king of heaven.
- "He who desires children worships the lord of progeny, Prajapati.
- "He who desires luck worships the Power of Illusion, Maya.
- "He who desires intelligence worships the Sun (Surya).
- "He who desires wealth worships the spheres of the elements, the Vasus.
- "He who desires virile power worships the divinities of life, the Rudras.
- "He who desires food worships Aditi, the mother of the gods.
- "He who desires a place in heaven worships all the gods.
- "He who desires a kingdom worships the Universal Principles, the Visvadevas.
- "He who desires power worships the Means-of-Accomplishment (Sadhyas).
- "He who desires a long life worships the celestial physicians, the Asvins.
- "He who desires strength worships the Earth (Ila).
- "He who desires stability worships the World-Mothers (Loka-matas).
- "He who desires beauty worships the celestial musicians, the gandharvas.
- "He who desires a woman worships the nymph Urvasi.

- "He who wishes for domination worships the Supreme-Ruler.
- "He who desires fame worships the lord of the sacrifice (yajna).
- "He who desires a treasure worships Pracetas [Varuna, the lord of the waters].
- "He who desires knowledge worships Siva, the lord of sleep.
- "He who desires a happy married life worships Peace-of-the-Night (Uma), the consort of Siva.
- "He who desires [firmness in his] duty worships the Highest-Praise (Uttama-sloka), that is, Visnu.
- "He who wishes for numerous descendants worships the Ancestors (pitr).
- "He who desires protection worships the virtuous-ones (punyajana).
- "He who desires strength worships the divinities of wind, the Maruts.
- "He who desires a throne worships the Lawgiver, Manu.
- "He who desires magic powers worships the goddess of witchcraft, Nirrti.
- He who desires lust worships the Offering, Soma.
- "To be free from desire, a man should worship the Supreme Person, Para Purusa.

"Whether a man is realized or is a seeker or is still in the grip of attachment, he should, with intense devotion, worship the Supreme Person." (Bhagavad Purana, 2.3.1-10 [616])

120

The Stages of Worship

WORSHIP can be of different forms. It can be mental or external, collective or individual. It can begin with abstract contemplation and end in outward ceremonial or the reverse. The external worship of the yogi is only the instrument that leads to abstract contemplation.

> *"The highest stage is that in which the Immense Presence is perceived in all things. The middle stage is that of meditation, the lower that of hymns and rosary. Still lower is the stage of external worship."* (Mahanirvana Tantra)

> *"The worship performed by the initiated is of two kinds, internal and external. Internal worship is ordained only for those who have renounced the world. Both internal and external worship are necessary for others."* Tantra Samhita [617]

> *"The worship of images of stone, metal, jewels, or clay leads the seeker of liberation of rebirth. Hence the man who wishes to renounce the world should worship only in his own heart and fear external forms of worship so that he may not have to live again."* (Silpa Sastra, p.27 [618])

In the final stage of realization, the yogi does not perceive anything but an Immense Presence pervading all appearances. At this stage no outward ritual exists any more. All physical and mental functions have themselves become ritual, that is, have ceased to have any purpose other than to support the contact between the yogi and the object of his contemplation. When life itself becomes a hindrance, the lingering remnant of an already past existence, the yogi has ceased, for all practical purposes, to be a human being.

Chapter 14
Kali Church and Kal Bhairo Worship

S wami-Ji, I am confused. If Kali is one of the 9 forms of Mother Durga, why is the proliferation of Kali churches in places like Guyana and Trinidad so bad for the people? "This question was posed to my Guru-Ji recently. He looked over at me and smiled benevolently as he rummaged in his carrying bag and fished out a copy of his Book on Hindu Gods. This was my cue that I should be paying full attention to his answer.

With that, Swami-Ji opened the book to the page depicting the image of Mother Kali dancing When the evil man is about to destroy the universe, Kali, the destroyer of evil, steps in and stands over the man to bring him back in line. You are right that Kali is one of the 9 forms of the Mother of the Universe. She is the representation of Mother Durga in Her destructive form - the form in which she destroys evil. It is for this reason that Mother Kali is represented as darker in color with her tongue hanging out and blood dripping from the beheaded skulls of the monsters that she slew. You must remember that a lot of the scriptural writing is based on Hindu mythology and you must not take the words in their literal meaning but rather allow me to put this in perspective for you.

Look over at the upper floor of that building next door. See the group of men?"

You mean the ones on the verandah of the banquet hall?"

Yes. They were congregated there since Friday evening and most likely will be there until Sunday night when they will return home to get some rest for their return to work on Monday morning. They are drinking, smoking, swearing and cavorting with females who are not their wives. They seem to have no real purpose in life. A number of them are married with children. Where are their wives? Where are their children? Who is providing the care, love and respect for their families? And if this continues for years we seek Bhairo Land?" Yes. The area is nicknamed after the dark force or Kal Bhairo. This is the land where a silent killer lurks in the darkness, a killer known as incest. A killer that has its origins in the generation that began the worship the dark force of Kal Bhairo, or the worship of Satan, as we know it in the Western world. You look so shocked my young friend. Why? Don't you think that incest occurs within our Caribbean immigrant society?

.

The Cycle of Incest - Its Impact on Health, Happiness and Prosperity

I have come across hundreds of cases in the past few years and the occurrences seem to be surfacing with greater frequency. Husbands with sister-in-laws; father-in-laws with daughter-in-laws; fathers with daughters, uncles with nieces; brothers with sisters; and the list goes on and on. There is a tremendous negative impact on the female. During the forced and traumatic event, her womb

124

becomes twisted and the spinal column becomes affected causing brain functions to be altered. To the person who is subjected to the abuse of incest, attentiveness, concentration and focus diminish, their mind is in constant emotional turmoil and sexual intercourse becomes painful and less enjoyable. Such an individual finds it difficult to focus on a good education and may end up in low paying jobs in warehouses and factories. At home, their love life suffers and they become quite unhappy. All the mental anguish and suffering tend to lead to health problems which often manifests itself as pains in their body

I'm sorry Swami-Ji but I don't see the relationship between the Kali Church and incest."

Be patient my young friend. Let us now focus on the men who prey on these young and vulnerable females. In our civilized society, they are criminals. But there is also a Spiritual connection here. In my research and analysis of the live case studies that come to me, I find that incestuous relationships exist in multiple generations.

You mean it is sort of hereditary?"

Swami-Ji paused for a brief moment to consider the question. "A hereditary or genetic explanation is based on scientific fact. It is based on the premise that it is a trait carried within the cellular make-up of the individuals. However, although incest is inter-generational, its causative factor is not scientific based. Neither is it random acts of violence perpetrated by criminal minds. But rather, each act of incest seems to follow a previous act in a past generation. However, I must caution you that whether you like it or not, the answer will be the truth.

How do you mean?"

Let me try and relate this in a story form. I have come across a case where a newborn baby began to gasp and suffocate as soon as it exited the mother's womb. It was as if the baby was being strangled by some unseen rope or cord around its neck. The father rushed to the village pundit who advised that a special sacrifice had to be done immediately in order to save the child's life. A goat was bought and taken over to the local Kali church where the sacrificial ritual began. Shortly after the ceremony, which involves the taking of an animal life and sacrificing it to the Demonic forces, the father of the child realized that what really happened here is that his father (grandfather to the child) practiced Kal Bhairo worship. At the time of birth of his son, Kal Bhairo forced the father to offer a sacrifice or else he will take his newborn child instead. But as a result of the sacrifice, the spirit of the goat, imbued with the negative force of Kal Bhairo comes into the baby and subjugates the old spirit with which the baby was born. Thus the boy grew up with twin personalities.

However, the negative spirit was stronger than the positive one and…

You are right Swami-Ji. This does sound like a non-sense story as we know it in the Western world

But there is more. I still have to tell you about the Kali Church. You see, the sacrifice was not made to Mother Kali at all. It was made to Kal Bhairo. So in essence, the churches you mention are not Kali churches.

The word 'Kali' in the name of the church is really a misnomer. They are Kal Bhairo churches - a place where devil worship takes place. The Mother of the Universe does not need sacrifices. She comes to destroy evil in your life. She comes into your life as your Universal Mother through the Durga

I know Swami-Ji. The 10th plate must be offered to Lord Shiva. You drummed that into my head many months ago."

Good. Then you have learnt something valuable my young friend. This brings us back to the issue of incest. When men commit such heinous acts of violation of innocent women, it is the dark force of Kal Bhairo working through them. Kal Bhairo likes meat, rum, cigarettes and forceful sex. Once the devil sacrifice was done in one generation, someone in that generation will have forced sex with a family member. In the next generation, again a male will have forced sex with a family member. And so on for many generations.

Why does God allow this to go on?"

He doesn't. You will notice that girls who have been forced to have sex with a relative cease to enjoy a love life and very often do not have beautiful children. It is God's way of ceasing the propagation of the evil forces.

Mother Durga steps in as Kali and sets the stage for the destruction of the man. He may get into fights during his drunken sprees and end up in prison, get maimed or killed, lose his job and family, or have some major crises in his life which will cause him to stop and reflect upon his past. This makes him pay back the karma of what was done.

I truly feel sorry for those young men on that verandah across the way."

You are right my young friend. You feel sorry only because you know what lay in store for them. But to all outward appearances, they are having a good time. However, as the saying goes, 'the chickens will come home to roost very soon'.

And you will be here to catch them when they fall Swami-Ji?"

I hope so, my young friend. I truly hope so. Their journey will be hard and rigorous. Remember that they are coming from the depths of Patal [Hell] and must make the transition to the Astral Plane. But for everyone who crosses over, it becomes one less in the domains of

Kal Bhairo." "If we take off the letter `a' from the end of `Kala' we get `Kal'. And if we replace the `ava' from `Bairava' with the letter `o', we get `Bhairo'.

Quite an ingenuous plan on the part of the swindlers who want to make money from innocent people," I surmised.

Chapter 15
Katari - The Demoness – Not To Be Worshipped

K atari is a name given to the soul of an animal or human which has ended its life abruptly. This soul becomes a lost soul because of the sudden death of the body and wanders about in limbo between the earthly plane and the astral plane. The soul becomes angry because it was not allowed to exist long enough in that specific life form to help it pay back its karmic debt. Each life form, whether plant life or animal life, is a soul in a re-birth phase depending on karmic debt. A reborn soul may take the highest form of plant life as the Tulsee plant; or as an animal anywhere in the range from oceanic life forms through slimy creatures and worms up to the sacred cow. In human birth, a person's life will be one of poverty and suffering to one of wealth, health and happiness. Again all of this depends upon the karma of the individual. In this context, when animals are sacrificed by humans, the soul of the animal becomes angry and so it will inhabit the body of the person who committed the act of sacrifice. This is called spiritual possession. This kind of possession can cause the possessed person to experience the following:

1. Insanity.
2. Financial problems.
3. Suicidal tendencies.
4. Shaking or vibration of the body.
5. Pain in the knee cabs.
6. Twisting of the female uterus.
7. Female menstrual cramps.
8. A blockage of progress to a person's life.
9. Depression.

In other words as can be seen from the above, Katari can be referred to as the female devil or the wife of Satan. In Hinduism, Satan is referred to as Kal Bhairo in the West Indies and parts of South India. The following actions or Karmas are responsible for bringing Katari or female Satan into your life.

1. Wearing black clothes.
2. Eating red meat, especially beef, duck, goat.
3. Visiting the rituals or temples of Kal Bhairo or Katari.

Katari, Koteri, Kateri or Demon Goddess of the Rakshas Race

The Vedic texts define the word "Koteri" as a demon that eats flesh and an evil force that causes women to have excess bleeding of the menstrual cycle so that it can feed off of it.....usually removal of this demon cures the excess bleeding problem......see Swami-ji on this.

There can be no such thing as a *SMALL MOTHER* and *BIG MOTHER*. One cannot have more than *ONE MOTHER*. Each woman can be a mother but a person can be born only out of One Woman. Each woman is represented by the Universal force called *DURGA*. Durga represents all women as mothers; simply because *each woman can have enough children to create this whole world.....if there is one abortion or miscarriage the whole world is affected*...It could be Einstein, Newton, Osama Bin Ladin, Bush or Clinton, etc.

Kateri – Not a Force to Be Worshipped As a Devta

The birth of children is represented by the symbolism of Durga. A look at the picture of Durga reveals the circular wheel of time indicating that without a woman no person can be born into the world without a woman's womb.....all of our reality comes as a result of being born and molded from children to adults by the female energy. Our whole life requires the woman in one form or another thus the nine pairs of hands in the picture of Durga reflects the nine forms of womanhood. The ancient Hindus knew the importance of each birth of each child and the impact it would have on the whole world and the rest of us so they developed a great deal of scientific formulas that can help us be aware of the type of child that is being born. Every time a woman has an abortion it changes history for it could be the next Mahatma Gandhi or the next Adolf Hitler. Every time there is an abortion the history of the world will change because the paths that would have been developed in that couple's life will never occur.....it could have been you or me, Krishna or Christ.

Children are nature's gift for the happiness of a family. When a native is devoid of a child, the life becomes HELL. A True Hindu woman is a symbol of sacrifice, service and sacrament. She adores her husband in all walks of life; whether the husband is poor or wealthy, she loves him like God. The peace of mind in spite of having all comforts of life or otherwise becomes upset if there is no child or any issue out of the couple. People hanker after the quacks, savants and other places of their interest to achieve the goal but are usually robbed and remain disappointed. Astrology in such case comes to the rescue of such couples. Careful study of their horoscopes indicates whether or not they will have an issue in the form of a child. Whether husband or wife is devoid of virility and above all medical Astrology can help the couple to shape their action and life according to the advice of an astrologer. In case the horoscope indicates children or issues but are delayed, upayes through occult science are adopted which is an indirect way of prayer and the sadhaka is blessed with his or her desires. Yantra and Tantra are the two ways out of the occult science where a number of yantras are available for getting success in this respect. Such mantras have been detailed in author's famous book, MANTRA RITUAL.

The "semi-god" or deity representing the problems with childbirth, and abortions is known as "Katari" or dark mother. She works together with the planets Rahu, Ketu and Mars to affect the womb so that children may not be born. Generally women affected by "Katari" tend to wear a lot of black clothes, and experience pain in the uterus constantly. Rahu or the ascending node of the moon affects the womb by making the male partner intoxicated with alcohol or drugs thus enabling the injection of negative energies into the sperms which are injected into the womb, causing miscarriages. Ketu or the descending node of the moon does the same by creating infections in the womb. Mars creates accidental favorable childbirth and women are advised to always dip themselves religiously in the waters of the Ganges. The planet Venus, sun, and moon are favorable for childbirth; prayers to the sun everyday and the full moon are beneficial to protecting the unborn child.

Chapter 16
The Correct Way to Worship the Mother Energy Known as Navraatri Puja

Worshipping the Female Consort of Shiva the Shakti- Rebirth from Mother

There are nine forms of female energy in the universe. Before the birth of the Universe, the first Energy after Time (Shiva) was Heat (Shakti). Then after Creation (Brahma) came subsequent to the Universe (Vishnu), the various energies of Heat or Shakti were created. Since Brahma got knowledge (Saraswaty) as his consort, and Vishnu got Light (Laksmi) as his consort, they both approached Time (Shiva) and asked him to get a consort. However Time or Mahakali hesitated since Time is above everything it would be difficult to be subjected. In spite of this the Universe and Creator (Brahma Vishnu) insisted that Time has a consort or else there will be no Motion (Kali) and thus Reality (Laksmi Narayan) will not be sustained.

Shiva (Time) was persuaded to get a consort, but to complete the proper propagation of the Universe and its creations, Shiva (Time) had to consider all NINE LEVELS of the Universe. To make all these levels work in harmony, Shiva (Time) had to link all these levels by merging the NINE Forms to achieve the universal Shakti or Energy, thus Time would be able to create all NINE dimensions of this Universe.

The **first** form Shiva (Time) wanted to marry was Devotion (Sati), however, Ego (Daksa) had a problem with Time and because of their disagreement Devotion did not listen to Time, and so Devotion was burned in the Yagna fire.

The **second** form Shiva (Time) married was Motherhood (Parvati) who was the mother of Ganesh, but mother did not reveal all things to Time so when a battle took place over the death of their son, Ganesh (Obstacles), Mother placed more importance on Obstacles (the son Ganesh) rather than Time, (Husband).

The **third** form Shiva (Time) got married to was Knowledge (Gayatree) but knowledge was always studying, playing, and entertaining, so Knowledge paid very little attention to Time.

The **fourth** form Shiva (Time) married was Work (Rudrani). However Work spent much time cleaning, cooking and other household duties, that there was hardly any time for Shiva (Time).

The **fifth** form Shiva (Time) married was Lover (Narayani) whose demand for attention and love was so great that Time had to stop and change many times over for Lover. Because Lover demanded changes, Lover was then left alone.

The **sixth** form is Katyaeni (Chamunde). Power had a lot of Energy. Power was very commanding and constantly frustrating Time over following rules and regulations. Time could not cope with these rules.

The **seventh** form Shiva (Time) was married to was Emotion (Ganga). Emotion was a "cry-baby", demanding that Time paid more and more attention to

Emotion and feelings. Emotion wanted to constantly affect the head of Time so Time demanded that Emotion flowed out of Time's head.

The **eight** form Shiva (Time) was married to was Wealth (Laksmi). After marrying Time, Wealth demanded materiality constantly, had great attachment to material reality. Since Time could not be attached to materialism Time was not able to cope with Laksmi.

The **ninth** form Shiva (Time) was married to was Destruction (Kali) who had always been with Time but was never able to exercise Destructive power until Reality came into being. Since Destruction was always trying to step on top of Time, and sometimes Time (Shiva) had to play dead so as to deceive Destruction, it was difficult for Time to get Respect, so Time was unhappy.

Since Shiva (Time) was unhappy with all the individual forms of Female Energy, Time decided to fuse them together as One, so that Time would have some Devotion, some Knowledge, some Motherhood, some Work, some Love, some Power, some Wealth and some Destruction (portions of all the qualities, in one) to have a complete female called NAV-DURGA.

The 9 days of Nav-Raatriri is the worshiping of the nine forces or components necessary for the perfect woman to sustain the Universe. When there is a failure in any of the components, it creates a breakdown in the system of the home. As NAV-DURGA - THE COMPLETE WOMAN, who may be the wife, mother, sister, aunt, mother-in-law, sister-in-law, maid, daughter, cook, all the forms are needed to have a complete and blessed home.

Forms of Durga - Navraatri Puja

Day	Form of Durga	Represents
First	SARASWATY	Knowledge
Second	PARVATI	Motherhood
Third	GOWRIE	Romance
Fourth	RUDRANI	Home Care
Fifth	RADHA	Pleasure
Sixth	SHAKTI	Power
Seventh	GANGA	Emotion
Eight	LAKSMI	Wealth
Ninth	KALI	Destruction of all evil

Procedure of a Durga Puja Priests Should Follow

Having received permission from *Mother Earth*, removed the obstacles by *Ganesh*, obtained permission from *Gowrie*, crossed the *Seven Oceans*, requested the blessings of *Laksmi* for more light, and visited each planet in the *Solar System*, we are now ready to ascend to *Mount Kalash* (after Pluto) to perform complete puja and requests to Lord Shiva or the Goddess Durga for fulfillment of our desires to change the world and re-arrange the universe to suit our purpose. Lord Shiva is known as the Lord of Time and Durga is the Goddess of Procreation of the world. After going to Lord Shiva, Lord Brahma made the request for Lord Shiva to get married (see *Shivapuran*)

PLEASE NOTE:
At this point in the puja procedure the 10th plate of Prashad is given to LORD SHIVA, and NOT KAL BHAIRO. .SHIVA is the true Pati Parmeshwar of Durga, not a demon. After this 10th plate is given to LORD SHIVA then the nine forms of Durga are invoked as follows...

- Inviting the 1st female half Lord Shiva - Sati, also known as BRAMHA CHARINI
- Inviting the 2nd female half of Lord Shiva - Parvati, also known as SHALPUTRI
- Inviting the 3rd female half of Lord Shiva - Gowrie, also known as CHANGRAGANTA
- Inviting the 4th female half of Lord Shiva - Rudrani, also known as KUSHMANDI
- Inviting the 5th female half of Lord Shiva - Ratty, also known as SKANDAMATA
- Inviting the 6th female half of Lord Shiva - Kali, also known as KATYANI
- Inviting the 7th female half of Lord Shiva - Rohini, also known as GANGA
- Inviting the 8th female half of Lord Shiva - Shakti, also known as MAHAGAURI
- Inviting the 9th female half of Lord Shiva - Indrani, also known as SIDDIDATRI

Bringing all the 9 forms into the form of Nav-Durga

- Ritual to the procreative energy of the universe called Durga
- Marrying Durga to Lord Shiva
- Releasing of the egg - Cutting of the nutmeg
- Protecting & growing of the egg - Hirany Garbha

- Breaking of the egg - Birth from the mother
- Cutting of the banana flower - A symbol creation for children
- Blessing the child with worldly prosperity
- Marrying Durga to Lord Shiva
- Ritual to install the flag of the Deity
- Contemplation on Nav-Durga - The Slokas
- Havan or Fire Ritual to conclude puja
- Closing Prayers before Artie

Preparation of an Altar of the Gods

Your Must Have an Altar or Location for praying in the House

This place is where you can communicate with God. This location when you pray every day will become charged with Holy Energy. You will benefit from this energy of the gods when you pray everyday. It's like tuning into the same special radio station everyday...

It is stated that where an altar of God is present, that home will never be affected by theft, evils sprits or enemies.

To start you Altar you will need the following items......

1.   Picture/Murti of Lord GANESH to remove all your Obstacles

2.   Picture/Murti of Lord SHIVA to protect you from all evils

3.   Picture/Murti of Lord KRISHNA to bring Bliss and Good feelings

4.   Picture/Murti of Goddess DURGA to obtain blessings of Mothers

139

5.   Picture/Murti of Goddess LAXMI to Obtain Wealth and Prosperity

6.   Picture/Murti of SARSWATY to obtain Knowledge & Wealth

7.   Picture/Murti of Lord VISHNU to Obtain Comfortable Environments

8.   Picture/Murti of Lord HANUMAN to be blessed with Health/Strength

9.   A Dark stone (attached) LINGAM to create pleasure in love/ marriage

PLEASE NOTE:

Do not have more than ONE Ganesh Murti on Altar. Do not worship more than ONE Durga Murti on altar (Only ONE mother.) The TOP MOST picture of your Altar cannot be LAKSMI. Do not buy a loose Shivling or White Shivalingam if your are married

Chapter 17
The Controversy: Which is the
Correct Day to Celebrate a Holiday

The correct day on which a festival is celebrated is based according to the rules of the Shastras by our Rishis or ancient scientists.

As a (tithe) LUNAR DAY generally covers a portion of two days, it sometimes happens that, though for civil purposes the tithe of a day is that which is current at sunrise, yet for religious purposes, the tithe may have to be celebrated on the (previous) day when it begins. When a tithe is appointed for the celebration of a feast or fast, to be kept at forenoon, midday, late afternoon, midnight, etc., it is obvious that the feast or fast must be observed on the day when the tithe covers the prescribed part of the day. The day for such purposes is divided, first of all, into five portions between sunrise and sunset.

Please Note: 2.5 Ghatikas = 1 Hour

1	Pratahkala	Early forenoon	6 Ghatikas from Sunrise	2.4 hours from Sunrise

2	Sangava	Forenoon	6 – 12 Ghatikas from Sunrise	4.8 hours from Sunrise
3	Maadhyahna	Midday	12 – 18 Ghatikas from Sunrise	7.2 hours from Sunrise
4	Aparahna	Afternoon	18 – 24 Ghatikas from Sunrise	9.6 hours from Sunrise
5	Sayahna	Late Afternoon	24 – 30 Ghatikas from Sunrise	10.4 hours from Sunrise

(a) The 4 ghatikas before sunrise are called arunodaya or rise of dawn.

(b) The 6 ghatikas after sunset are called prasosha or evening.

(c) The 2 ghatikas in the middle of the night are called nisitha, midnight

(d) A festival marked as PURVAVIDDHA is celebrated on the first day of the tithe, not on the second. A festival celebrated on the second day on which a tithe is current is said to be PARAVIDDHA.

Amavasya- the Tarpana or minor Sraddha should be in Aparahna. If it occurs in Aparahna on two days, and is less than 60 ghatikas in length, it is kept on the first day; otherwise (i.e., if of normal length or longer) on second day. If not occurring in Aparahna of two days, it should be kept on the first day. The same rule is observed for Sraddhas.

Suklayajurveda - Amavasya is kept on the third day, before moonrise.

Time for **Yugas (Yajna Kala**) - The last fourth part of a parva (i.e., either amavasya or paurnami) and first three parts of pratipad are suitable as yagakala. If there is yagakala on two days, then the day on which the kala is current at noon is the proper day.

Chaturdasi (14th tithe) - Krishna chaturdasi in every month is Sivaratri, but Mahga - KRISNA PAKSH

Chaturdasi (14) is Maha Sivaratri.

Chaturmasya Dvityas- Bhadrapada Krishna Paksh Davityas; Phalguna Krishna Paksh (2) & Karttika Krisna Paksh (2).

The Krishna Paksh Dvitya in Ashadha, Sravana, Bhadrapada and Asvina is called Asunyasayana Vrata and the fast is broken at moonrise.

Ekadasi - (11th Lunar day) - Every Ekadasi is sacred, like every Amavasya, and receives a special name. It is called Vijaya when joined with the nakshatra "Punarvasu." The following are the names of the 24 Ekadasi: (12 in bright halves and 12 in dark halves of the 12 lunar months).

The following Table shows the different Ekadasi for the months in the year...

MONTH	SUKLAPAKSHA	KRISHNA PAKSH
Chaitra	Kamada Ekadasi	Varuthini ekadasi
Vaisakha	Mohini ekadasi	
Jyeshtha	Nirjala ekadasi	Yogi ekadasi
Ashadha	Vishnusayanotsava; Sayani or Vishnusayani ekadasi (i.e. going to sleep)	Kamada ekadasi or Kamika ekadasi
Sravana	Putrads ekadasi	Aja ekadasi

Bhadrapada	Vishnuparivartanotsava or parivaritini ekadasi (Vishnu turning on his side) called Vishnusrinkhala, when 11th and 12th tithes meet in nakshatra 'Sravana	Indira ekadasi
Asvina	Pasankusa ekadasi	Rama ekadasi
Karttika	Prabodhini ekadasi (walking of Vishnu), Bhishma panchakavrata commences.	Utpatti ekadasi
Margasirsha	Mokshada ekadasi	Saphala ekadasi
Pausha	Putrada ekadasi or Mukkotti or Vaikuntha ekadasi	Shattila ekadasi
Magha	Jaya ekadasi	Vijaya ekadasi
Phalguna	Amalaki ekadasi	Papamochini ekadasi

Vaishnavas - If dasami ends after 56 ghatikas, the fast is on dvadasi day. If on ekadasi day, there is any part of navami or dasami day, then also the fast should be kept on dvadasi. If dvadasi touches three days, then the fast is on the day which is wholly dvadasi and paranam on the next day when dvadasi ends. In any other case, ekadasi is the fast day and dvadasi the Day of paranam. Sanyasins and widows of all creeds observe this rule for Ekadasi.

    Smarthas - Even if dasami ends after 56 ghatikas, the fast is kept on ekadasi. If dvadasi touches three days Smarthas observe the first dvadasi day as Ekadasi.

Kamya Ekadasi - Those who observe ekadasi for Kamya purposes (begetting children, etc.) observe the Smartha rule: those who observe ekadasi for moksha (like Sanyasins) observe the Vaishnava rule. If a DEATH occurs on the day of ekadasi fast, whether it be Ekadasi or Dvadasi tithi, then the Sraddha is on the next day. Only Madhvas and Tengalai Vaishnavas observe this rule: Smarthas and Vadagalai Vaishnavas observe the Sraddha on ekadasi fast day also.

Grahana - For 9 hours before commencement of a lunar eclipse, and for 12 hours before commencement of a solar eclipse, neither Sraddha nor meals are allowed: they are allowed after Moksha, i.e., release of the eclipsed body. On the occasion of a grasthodaya eclipse of the moon (when moon rises in an eclipsed condition), neither Sraddha nor meals are allowed during day, and after Moksha, performers of Purina Sraddha must fast and perform Sraddha next day but others may have food at night. If the moon sets in an eclipsed condition, (Grasthasthamanam) meals are allowed only after next moonrise, except to the performer of Sraddha, who must fast in the night and perform Sraddha next day. Pregnant Women are not allowed to use knives to cut any thing during this time. According to Manu, no Sraddha on account of a tithe can be performed at night, but Sraddhas on account of eclipse must be performed during the time of eclipse, even if it be at night.

Chapter 18
Which is a Good Day to Perform the Right Puja?

There has been a lot of confusion regarding when is a good time to do a specific Puja and whether your Puja will be done on the right day and so on. Usually Pundits and Hindu Priests will tell a Yagman that a specific Puja has to be done on a specific day or else the Puja would not be blessed—however, this is *incorrect and misleading.* If such is the case, then why do all the temples do Pujas on Sunday mornings?

Nowadays, some Hindu Priests do Pujas according to their own convenience. They do not check whether it is a good day or time to do a Puja, rather they do it according to appointment. This is not good because the results of blessings from a Puja can last longer when done on certain days, times and months. Some priests may tell a Yagman that he needs to do a *specific puja* every year, however, this is not true. It is good to do a puja every year, but does a car break down in the same place every year? Does a person have the same problems in their life every year? Of course not!

When a person has problems with money they would have to do Laksmi Puja, when they have education problems, a Saraswaty Puja will be needed, and when a

146

woman has marriage problems a Shiva Puja is needed. As you can see the Pujas are done every year according to the need. If you wish to perform a specific Puja every year, consult with your Hindu Priest. Such a priest must have knowledge of Vedic Astrology or Jyotish; if not he will not be able to tell what kind of Puja is required for you to do.

Usually any Puja can be done anytime or any day because prayer to God can never be bad. However if a Puja is done at certain times, certain results can be obtained and the benefits can be increased if it is done at the most auspicious time. *How does a person know which is the most auspicious time for a puja?* Well, here is a simple table that may guide you to know if your puja is being done at a good time. The day you perform a puja will determine what your desire is, and what blessings you will receive, *the time* of your Puja is auspicious according to your Birth Time and so on...

Chapter 19
Rules & Discipline to Observe Prior to the Puja Day

The following are the basic rules and discipline that must be observed prior to a puja:

1. You must clean the house or Temple thoroughly at least a week before a puja.
2. Do not eat any fish, meat or eggs at least TWO weeks before the Puja day This is because the Lunar Fortnight or Moon phase lasts at least 14 days
3. Try to live by the following rules at least 5 days before the Puja day
   - No drinking of Alcohol, taking of Drugs
   - No Sexual contact with the opposite sex
   - No quarrelling with family members
   - No coming into the home after Midnight (unless you are working)
   - Welcome all visitors to the house and serve them good food
   - Invite Religious and Spiritual people(Bramhins) to the home

- Listen to the religious songs and recitation of Mantras at this time
- Avoid listening to Rock music etc...music must be classical in nature

4. On the Day of the Puja:
    - Do not eat or drink anything salty in the morning
    - Make sure you go to the bathroom prior to the Puja, as you cannot get up and go to the washroom once the Puja has started
    - Do not taste the food or prasad before the commencement of Puja.

Chapter 20
How to Select a Holy Guru

This chapter is intended as a first aid manual for all those who need a *Guru* or *Spiritual Leader*. First aid has its limits, and while it can be used to alleviate basic problems, more severe ones must be directed to a trained professional. Many difficulties which might be encountered in the metaphysics realm cannot be solved by the average individual, as these difficulties really involve the work of a specialist. There are a number of factors which influence the location of an honest and competent guru. Generally speaking, gurus are hard to find for several reasons: your own attitude toward astrology, the paucity of good gurus, and the ready availability of fraudulent ones.

First, let's discuss the attitude you may bring with you as a client. Many people have a mental block when even considering the idea of astrology. Our culture has instilled in us a belief that all existence is on the material plane, that there is no such thing as "metaphysical energy." Because most of us have "programmed" ourselves to accept this belief, we refuse to consider seriously that any other form of existence is possible. We can't accept the work or the energy of any guru when we believe in manifestation only on a material or physical level. Some people may outwardly reject the permeating western cultural belief that all existence occurs on the material plane, but the belief is still held deep within them. These people will also reject any real astrology predictions. It can be difficult for those who outwardly or intellectually think they have rejected childhood beliefs, for the predictions may not be positive, and they really won't know why.

In order to successfully change negative events, the guru must work within the boundaries that the client will accept. When a guru is from another culture, or works within a practice which is unacceptable to the client, the client may not allow himself to accept the help. This means that the guru must personally analyze every client, to the extent of whether or not the client can accept the work. If the client can't accept the help there is no point in the guru making an appointment. If you call a guru, and for some reason he doesn't wish to see you as a client, don't take the rejection personally. It merely means that he realizes he cannot work with what you need. A rejection of this sort usually means that you should continue your search for a competent guru who can work within your cultural background. You might start your search by looking for someone who works in a way compatible with your own religious tradition - the religious practice of your youth.

People are afraid to work with a guru for many different reasons. For example, some people believe that all astrology is limited to afflicted persons.

Those who believe this way should seek a priest, minister, or Christian Scientist Practitioner to pray for them. They will attain as much from the prayer of their priest or minister as they would from anything a trained guru can do. Christian Scientist Practitioners are gurus, as are those of the Religious Science church who "treat" people. Neither of these groups may like to be classed in this way with Hexenmeisters and Witches, Santeros and Strega, but the cures of Christian Science are just as real as those of the others. Other people, particularly the Protestant Fundamentalist believers, think that astrology involves some kind of pact with the devil. Holding these beliefs makes valid astrology for these people an impossible alternative. Those who believe this should return to the church of their childhood and ask the minister to pray for them. The percentage of people open to work with a guru is very small. These are the people who will allow the guru to diagnose and prescribe for them in accordance with the requirements of their particular case. These people will attain a satisfactory solution to their problems.

The next obstacle in your search for a guru is the problem of finding a good one. There are many fraudulent gurus in the field. Palm, card and tea leaf readers often pretend to have knowledge on astrology. Some assure the client he has been cursed, and only large sums of cash will free him of it. Usually the client has never been cursed in the first place. An easy way to avoid this type of fraudulent guru is to notice how he advertises himself. Store front signs, flyers on the street corner, any kind of a "hand-out" advertisement will usually be your clue that this person is not a professional. Gypsy fortune-tellers will not be any help in solving a serious problem, or having a serious reading. The flamboyant personality, the psychic showman is not the kind of worker you need to look for. If you hear of someone who works as a guru, and you hear he is booked months in advance, or that he has a waiting list of the best clients, people in show business and the social register, then you know that this person is not really a guru. He may be a guru but a sincere guru does not let people, even other clients, know who his clients are. If he is "counselor to the stars" other people don't know it, and the stars don't tell.

Don't confuse the guru with the average psychic; gurus are not psychics. The information that a guru provides has a deeper meaning and impact in a person's life and spiritual future. Psychic readers basically cater to the "unwashed public", people who don't know much about the occult, and who want to learn some deep dark secret about themselves. Many people have had readings from various psychics and readers. This kind of reading is often harmless, and they can be very useful in their own way. They can help someone break the bonds of the "life is only material" belief, for the psychic may know things that he or she can only know because of knowledge coming from some other plane. Don't discourage your friends from their psychic readings for it may be an interesting experience for them. But this kind of reader is not a guru. A guru will not do "psychic readings" for your entertainment.

The sincere guru is not a "psychic investigator." He may be disgustingly prosaic about his work, but he is also calm, efficient and to the point. He is usually uninterested in your psychic experiences, and will only tell you one of his to prove a point. The person who brags of his accomplishments, or who brags about the fame and social standing of his clients is usually not a valid guru. If he talks about how he suffered to learn, and how eternally grateful you should be to him, you might want to avoid him. If he talks about his power, and how he can use it over the people, he is usually not serving the truth. Anyone who gloats over the spiritual accomplishments or the wonders he has performed is not who you are looking for. There are a few sign-posts along the way when you search for a sincere guru. It doesn't really matter what practice the individual follows or what format he uses, but there are a few things all gurus share in common. By

153

following these sign-posts you may find the needle in the haystack - the compatible Guru.

1. He doesn't advertise in any way. Clients come by word of mouth recommendation. Occasionally a client may simply walk through the door, not really knowing why he came. The guru is not to be found in the yellow pages; he may not be listed in the white pages either. `He maintains a low profile in his neighborhood - although many people may know that he is there.

2. The guru does not live alone. He or she may be married or otherwise mated, or may live with a friend or associate. Gurus rarely live alone for they are unable to work effectively without the "earthling force" provided when living with another person who does not do the same work.

3. You will feel completely at home with the guru the first time you meet. In order that the work you need be effective, you must have an innate sense of trust in him. You must be open and feel comfortable. The trust you feel will be an intuitive and an instinctive one. If this feeling does not take place shortly after or as you meet the guru, he won't be able to help you. If the guru senses your hesitancy he will try to put you to at ease. However, this will mean that you will have to visit him several more times before you will be able to accept any work he does. Trust is an interesting feeling. We immediately trust certain people - and the trust seems to take place somewhere in our guts. Trust doesn't happen when we use the intellectual mind too much, for then we begin to trust based on an intellectual appraisal of the situation. We are sometimes afraid to admit our "trust or distrust" to ourselves, for we may think that to immediately like or dislike someone intuitively is judging that person. If we listen to our "gut" the intuitive feeling inside ourselves can

guide us, and help us know what we need to know, without judging others.

4. The guru will instantly "know" you. He will look at you with a glance that your spirit may feel piercing to the core of your soul. If he has been in practice a number of years, knows you and will tell you things that strike deep chords within you. Eventually you will learn that you cannot deceive a true guru! It is impossible to lie to a true guru.

5. A sincere guru may not be readily available when you phone. You may get an answering machine when you call. You may speak to someone who takes a message for you, and this person may ask you for your name, birth data and for some brief description as to why you are calling. You may then be asked to call back in a few days in order to make an appointment. The delay in making appointments usually occurs to avoid the potential client who wants to handle an emergency. When people allow their lives to hang on a thread of time they are indicating that they do not want to take responsibility for their own life. They are really asking that the guru save them from something that they have let build up until it becomes an emergency. The guru is put into the position of taking responsibility for the person, something that they must refuse to do.

6. Usually gurus are very warm and receptive to you. They are also non-judgmental. When you come to visit for the first time, you are shown warmth and friendliness because you are completely accepted by the person who will help you. The guru is not cold and arrogant - for you are there to change your consciousness for the better. If you find it difficult to accept warmth or if you are suspicious of someone who is warm and friendly, this will serve to discourage your further interest in this kind of work. Genuine warmth and sincerity usually go together.

If you are searching for a guru for curiosity's sake, you may be taken for a "roller coaster ride" which will be good for your soul, but which may leave you a bit shaken. You may even receive all kinds of deceptive mystical information that may help you spiritually, but which will eventually expose your motives to yourself. The self-awakening may be rather unpleasant.

In your search there are also three things to beware of; they are not immediately noticeable, but will develop over a period of time while you are working out of your difficulties with the guru. They usually indicate a guru who has not really developed beyond certain point. The work may be effective, but the worker's self development may have flaws. The three things are:

1. Beware of gurus who try to "lay a trip" on you. They belong, morally, to the same school as they gypsy fortune tellers. If they stress overcoming your problems with willpower, if they want you to consider yourself a failure or if they make you feel guilty about anything, they are laying a trip on you, not helping you. Any person who judges you and finds you lacking, who makes you feel guilty, or who places you in fear of the unknown is putting you on some kind of mental trip for their own benefit. They are not helping you. Avoid these moral frauds and keep looking for one who is ethical.

2. Beware of dependency. When a guru tries to make another person dependent on him he is not helping but rather enslaving the client. When a person encourages your dependency he may have negative motivations. This also happens when a worker lays a "holy trip" on you. He makes you feel guilty because he is "holy" and you are not. This does not help. No true guru will do this, as he knows the moral consequences of claiming holiness. False ones will, and frequently do.

3. Beware of immediate acceptance as a student. You are coming for help from a disadvantaged position. Why should anyone want you to join a class until you have your act together? If the request is real you will get a meaningful explanation. Otherwise be suspicious. This is also true of those who inform you on the first visit that you need to be initiated. Initiation is never properly done to solve a problem in a person's life, it must be done only when someone has assumed responsibility for himself, and grown to the point where initiation can be accepted. Look for another guru in these cases.

Now that you've found a guru, let's take the relationship between you a bit further. When working with someone who can help you rid yourself of any problem you may wish to remove, you can expect to have a relationship which varies with each case.

In fact, each guru will have a unique relationship with each client. Usually on your first visit you will discuss the case, and the guru will tell you just what he feels has to be done to solve the problem. This may involve anything from his praying over your head, blessing you, recommending a bath for you to take or giving you a prepared bath, giving you some incense to burn or maintain a special diet, fast or period of holiness.

If the guru feels that further work may be necessary, you will be (usually) asked to purchase an assortment of materials, or to obtain them on your own.

At your fist meeting you will set up a new appointment for the next visit. If you have been told to bring things you should bring them with you. In some cases you may be asked to bring a friend, or husband or the person who referred you to the guru. Certain gurus will not see a client alone, in some cases although the discussions are always done in private.

Usually, after the second or third visit, the guru will give you an appointment a month or more in the future, or will simply suggest that you call him if you continue to have any difficulties. This is an indication that the therapy he feels necessary for your case is over. Your problem will probably have vanished, and the solution is in sight, if not at hand. Unless you know that your guru teaches and accepts clients for long range therapy, do not be disappointed if he does not ask you to become a student.

Some gurus teach and some do not. Some do long range therapy for clients who need it, and others do not. The therapy is not psychology, and usually has no referents to psychology, either in terms or method. In any case the guru will suggest that you study with him only if he feels that it will be of benefit to you. Unless the guru feels that you should be doing the same work he is doing, he will not even suggest training you. It is not very often that one sees a client who has the capacity as a student. My best student was almost literally dragged in off the street, and after spending six months telling her she should be helping people, she finally agreed to let me teach her.

If your are having either a short or long term relationship with a guru, sometimes the relationship is marred by sexual overtones of some kind. Usually this occurs during the first two or three visits. Should you want to date your guru, or should you feel a sudden urge to have sexual intercourse with this person, you must doubt both the guru's motives and your own. You should suppress the desire and examine it later on your own - in private. If the suggestion originates from the guru, his or her motives are in question. Why would a helping person want to have a relationship with anyone who needs help? A relationship, by definition, involves a sharing on an equal or almost equal basis. A guru cannot really share anything of himself with a client - except a body! He or she can't share any life experiences or real thoughts or knowledge with you if you are in the process of solving

158

problems. Why isn't your guru looking for a relationship with a peer? If the guru is really interested in you why not wait until you have your act together, and then introduce the subject verbally?

If the urge to have a sexual relationship with the guru originated from you, it's time to question your sincerity. Several things could be operating here. Some people want to drag the person who helps them down to their own level. If the guru will have sex with you, then you can't be all bad. At least you are attractive. Some people think that when you seduce a helper you can prove this person wrong. Very insecure people feel that sex is one way to overcome having to face some of the other facets of personality that are not too attractive under close personal scrutiny. The desire to have sex with someone does not always mean you like that person. Sometimes it is used as a means of control. Any desire to have sex with a guru should be examined closely, for it is not a mature response.

Before beginning your search for someone who can really help you, it's important to realize that the sincere guru is not working just for your benefit. The true guru is working only for God - and he is primarily concerned with his own knowledge and spiritual evolution.

Your importance as a client is secondary to his primary dedication. Gurus help others because they know that by helping you they are renewing the blessings of the universe. In other words, they help you as they walk a private path.

Money is another issue here for often the most dedicated person is not rich. The person dedicated to helping others doesn't charge tremendous amounts of money to do his work; and if you have a problem you can work on clearing up that problem even if you don't have money. Some day you will have money, and at that time

159

you can help him buy his food and pay his rent or living expenses by donating what you feel the help he gave you was worth to you. In the meantime, you should pay him whatever you can afford, no matter how little it is. A truly dedicated guru will not refuse to work with any sincere client.

Sometimes a guru will quote a fee for work, sometimes not. If a fee is quoted, and you really need to have the work done you will have the funds to pay him. Some people have lived life in a negative manner, and only by paying a fee are they entitled to the work. Occasionally the guru will quote a ridiculous fee because he feels that is the only way you will understand he does not want to work with you. Gurus tend to refuse work that is requested for the wrong reasons, and they sometimes refuse it in rather peculiar ways.

Locating a guru can be difficult because the real work is unsung. The person on this path has not chosen an easy and lucrative life. For this reason, competent workers in the field are not easily found. Keep looking. When the time is right, when you are truly sincere, the Devtas will direct you and help you find your Guru.

Finally, when the true Guru-Disciple relationship forms, a bond of love develops. As the disciple improves his or her knowledge and develops a better understanding of the scriptures, questions will be raised and the disciple will crave contact with the Guru. Some of the reasons the devotee will have for seeking the attention of the Guru will include:

- Asking questions about the mystical meaning of a certain stories or passages in the scriptures
- Letting the Guru know how well they are progressing with their learning
- Providing feedback to the Guru about how well the blessings and mantras worked in

healing or in changing some aspect of the devotee's life.

- Seeking help from the Guru in interpreting the dreams of the devotee.

No matter what the rationale is in the minds of the devotee for making contact with the Guru, the often hidden or underlying reason is simply to feel the touch of the Guru's love. The voice of the Guru instills confidence, creates a feeling of warmth, reinforces a sense of belonging and provides inner meaning to the life of the devotee. Such love knows no boundaries and the life of the Guru becomes enmeshed with the lives of numerous devotees spread over many countries all across the world. It is for this reason that the Guru establishes multiple ashram centers where devotees can go and feel the presence of their Guru. So whenever you feel the urge to contact your Guru, close your eyes and imagine his form and his presence will be with you. You will then begin to feel at ease knowing that he is close and is aware of your inner turmoil.

Chapter 21
The Power of the Number 9, 666 and 18

Vedic Code #9 –The Vedic Code of Indra

Before we proceed to the next chapters, it is important that you understand the tremendous power of Vedic Code #9. As we discussed in the Introduction, any number added to 9 does not lose its Vedic Code identity. Any number that is a multiple of 9 retains its identity as 9, also. The number 9 can have a tremendously negative effect on a situation or an extremely positive effect depending on the connection or path it is related to. Many famous criminals have Birth Code #9. (See Appendix 2 for Birth Code Information)

Six hundred and sixty-six (666) adds to 18, which adds to 9, which symbolizes (at least) a tremendous number of curiously similar coincidences. In the New Testament, the Book of Revelation (13:17-18) cryptically asserts 666 to be "the number of a man," associated with the beast, an antagonistic creature that appears briefly about two-thirds into the apocalyptic vision. In modern popular culture, 666 has become one of the most widely recognized symbols for the Antichrist or, alternately, the Devil. 666 is the magic sum, or sum of the magic constants of a six by six magic square, any row or column of which adds up to 111.

A Great Sidereal Year is 25,920 years. This is how long it takes for all the planets to return to their same positions and relationships to each other. It has to do with the precessions of the equinoxes. This means that spring and fall equinoxes occur just a fraction earlier each year. It takes 72 years to complete one degree of equinoctial advance (7+2=9).

If you add the digits of the Great Sidereal Year, you find they also equate to 18 – and, of course, 1+8=9. Two and a half degrees of equinoctial precession occur in 180 years (1+8+0=9), a period, which cycle experts have shown to be extremely important in political changes.

In the monthly bulletin of the New Jersey Astrologers Association, editor George J. McCormack published many series of cosmological cycles, all of which equate to the number 9 – and to man. "The added digits of various cosmic cycles," he wrote in the November 1958 issue of *Astrotech*, "when reduced to 9 shows a striking relationship between macrocosmic and microcosmic cycles. The Grand Year of Equinoctial Precession – 25,920 years – equates to 18 or 9. The 360 degrees of the zodiac and of terrestrial longitude also equate to 9. Whether you add all the minutes in a day (1,440) or all the seconds (86,400), the digits always add to nine. One degree of equinoctial advance takes 72 years."

Any number of degrees of equinoctial precession equates to 9! Two degrees take 144 years; 3 degrees take 270 years; 10 degrees, 720 years; 5 degrees, 360 years. Or the entire 360 degrees of precession take 25,920 years – both of which, as we have seen, equal 9.

The mean normal respiration rate in humans is 18 times a minute; the normal human heart beat or pulse rate is 72 times a minute. Both equate to nine. The average number of heartbeats in one hour comes to 4,320 – or 9. The average number of breaths in an hour is 1,080 – also 9. In 24 hours the heart beats an average of 103,680 times, all which add to 18 or 9.

It takes 270 days or 9 months to complete the period of human gestation. Is this also a coincidence? It hardly seem coincidental that the harmonious angel of 30 degrees, 60 degrees, 120 degrees and 150 degrees formed between planets equate either 3 or 6, while the adverse or discordant aspects of 45 degrees, 90 degrees, 135 degrees and 180 degrees, each total 9!

Historians and cycle experts have concluded that great political, dynastic, and historical changes occur in cycles, which all equate to 9. These are exactly the number of years during which any number of degrees (or fractions thereof) of equinoctial precession take place. It takes 2,160 years for the equinoxes to proceed through 30 degrees of the zodiac or 1 sign. The equinoxes proceed through the 90-degree (3 signs) in 6,480 years. It moves one half of a degree in 36 years, a quarter of a degree in 18 years, and eighth of a degree in 9 years.

The 6,480-year period (3 signs) is kabalistically called an Age, and the centers of world civilization have gradually moved westward in phase with this precession. Ancient records of the cradle of Western civilization indicate that these 6,480-year cycles are traditionally believed to end in global catastrophe.

One of these kabalistic observations was that the reduced sum of all digits is 9. Thus, 1, 2, 3, 4, 5, 6, 7, 8, and 9 added together equals 45 (4+5=9). *Nine is the basis of the unit value of all numbers!*

Nine is also the fantastic number that figured in the death of Maximilian, emperor of Mexico – and in the silver peso that was coined in his honor. He reigned for three short years, between 1864 and 1867. When the last coinage was struck during his reign, the die broke. The last piece was badly mangled, and there hangs the thread of a fantastic story: as soon as the die broke, a tiny chip (something like a gash) appeared on Maximilian's forehead. As each peso was minted, the crack grew a little bigger and the die became progressively worse. By the time the 32nd piece was minted, the damage was clearly evident. (Maximilian was only 32 years old when he became emperor.) The next three coins were badly broken, and the final (36th) piece was mangled almost beyond recognition. Indian workmen took this as an omen that the emperor would die violently of a head wound at the age of 36 – killed either by a sword or bullet wound. The American officer in charge of the Mint rejected the Aztec, Miztec and Toltec superstitions of his Indio workmen, but they were right! Napoleon III placed Ferdinand Joseph Maximilian, brother of the emperor of Austria, on Mexico's throne on June 12, 1864. Despite appearances, Maximilian was a true humanitarian, who really wanted to help the Mexicans. But he was executed on June 19, 1867, at the age of 36. Bullets horribly mangled his whole body but only one bullet entered his head – and at the exact spot designated by the chip, which appeared on his likeness on the silver peso! Was this the power of 9 operating in his life?

All cultures in all history reflect this value of 9 as adverse to human kind on this planet. The 144,000 saints gathered from the 12 tribes of Israel equal 9.

The Masonic Order of the "Elect of Nine" incorporates 9 roses, 9 lights and 9 knocks in the ceremony.

Ancient Jews were forbidden to wear either the Talleth or the Phylacteries on the 9th day of the month of Ab.

In the story of the Kilhiveh and Alwen, the castle was built with 9 gates and 9 portals beside which sat 9 dogs. King Arthur symbolically fought an enchanted pig (his baser nature) for 9 days and 9 nights.

Receiving the Holy Eucharist on the first Fridays of 9 consecutive months is believed by Roman Catholics to be assurance of dying in a state of grace. Novenas are celebrated for 9 consecutive days.

In Grecian mythology there are 9 Muses, the daughters of Jupiter and Mnemosyne (memory). When Roman male infants were 9 days old, a Feast of Purification was held for them. Romans were buried on the 9th day. A "Novennalia" or Feast of Death was held for the deceased every 9th year.

There are 9 mother Goddesses in Hinduism. A woman is considered perfect when she is able to perform the 9 functions of a woman in life. Most of the Gods in Hinduism are considered to have 9 different functions or forms. The deity known as Ganesh has 9 forms and is considered the Remover of Obstacles.

The most interesting correlation to the 9 is the goddess of wealth in Hinduism called Laksmi. She is considered the white light that exists in our Universe, and it is stated in the Vedic text that Laksmi has 9 forms, which can be exactly compared to the 9 forms of electromagnetic energy found in the white light coming from the Sun. This includes the 7 colors of the rainbow that we see as well as the 2 we don't see – ultraviolet and infrared.

The 9 is the number of Yamraj, the God of Death and also represents the Hindu God Dharamraj, the God of Truth. The God of Death is considered the guardian of hell and burial grounds. It may appear to be coincidence that you will find most burial grounds are on a street that adds up to a 9 or at an address that adds up to a 9. The location where truth is tested and tried – courthouses – usually have addresses that add up to the #9.

Famous missionaries, priests, great swamis and gurus, such as SAI BABA, have Birth Codes that add up to the #9. One of the most loved U. S. presidents, Bill Clinton, has a Birth Code of 9.

Due to its highest position in the number system it is considered the limit at which our present Universe ends and the next Universe begins. It is the limiting point between parallel universes. After the 9th form of electromagnetic energy, which is the limit of the speed of light, the Universe enters into another dimension where no laws of physics are able to work.

Because of its encompassing effect on life in the Universe, the 9 is closest to God, but also closest to 0, the companion of what is considered negative or evil; thus in Vedic Science, we see 9 and multiples of 9 occurring frequently in the Vedic scriptures.

There are 18 (1+8=9) chapters in the Bhagavad Gita. A normal person takes 21,600 (2+1+6=9) breaths in day. There are 792,000 (7+9+2=18, 1+8=9) nadis or energy centers in the human body. Vedic hymns are written in meters of 9. However, like the odometer on a car, when the highest level of 9 is reached, it rolls over to 0 to begin its cycle all over again.

Because of this proximity or closeness to 0, the number 9 is also farthest from God. Thus 9 acts with confusion in its normal state because it does not know if it belongs to God or to Yama (God of Death). If it is well grounded and follows the Satvic path (path of goodness) consistently, 9 can achieve the highest level of spirituality. If it follows the Tamasic path (path of ignorance and darkness); 9 can end up in the deepest levels of Patal (Hell). It is because of this multiplicity of behavior that confusion reigns in our true understanding of this number.

John Lennon: How the #9 Affected His Life

John Lennon, the musician and songwriter, believed in the influence of the 9. He was born on October 9, 1940. His mother's house was 9 Newcastle Road in Liverpool, where John wrote at least three songs with 9 in the title. The three songs were: "One after 909," "Revolution No. 9,"and "# 9 Dream." The song "Imagine" starts with the 9th letter of the alphabet. The Impresario Brian Epstein first saw the Beatles perform live when he attended one of their lunchtime gigs at the Cavern in Liverpool on November 9, 1961. He quickly became their manager, signing their EMI Parlophone record deal on May 9, 1962.

The Beatles' first song, "Love Me Do", had the number 4949. John Lennon first met Yoko Ono on November 9, 1966. The Beatles' legal partnership was ended on January 9, 1975. John and Yoko's son Sean was born on John's birthday, October 9 1975. They lived in an apartment on West 72nd Street, New York (7+2=9). Their apartment number in the Dakota building was also 72 (9).

John was shot and killed just outside that building on the evening of December 8, 1980, when it was December 9 back in Liverpool. His body was taken to a hospital on 9th Avenue. Using only the consonants of Beatle, the number comes to 'his' number, 9. Using only the consonants of Lennon, the number comes to 18, 1+8=9. Add the two – 9+9=18, 1+8=9 – and we have the numinous power of 9 reproducing and just as supernaturally returning us to Lennon's birth number.

Chapter 22
The Power of the Number 6 – The Form of Kali That Destroys All Evil

Special Note on the Power of Vedic Code
#6 –The Vedic Science Code of Kali

Small droplets of water condensing into storm clouds and falling earthward through cold layers of the atmosphere cannot "think." Yet one of these droplets, when it freezes, forms a flat hexagonal crystal. Countless billions of them comprise tiny snowflakes, each with six sides or arms – and each one different than all the others. No two ever alike, infinite variation and endless beauty. How does this happen? Why don't they sometimes have eight or ten sides or four?

A snowflake is a crystal of frozen water; a diamond is a crystal of "frozen" carbon. One is formed in the atmosphere, the other within the mantle of the Earth. One has six sides, the other 12. Each seems to conform to the geomagnetic field and/or celestial magnetic field. They cannot "think." They have no instinct, let alone reason; therefore, exogenous forces must act upon them.

Distant stars, great nations and tiny snowflakes all are inextricably intertwined. Weather conditions are strongly responsive to the crystallizing 60-degree angle between planets. This 60-degree (hexagon) was considered by all ancient civilizations to be "sacred." Two perfect triangles of 120 degrees when placed together form the symbol of Judaism, the Star of David. Each point of this star is 60 degrees to the next.

Bees all over the world build hexagonal honeycombs. It is "unthinkable" that bees, of their own intelligence, consciously agree to this standard. Only recently have engineers discovered that the hexagon is the strongest, most economical storage bin imaginable. Yet bees have always "known" this, but how? By instinct? If so, exactly what is this instinct? How does it differ from free choice?

How do bees all over the world (ever since bees were "invented") build six-sided storage bins for their honey? They've always done it and probably will continue doing so for as long as they are bees.

In the Vedic Code of Science, 6 is considered a code that represents power, destruction, frustration and great emotional upheaval in relationships between all things. The Vedic Code of 6 represents the influences of war, conflicts between people, war between countries, separation of couples and such things as mortgages, debts, credit cards and loans. You'll find that the police or security forces of a country are represented by the Vedic Code #6. An analysis of the Birth Codes of all the police or military members would reveal a predominant number of them that add up to the Vedic Code of 6.

In the Vedic Code of Science, the God of negative time and destruction of evil is known as Kali, the sixth form of the female goddesses. She is known as the caretaker of the rules of the Universe. When the rules are broken and evil thoughts, acts or intentions threaten the Universe, Kali is the one who corrects the person or destroys the evil permanently.

170

People with Birth Codes that add up to the Vedic Code 6 usually experience a lot of traffic tickets in their life, court problems and accidents, if they live a negative lifestyle. If they live a positive lifestyle, they will experience power, luxury, family inheritance, popularity and great reputation in their career. Usually getting a government position helps to uplift the life of Kali people in a positive manner.

The year 1961 is made up of the numbers 6 and 9. When turned upside down, the numbers remain the same.

The number 9 has remarkable inversion properties. When reversed, it becomes a 6. When added to 6 it becomes 15, which if you add 1+5, you get 6. If we take the number 133335 and add up the digits, the result is 9. If we take the reverse of this number 533331 and add them to the original number, the result is 666,666, a double form of evil.

The 6th planet from the Sun is Saturn. The number 6 also rules Mars. Both of these planets are considered negative planets in astrological science.

The Vedic Code of 6 rules such things as violence, assassinations, violent deaths and separations. Interestingly, the highest office with the most power is the office of the American President. The First President, George Washington, had a Birth Code of 6 (February 22). President Harrison had a Birth Code of 2 (February 9), when added to April 4, 1841- when he died in office - you get the Day Code of 6.

President Abraham Lincoln was assassinated and died in office. His Birth Code was 5 (February 12), and the day he died, Vedic Code 1 (April 15), when added to his Birth Code, gives the Vedic Code of 6, which indicates violent death. President William McKinley had a Birth Code of 3 (January 29), when added to the day he was shot in office (September 6), gives the Death Code of 9. McKinley died 8 days later on September 14, 1901.

President Warren Harding's Birth Code was 4 (November 2). He died in office after a heart attack on August 2, when added to the Day Code (4+ 2) gives the Vedic Code of 6. The Vedic Code of 6 (November 22) was also ruling at the time that President Kennedy was shot.

The first President Bush, elected in 1989, has a Birth Code of 9 (June 12). He was the first US president to take America into war after Vietnam. If you remember also, President Lyndon Johnson, the 36th (Vedic Code 9) US president, started the Vietnam War. His Birth Code was 8 (August 27), he was elected in the year (1963), which when added to his Birth Code results in 9 (code of struggle).

Bill Clinton, whose Birth Code is 9, was troubled by terrorist bombings throughout his term in office. He was also the first president to be impeached by the House of Representatives.

President George W. Bush (2001-2009) has a Birth Code of 4 (July 6), when added to the birthday of America (July 4) comes out to the Vedic Code of 6, the code of war. He restarted his father's legacy of war in Iraq. Please note his inaugural Day Code 2 (January 20), when added to his Birth Code, results in the Vedic Code 6. As I predicted, the United States was at war as long as he was the president.

It will take a strong personality like Hillary Clinton to take us out of all the wars. Please note that the planet Mars, which started its journey toward Earth when George W. Bush took office, is going to recede after the 2008 elections, and eventually ends its cycle by 2012 hence the return of the troops.

Obama is a number 3 Lifecode just like John F Kennedy. When you add their Lifecodes to that of the

United States (July, 4= 7+4= 11= 2) it comes out to 5 which means changes that are demonstrated in things such as change of party and change of direction for the country. Five also shows the presence of global confrontations. The global disputes of Kennedy were with Russia, and Obama's are with Iraq and China. Names are powerful mantras that identify and individual and are repeated; notice the similarities between Obama's name and Osama. The difference is one letter. The first vowel O is common not only with Obama and Osama, but also with John Kennedy. They all denote that there is secret ego-need for power in all these personalities. In each case also the American public was not fully informed about their actions. Obama's Lifecode three was running a 6 in 2010, and the American public was very disappointed and disenchanted with him during that year.

Chapter 23
When Spirits & Ghosts Have Sex with Women and Men

...Is It Created By The Location Or The Person?

PLEASE NOTE: Many women have consulted me on this subject, and in my research, I have found that many of them had some common factors that may have created this problem. Most of them were lonely, or her husband died for a while, or they were abused when they were young. Please keep this in mind and also understand that is a real problem that needs to be addressed as it is one that needs curing, which I will indicate at the end of this chapter.

Ranee came to me back in 1995. She he was crying as she spoke. She appeared very distressed. She was dressed in black and there were dark rings around her eyes. Her complexion seemed to have darkened over the years and there were dark spots on her cheeks and neck. She claimed that she was having lots of back pain, she was bleeding heavily in her menstrual periods and that she could not sleep at night.

She also said that she was constantly having problems at her job with co-workers and that nobody seemed to like her. She and her husband would fight constantly and he would refuse to sleep with her in the bed most of the time. Their sex life was almost dead and she has a lot of bloating and pains in her stomach around her navel.

After looking at her Vedic Chart, I asked her if she felt any pressure in her chest at night while sleeping. She nodded her head and then I asked her if she would feel like someone is having sex with her at night. She raised her head up quickly and looked at me', "How did you know that?" she said appearing startled, "Yes, its true but I have never told anyone."

"Do you get up in the morning, tired and exhausted as if you have had sex all night?" I asked.

"Yes, that's true" She answered now appearing shocked at my questions.

"Do you skip your menstrual cycles sometimes and do your have a lot of Cramps when you do have your cycle"

"That is true"

Do you notice a white streak in the menstrual blood during your cycle?"

"Yes, most times" She answered

"Does the love making start with you dreaming of your husband as the lover and then the person turns into a dark person at the end of the session of the sex?"

"Yes, that is true. That is exactly what happens" she shouted back.

"Alright stay calm, Ranee" I assured her

"Do your parents perform sacrificial prayers at any temples?"

"No, Swamiji, my husband does that at the Kali temple every once in a while" She continued, "The family priest would advise him to do that, so that our business can bring in more profits."

175

"Do you eat the meat that has been sacrificed at the temple?" I asked.

"When your husband actually makes love to you, it seems to be very painful and you actually do not feel any pleasure from his lovemaking. Is that right?

"Yes, the sex used to be great when we first got married. Now it's like a job for me sometimes" She said in a sad tone of voice

Well, it seems that your husband's way of praying is the cause of your unhappiness. The entity that is making love to you every night and draining your energy is none other than the spirits of the animals who have been sacrificed by your husband at the Kali Temple. If he continues to do so then your and his life will become more miserable and eventually all sexual desires will be lost and incurable illnesses will occur in your lives. You could have more problems with your children and you yourself will continue to feel the sprit making love to you every night. It could also cause you to lose your job and have more money problems than you have now."

"What can I do to correct this problem?" She asked pleadingly.

"Well, it is going to be difficult but in the end you and your family will experience great happiness, very little health problems and you will be able to enjoy wealth, love, great sex and family success." I said

"I will do anything to get out of this mess I have placed myself into. Please help me Swamiji, you are my only hope and I cannot wait to get started" She begged.

"What about your husband, will he follow all the rules I outline?"

"Do not worry about that. I will get him to follow later. First you have to help me and then I will be able to help him" She insisted.

"Ok! Here is what you need to do. You have to stop all red meat in your life for ever. For three months you have to avoid all meats, fish and eggs. Your husband will have to stop worshipping the devil and go to a real temple to worship God in his true form. He can see a real priest. He can accept Christ as his lord or perform charitable prayers as advised by the real priest. I will give you some instructions to take herbal baths, perform meditation and yoga exercises and some prayers to recite every day. You and your family have to give up all black clothes forever. That includes underwear, bras and socks. Black shoes and handbags are ok Make sure you are sleeping east west and not north south on your bed and you should be sleeping on the left of your husband. "

After working with Ranee for almost 3 months, her pains were gone, her menstrual cycles became regular, her complexion became lighter, her stomach was not bloating any more and her general health was very good. The love making sessions at night with the spirits were no longer happening and her and her husband were attending a nearby temple dedicated to Krishna where they did meditation and yoga sessions regularly.

One day her and her husband came to see me, they were very grateful to me and I began to explain some of the reasons why he and his wife went through this experience.

PLEASE NOTE:
From the above article you can see that our own karmas, experiences and actions create our own health problems and suffering in life. Following the wrong paths of life brings these negative things in your life. "If you live by the sword you die by the sword"

Are There Evil Spirits At Certain Locations? Can They Affect Your Life & Success There?

This problem needs to be addressed. *Many people move into homes without knowing that the previous owners might have performed evil actions there.* Thorough cleansing of the homes is needed before moving in. Inviting a priest and blessing of the home should always be done before moving in. The following chapter is narrated by a devotee of Swami ram Charran to illustrate that a person needs to look at their own actions before blaming location spirits for their suffering.

An Experience Described by a Devotee
Her name is VEEM

Veem:
"It's all true; all the dreams are very vivid. This apparition called SANGANI, whom I think is the devil comes to me in my dreams. I think he comes to take the dead soul to wherever it has to go. I saw him in my dream (very real life). His physical appearance was very strong looking. He had a shiny bald head and was walking around in front of me as though he was looking for something. He came to get something to take back. He looks at me and in a deep voice, said, I'm Sangani and walked away. Then I wake up wondering who Sangani was? But in the back of my mind, I knew he came to take a soul somewhere.

I dream of all dead friends and relatives shortly after their death; most of them never say a word—just always look at me or touch me.

I dreamed that I was driving my car and there was a big black snake in front of my car while I was driving. During this time in real life I was always inches from accidents that could have happened if I was ahead (in my car) a few seconds more.

I dreamt that my husband's father, who passed away years ago, was standing next to me by my bed with both of his hands on his waist. He was very mad at me. I saw this from above looking down at me sleeping and knowing that my husband was next to me. I saw him sleeping and was wondering why this man looks so much like him, but was shorter and smaller built. During this time in my real life, my husband left me and went to his family for many days and months each time

After seeing Swami Ram Charran, He gave me an Herbal Bath Mixture and I did that herbal bath procedure as he requested me to do."

My bath experience is as follows:

After the first bath from Swami, I woke up getting stronger inside (physically). I had so much energy, I ate twice as much and my appetite had come back. I love myself more today and feel happier with myself. Thank you, Swami, from the bottom of my heart.

The second "bath night" was very different from the first night's sleep. I didn't sleep at all. I felt as if there was someone there with me all night. This feeling was of someone as a soldier or guardian person who was strong and very protective over me as to make sure no one comes in that door to bother me. I felt his presence. He wasn't bad, just to guard or protect a special jewel. Again, I woke up feeling very energetic and not lazy or tired. My mind feels more clear, not as cloudy or confused. A good positive feeling was what was fascinating to me at the start of this morning. I haven't felt so confident and positive about myself—for today and for the future—as I do after taking the baths.

After the seventh day of the powder bath, I slept better, especially after I moved out of the house where KB dwelled—hence the bad dreams, pains, etc. I felt the evil spirits closer and everywhere, but they can't come inside of me or touch me. I can face them now instead of hiding from them.

Furthermore, while sitting upstairs in the altar/prayer room both mornings, the statues (murtees) and pictures look and feel as though there is life looking at me from their eyes. They seem so *real* as if they have feelings to them.

I see and feel the power of the love from their eyes and felt that now I was surrounded by angels. After moving out of the house and making up back with my husband, we took an apartment (recommended by Swamiji) and have lived happily ever since we moved there."

Chapter 24
Other Experiences from Men and Women I Helped

Letter of Testimony from a Devotee

We are very pleased and happy that we have sat with Swamiji, our preceptor, and our Guru, together in devotion to Lord Shiva, Lord Hanuman, and Mother Laksmi. I felt a sense of accomplishment with peaceful and loving thoughts running through my mind, most of the times since the day of the Pujas. I pray that these feelings will always be a part of us. Ever since then, the air that I breathe feels more pure, and my respiratory tract seemed healthier too. Everything seems so peaceful in our house and around the yard too. Even the plants and flowers in the yard seemed to be benefiting from the effects of the Pujas. Within one week they looked so different, strived so much, and are blooming so nicely too.

Swamiji has been very patient with us in every step with all of the intricate details, preparing the altar for the Pujas; he beautifully laid out everything within his reach during the Pujas. More importantly, Swamiji adored us as his devotees, as I can see and feel this connection. I felt that we are very open with each other, and as such it creates a very comfortable atmosphere, a homely and humble feeling among us. Swami has enriched our knowledge with his teachings, and not only that, we felt more connected with the gods spiritually too. We are so delighted, and also enlightened with the detailed and clear explanation he has given throughout the entire Puja ceremony. We have learnt so much from him, and have seen such great changes in our lives, since we have been a part of his life. We are very thankful to him for that. He has corrected so many situations for us, took care of so many problems for us, and is always there to guide us in the right direction. We are truly blessed to have met with him. I find that the more I speak to Swamiji, the more I am expanding my knowledge.

From the inception we had spoken to Swamiji about our Pujas, we were eager to sit with him to do it. Each day that passes by, we had our thoughts and mind set on it, and were constantly planning all the way through, for this beautiful day with the Guru and the Gods. We were happy throughout the period. The cleaning and tidying of the house, yard, shopping, and all other preparations were so much of fun. However, I must admit that there were few mishaps, some stress, fatigue and tiredness in between everything else, nevertheless, we still enjoyed what we did and we got everything done, the way we had anticipated, through the blessings of the Lord. It was like a miracle.

On the morning of the Puja, I woke up at 4:00am. I wasn't feeling well. I was dizzy, groggy, had a mild headache, and pain on my right side. I didn't have a good night's rest. I had a long and terrible dream, which I don't remember. I snoozed the alarm clock a few times trying to relax myself out of the tired feelings. I eventually got out of bed at approximately 4:30am; feeling very drained of my energy, and slowed down. I showered and went to my altar to pray, starting off with the outdoors dar, to the

Sun God. I went outside (in the yard) to throw the dar, and as I closed my eyes to concentrate, I had a weird and unusual feeling of slight fear suddenly, but I let go of that and tried to focus and concentrate through my prayers. At approximately 5:20am I lit the outdoor stove to start the cooking for the Puja, I felt like I was forcing myself to do all of this…I had no energy, but I know it had to get done. I was still with the headache and the pain was sharp on my right side too. I begged god to take this ill feeling away from me, for I know that I have to do it, or how else it will not get done in time for the Pujas. I felt like I didn't want to be bothered by anyone, irritated, sick, and out of place. For a bit, I felt like I forgot how to cook the food, or what I should cook first. My first dish was not cooking to my likeness, and this negative type of feeling was not leaving me, I said why me? Why today out of all other days, I need my strength, my thoughts, and my power to do this, oh god. I tried harder to pull myself together and to win the situation with my will power. I took another shower, and from there on the cooking went well.

At approximately 8:20am I was on the Belt Parkway, heading east to pick up Swami. The traffic was moving well, and I was saying to myself that I will get there in time, as we had planned a pickup time of 8:30am. As I drove another mile, I realized that traffic increased, but I continued on. Eventually, I was stuck in traffic as I connected to the Cross Island Parkway, cars were crawling, and there came a wailing fire truck, which made it worst, as it was trying to get past everyone, cars rode up the parapet to accommodate the passage of the fire truck. In my thoughts I said, oh god, this is not good, this is definitely a blockage for me today…Swami expects me there at 8:30am.

Suddenly my cell phone rang; I thought that Swami was looking for me. I looked at the caller's ID and noticed it was a call from my sister's home. I answered the phone, and it was my brother in law who rarely kept in contact, or rarely visited with me. I was surprised by his call. I spoke to him briefly. He mentioned to me that he would like to come over by my home to visit with my mother that morning. I asked him if he could come after lunch that I am having a Puja in the morning hours and we would be busy, preferably, after lunch would be good. He told me that he has some things to do on the road and that he will be at my place at approximately 10:00am, that he will not be able to come later in the day. I was embarrassed that I had not extended an invitation to him previously for the Puja, since we were planning a private Puja. Now to be faced with this situation...I said OK to him.

I eventually reached Swamiji's place at 9:00am, we were back at my home at about 9:20am. Swamiji attempted to start the Puja's about three times and was interrupted, as he explained that the evil does not want the Puja to be done. He also explained that our Pujas were delayed due to blockages or affection by evil spirits around. However, the Puja began and everything moved smoothly and quickly, with no other interference. Swamiji was amazed and said to us that our house was long waiting for this Puja, as it accepts everything so quickly. The Pujas finished after lunch, and my brother in law arrived just about then.

Days prior to the Pujas, there were flies entering our home; they were the big and black ones, with a mixture of blue and green wings. I knew our experiences in the past with flies, and I sense that it is not good to have them around. Once we noticed them around, we tried to get rid of them, by swatting them, or by opening the windows and chasing them out. On the morning of the Puja, a honey bee came into our house and flew

184

around for a bit and then went to our altar and sat on the altar curtain for sometime.

Over the past months, there were nights of different types of dreams too, some of which I remembered the next morning, and some of which I didn't. There were some peaceful dreams, and there were some very long, annoying, frightening, tiring, and horrific, dreams which drained my body of its energy upon waking up. For a few nights, while sleeping my wife would have to shake me awake due to me fighting up, screaming, or groaning, or like a loss of breath, like I am having a difficult time with someone, or chasing a demon, or thieves, or trying to avoid dangerous situations, or trying to protect my wife, or my children, or my families, or even strangers, or trying to care and preserve something from bad effects. Sometimes there are people in my dreams whom I have never seen, or interacted or associated with. Sometimes there are very friendly and beautiful sceneries, people, places or animals and sometimes it is such a nightmare. Cows, or snakes, or alligators, or even wicked spirit machines (actual engines, but has sense to find you) trying to haunt or hurt me or someone....most times I do win or over come them.

After the Pujas were completed that day, the entire house and yard was in great peace, and tranquility. Later on that day at approximately 4:00pm I went and took a nap, I woke up about 6:00pm and was still a bit sleepy, and like a vision and thought came to me that there were three monks standing by the entrance to my bedroom door, and they are wearing the similar clothes as Swamiji's. I got out of bed and walked around the house, and everytime I closed my eyes I envisioned Lord Shiva in a meditational form. In the night after returning home from dropping off my sister at approximately 10:30pm, as I pulled my car into the drive way and parked, and I glanced in front of my house, where my Puja flags are, I again visualized Lord Shiva there in a meditational form. At that point I recollect my thoughts, and said to my self that's a good idea, can I not put a Lord Shiva murti there? What's stopping me from doing so? Also that night while I was sleeping, I dreamt one of my previous tenants who was giving us a hard time. She was crying bitterly and she was saying that "we don't know that she has a lot of problems and that she has two holes in the center of her head". I felt concerned and I pitied her and went to feel where the holes were, and of course there were two holes in her head...and I was saying it loud to someone, but I don't know who it was.

In February of 2007, one night while my family and I were sleeping at approximately 11:30pm there were three knocks on my bedroom window (knuckle like sounds). Our room lights were off, but there are the outdoor sensor lights that should come on, upon sensing motions. However, the outdoor lights did not come on. That knock awoke me and my wife, and we were listening. We thought that it was someone in the yard (human being), so I got up and switched on an additional outdoor light and peeped through the windows around the house, I didn't see anyone. Outside looked very normal, the street lights were all on and bright, everything was calm. We speculated, maybe it was my little daughter sleeping in her crib next to the very window, might would have knuckled it, but her fingers are so tiny she could not create such an adult like knock. Apart from that she was sound asleep at that time too. I was scared that it might me a burglar, and at that time our house was under repairs, we had no one else living there, except for my wife, my two little kids (they were 2 years, and 1 year old then) and myself. I tried to be brave, but my wife dampened it a bit, she was very scared, and was worried about the neighborhood. She wanted us to sell the property, as soon as possible due to this and move "somewhere safe". I was also very worried and concerned about our safety, our children's safety and more. Anyhow, with heavy hearts we went back to sleep. The next day I went outside to do some investigational work, next to the window is a dirt patch with wet soil....I was looking for footprints, there were none. The window is a bit high up too from ground level, and it had a safety mesh that is a few inches away from the actual glass pane of the window, therefore someone knuckling the window would first hit the mesh, thus not creating the kind of sound we heard, or the person would have had to use a ladder, to reach the upper window (actual glass) to knuckle it. I walked around the yard; everything was there in place and normal. It was left unsolved.

In May 2008, the same incident was repeated in a very similar way, except that the rapping occurred at approximately 3:00am. First on our bedroom window...three loud knuckles, pause then three again. My wife jumped up in bed, and asked if I heard "that." I was wide awake from the very first knock and I replied yes. I instantly told her to hurry over to the kid's bedroom and check on them, since they are now sleeping in their own bedroom, (we have a monitor in our bedroom, for convenience). Upon her opening our bedroom door, there were three more knuckles on the kids bedroom window, with that my son started crying really loud, screaming and calling for "Mummy" as he is scared, my daughter started crying too. I sprang out of my bed quickly, and ran into their room to comfort them, along with their mom. The first and only thought that came to my mind is that "it was a spirit"....none of the sensor lights outdoors came on, at the side, or at the back of the yard. I again peeped through all four corners, the street lights were all on and bright...I saw no one...I left our backyard lights on for the rest of the night. Both my wife and I are now left to wonder, will this happen again next year? Why should we have to face this once every year?

Late March 2006, in one of our visits with Swamiji, he told us that we will be purchasing a house soon. I was impressed with this statement, and also couldn't believe what I had heard from Swamiji; for we have just used all of our savings to purchase properties in another state. I said, Swami, we cannot afford a house; we do not have any money to do it now. Swamiji assured me that I would be able to do it, and that we will see it happen soon. I asked him, where will we buy this house? He said right here in New York. I was happy to hear this, but wondered how it will happen. Where will the money come from to do it? I started to put my thoughts and thinking into what Swamiji said, and I began working on it.

First, we listened to all of Swamiji's advises. He told us that in looking for a house we needed to know which location codes are best for us. He gave us our numbers, and we started looking.

With the help of my wife, and from there on everyday we would look up properties on the internet. We would call up the agents, and ask for the property addresses, for the ones we were interested in. Most of the agents were hesitant about giving out the addresses, unless they accompanied us to the property. My wife and I talked about how we can do this transaction both emotionally and financially, with me leading. We are not professionals in home purchasing, but we used our knowledge and we did all research on our own. Everyday after work we would pick up our children from the sitter, and drive around the neighborhood, looking at houses, and doing the mathematical calculations on the addresses, to ensure that the house can really "work" for us. We went through many searches; we encountered many 9's and 6's on the market, and some looked attractive, while some looked very deceiving and haunting. Also, every time we saw a house that we liked for the price, it was not our number. Nevertheless, I pursued it and I called up a real estate agent about a property I liked that I saw online, luckily she gave me the address. My wife and I drove to the residence in the evening, and it was a perfect number for us, an 8. We saw the owners and asked for a walkthrough. We talked over it with the owners, and exchanged phone numbers and left for the evening.

My wife and I both liked it. I saw potential in it. I explained to my wife what I saw, thought, and felt about the property. She shared her views with me. I showed her my vision on how we can do financially, and the number of years I think it will take us to be back in a better financial standing. We both agreed with each other's ideas and we were very happy. We took our ideas to Swamiji and he advised us about the next step, we should take. We even drove by the property once with Swamiji, prior to purchasing it, so that he can let us know if it is a good place for us. He said it looks good to him, and that we may proceed with the purchase.

We kept in steady contact with the owners; I negotiated the price down a great deal. My wife and I would assign tasks to each other in between our jobs, and would cross reference information received from the Department of Buildings, Department of Finance, Housing Department etc., on the property. I took time off my job and visit the DOB several times in person, to obtain all relevant information and to verify the accuracy. We retained an attorney, who did nothing much for us, we did all the research on the property and had to feed it to him, which he should have given to us. He complimented us on our research on the property. It was like we paid him to be a figure to represent us at the closing table only; he was even 30 minutes late in the closing.

The purchase transaction did not move as smooth as I thought it would be on the seller's side, but I was fascinated by all that we did, and was amazed by how much we have educated ourselves through the buying process. As for the money, it just flowed in without us being worried where we would find it, but of course we had to make wise financial decisions. We found the house in April 2006 and "closed" in August 2006, running very close to my wife's grah. We moved in at the ending of October 2006, in the unfinished house, with all of our furniture covered up. We slept on bare mattresses on the bare floor for several months. Like this house would not finish.

Swamiji had warned us that we **must** move in the house by or before September 2006. Unfortunately we couldn't since the closing happened at the end of August. Upon which we started minor repairs and changes in the house. It eventually ended up being fully gutted, with all new electrical, all new plumbing, all new heating, insulation, sheetrock, and painting. Huge repairs and renovations - Repairs took at least 5 months, in which time we lost visits with Swamiji, due to the repairs of the house. We struggled with the repairs of the house, more than anything else. The contractors were "dragging" their feet on the work, while we were not there during the day. It was like a never ending project with these guys. It was very difficult, tiring, and stressful. We work all day, go there everyday after work and every weekend, to continue with whatever we can. I literally lived at the Home Depot and other hardware and plumbing stores, at all hours in the night. We had to work to pay all the contractors, buy materials for the house, and at the same time pay the mortgage for all those months on the same house, plus pay a rental for the apartment we were still living in, pay the baby sitter, our mortgages on our other properties, car insurance, credit cards, and groceries as well. We had little or no money left to do anything for ourselves, month after month. We were live less for a while.

But as all this was happening, I remembered that Swamiji had told us that we will have one year of struggle with the house, after purchase, and I based it on that. Not until later I went back to Swamiji, he then told me that we had not seen him for sometime (at least 3 months) and that we started the repairs on the wrong time, we moved in at the wrong time, and those were some of the reasons why we were suffering so much. By this time, we were drowning in debt, but we were still carrying on. He even told me that all of the contractors who worked there ripped me off, which is really the true. Swamiji came to our house, and he said that we had an awful lot of repairs done, that we should have consulted him prior to starting the repairs. The house looked as though a hurricane had passed through it. We forfeited a great deal, made a lot of sacrifices, ate less and tried everything to make it happen.

When we finished all the other floors, and advertised it for rent, we were not getting any renters; Swamiji again came and looked at the condition of the house and yard. The front fence was painted in black, the front storm door was painted in black, all the step rails were in black, Swamiji advised to repaint all in white, if not, we will experience further blockages, and hindrances. He told us that the black is preventing Mother Lakshmi from entering our home, and our lives. Black is also precluding us from seeing our way financially. I went to Home Depot, bought white paint and repainted all black to white, while it was below 40 degrees outside in January 2008, and about 3 weeks later we got the 2nd floor apartment rented. My wife, my kids and I were staying on the unfinished first floor; it was in very bad shape. We slept and moved from apartment to apartment, from top to bottom while fixing it. We were not afraid, sleeping there in such a huge house all alone. One winter night a water pipe froze, burst, and flooded our house from the top floor to the basement. The water penetrated the areas which were already painted and fixed. We were speechless and devastated, at 3:00am that morning. Water flowed through some of the electrical fixtures. To shut off the water I had to run through the water on the floor...I was scared of us being electrocuted and warned my wife to stay in a dry spot, while I ran through the water from upstairs then to the basement for the shut off valve. I felt as if I was alone, and what next is there for me to do. Who can I turn to for help at this hour? Both my wife and I became very sad over our hard work on the house, and to be faced with this flooding and destruction. It was very heart breaking and we were speechless. Nevertheless, we did not give up.

We then got another apartment rented on the third floor. This tenant lived there for a very short period. After she moved out of the apartment the apartment was invaded by flies, those big black flies. They were there for several weeks. I do not know where they came from, but they would not leave, and they kept multiplying. They were hesitant to leave even though I would open the windows and try to chase them out. Swamiji came to "bless" and "clean" the house. Amazingly, the next day all the flies were gone, some of which died and fell to the floor, and some maybe made their way out. During this time and experience with the flies, our finances and health were suffering. There were arguments erupting for no apparent reasons etc. Things were going the opposite way. No help from anyone to complete the house. My wife and I were even separated for a few months too, with me left alone to carry on.

192

After several weeks we got the last apartment rented by a family member. At first we were getting our rent on time, from all of the tenants. Eventually, one tenant started paying in pieces and this tenant was being very bossy and wanted to tell us how to do, or how it will be, and wanted to pay rent whenever she feels like. Eventually this tenant quit her job, and did not pay rent for a few months; she brought her daughter there and created more havoc than ever. They were unholy, and the daughter was also very bossy and demanding, and creating fights and scandalizing us. There was no prosperity. They were constantly gossiping about us. They did not like to work, and always expected us to accept their lazy and wrong doings. They didn't pay rent for several months, and damaged my new apartment too. The daughter had me arrested, fabricating and falsifying to the cops that I harassed her. In December 2007, this same tenant mentioned that her daughter had to go and do a "life" work…"that someone had put something on her and that she has to get it cleared and that she will return it". Of course the daughter went and did the "work". At approximately 10:30pm that same night the mother was possessed. She started saying and doing all kinds of strange things. At first we thought that she was only joking, and after some time she regained her consciousness. A few days later the same thing happened again, and this time my daughter was scared and was saying strange things too. I instantly contacted Swamiji, and he advised me what to do to protect my child and to get things under control.

This tenant eventually moved out of my place, but made a report to the Department of Buildings and had me investigated. We carried more losses than gain from this tenant, for the time they were there. I had to spend a lot of money to correct all that they had done. I went backward financially due to this tenant. We were very depressed and were loosing a lot financially, after consulting with Swamiji; he told me that they were not suitable tenants for the house. That they had brought a lot of negative energies into my house and our life and it is affecting us badly. I used to fall sick very often, out of focus and more. My wife and I were having many problems too. After taking Swamiji's advises and doing everything that he told us to do, we started to see great improvements again, and after that moment it's like we were on the road to recovery, from that dark era.

I must thank Swamiji so much for his advises and his predictions. In fact, everything that Swamiji predicted for us came to pass. I believe that Swamiji can really help you to change your life. However, as a devotee, you in turn must be prepared to make this change as well. My wife and I have been seeing Swamiji, for approximately 6 years now, and have received much help and blessings from him. I feel that we are reaping the good fruits from god, and we hope and pray that we continue on the path of righteousness.

Many things have changed for us for the better, and I feel that our bad dreams are coming to an end, through the great blessings from the Lord, and help from Swamiji.

Shesha

Dreams by a Devotee as Related To Swami Ram Charran

Dear Swamiji,
Ram Ram,
I would like to share with you the following dreams I had last night and the night before.

Last night (11/23/08) I dreamt that I am in a house and this house is old and it needs lots of repairs. I never saw this house or place before... It feels like I bought it, or I m going to buy it soon. I am on the first floor (empty) and I was trying to get to the second floor. I saw a step (right hand side of the house) leading to the second floor, but this step is shaky and old with missing boards to walk on. I am trying very hard to climb this step to reach to the second floor, because I wanted to see what is going on up there. I had to cling onto one side of the thread board of the step, I am holding on to it and I was basically pulling my own weight upwards to get to the top. The step was not too long but steep, almost straight upward (small and tight step area). Upon reaching to the top I realized that this board that I am holding on to, might rip off with me since it is old. Then there is like a gap that I had to jump (across) to reach to the 2nd floor...I did not jump, as the board was shaking with me. I was afraid that I will fall with it. I looked around and I saw another step at the other end of the house. I had no choice but to get down from this step, I had to take my time, slowly, and bit by bit, so that this board will not rip off, from shaking. I came down from this step and went to the other step. This one was stronger, but I still had to be careful, as I had experienced the other step, it was still somewhat steep/straight and difficult to climb, it was short (maybe 3-5 steps). I went upstairs and I saw that the area had beige rug, all empty space and in OK condition. To get back down the step is still straight, and it is now a metal ladder step, black in color, it was very tight and difficult for me to get down. I had to squeeze and force my self, being very careful; I eventually got to the bottom. I heard one of my aunts, saying that Swami is coming. I indeed saw you in your orange outfit, and you were there to do my puja in the same house. I woke up.

Again, after falling asleep, I dreamt that we owned a trailer home and we are going to live in it. We bought it and it is in better condition (I don't know why I thought so), that we are moving it and placing it on a bigger lot, not very far (I never saw this place before). After we set it up there, I began to clean up the surroundings. The yard was muddy due to rain. I was wondering if the doors and windows were strong enough on the house, as I was concerned about the safety of our kids. My main focus was to fix up the yard, as you are coming to do a puja for us. Eventually this trailer house looks like a permanent structure painted in white. I woke up.

The night before (11/22/08) I dreamt that my uncle bought a house (I never saw this area/place before). This house is very big in length not height, and looks good. In front, it is a brick structure. I did not see all of it at once but by walking through it, I realized that it is a very big place. It seemed that no one lived there and it is old, internally. It is an upstairs and downstairs (basement). It seemed there were more people there whom I did not see. Eventually, it is me who is buying this house. I saw a step leading to downstairs, I looked down and it was deep and steep. I went down the step slowly and carefully, it seemed short, but was difficult making it downwards. I took a tour throughout and I had to climb up another step to get back up. Again, it was very tight and difficult coming up the step, as they are very steep/straight, metal ladder steps. The flooring boards in some area were old, and that was a concern. At one point I was thinking who needs such a big house. It took a long time to walk from one end to the next end of the house. The outside of it is brick, and there were lots of trees around. There were sucker trees, and other types of trees too. The yard was big and some what bushy. I eventually finished the tour and came back out and we left. I woke up.

The same night I dreamt of the home where I grew up (true existence). I went back there after a very long time. My wife and I were in a bamboo basket boat (small and circular) in the trench, (there is indeed a trench there) beautifully floating, the water was calm, with her paddling and me relaxing. Eventually, we were walking on the dam to get to my childhood house. The dam was bushy, since no one was really dwelling there. The fruit trees are all there, mangoes, guavas, tamarind tree, green grasses, green beezie pastures, and the area where the calf pen was. On one of the heaps I saw the huge tamarind tree loaded with ripe tamarind. We had to walk under it, and I was cautioning the person with me (not my wife now, but another female from my school – like this person was also fetching me) lets not pick, or pull the tamarind limbs, as snakes might be living on the tree and can jump out and bite us. So we went pass easily, and approaching the calf pen area I saw several pepper trees, loaded with green peppers, we stop and examine it, but we did not pick any, we were enjoying the atmosphere there. Eventually I was looking at the rear of our house, the back window was open, and I saw you upstairs, and you were doing puja. You had a white shawl around your neck, but no shirt on. Like you are dressed like and ancient sage, but you were a bit darker. As I went under the house (house is about 12 feet high from ground), I saw a white human plastic skull, and it was placed up on one of the beams. I was not happy to see that and was a bit alarmed, but it wasn't a big concern, as I felt it was a toy skull. I eventually heard Lakshmi bhajans playing upstairs. Even though the place was abandoned for many years, it was like the same way we left it from then to now. I knew that you were upstairs, and I was eager to go up there to reach with you, as I walked up the steps, the bhajan was still playing. However, when I got upstairs, no one was there and I am saying "hello" "hello". I saw movements in one of the two rooms, like someone pulled a bamboo basket cover. It was all just plain and empty. I was shocked as to what

happened, no one there...bhajans stop playing...I woke up.
Swamiji, can you please let me know what your interpretations are.
Thank you,
A DEVOTEE

Chapter 25
Some Comments Found on the Internet about Kal-Bhairo, Katari Etc.

You Judge For Your Self from These…

P lease note that your can find these comments on the internet and more just by going to Google. Command: enter these names. Swami Ram maintains only one comment on these, and that is from experience after helping more than 36,000 people make their lives better. Swamiji has made all people obtain their desires by telling them to abandon TAMASIC WORSHIP and doing SATWIK WORSHIP….it's always their choice, but desires obtained by Tamasic worship are temporary not permanent.

You have to understand that Madurai Veeran and Kal Bhairo ARE NOT THE SAME. Madurai Veeran, Sangilli Karuppan, Karuppusamy, Kuthandavar, Kathuvarayan, and such deities are basically sub-deities who are essentially martyrs. They were once warriors/kings who were revered by the Tamil villagers and they became so popular, they evolved into sub-deities.

199

Muniswaran is another incarnation of Siva; his sub-deity form is Muniandy, or Muniappan. Other deities as incarnations rather than subdeities are Virumandi, Karumandi, Mayandi, and the most common Kaaval Ayyanaar, who is the one with the white horse and sword drawn.

Some head Pujaris that I have seen are so threatened by the youngsters, that they do not teach them everything because they are afraid that the young Pujaris will go out there and open their own temples and put them out of business. Whilst visiting Lewis Pancham temple on Inwood Street, Jamaica, Queens. When they give their Kata's he mentions that the people that open their temples in the bottom house or garages don't know anything and are leading people astray. How does he know that? This just goes to show how IGNORANT his way of thinking is. He is not saying that they are taking money out of his pocket. When you are secure with whom you are: there is no reason for condemnation. If Papalo did not edify him how would he have had that knowledge?
There is a saying about Indian/Culley people, they are like crabs in a barrel when the other is trying to reach the top, and there is always another crab that's trying to pull him down

I attend a Kali Temple in Trinidad and a Pujarin and The Guru Manifest Bhairo and Katyaeni/Katari. But I am unsure if that is the True Shakti; and I am unsure as to whether the Justice that is given or the reading is true and correct. Can someone please heed my plight? I need to know How to recognise [sic] A Real Manifestation and the right readings.
Thanks

This is to my brother from Trinidad, when you are manifesting, sometimes you are gone and do not remember anything that is happening. Sometimes, you are fully aware and cannot control what is happening. In order for you to know who is within you, you have to manifest in the presence of someone that is willing to tell you what you did and also when in the manifestation mode you will be asked to take an oath with the lit camphor to let the Pujari/Priest know who this entity is. Then, when you regain your full senses, they will in turn let you know. I do not know if you live in New York. There are many temples, but you have to judge for yourself which Ma Kali temple you wish to be a part of. I travel to The Bronx to a Kali temple. The Shri Durga Bhairo Mandir, at 2261 Watson Avenue, between Havemeyer Avenue and Castle Hill Avenue. The Head Pujari name is Kumar. I use to visit the temple on Inwood Street, but I stopped. I also attend the extention of The Shree Maha Kali Temple on Linden Blvd. It is opposite McDonald's. Right off Supthin. Davo the son-in-law of the head Pujari on Inwood Street is over there. I find it much more relaxing. I find the people are very nice. There us no argument, confusion, disruption and gossipping. It is very nice. Please, you have to find a Pujari that is willing to teach, and most importantly share his knowledge. Good Luck in your endeavours.

Caribcook 5810, I would like to know why are you are personalizing everything someone has been writing regarding the Shri Maha Kali Temple on 107-34 Inwood Street, head Pujari Lewis? The person did not mention anything about Dave and his wife's separation. I have been attending this temple for approximately six years and have seen it going from bad to worse. Many of the devotees went elsewhere. I have since left also. For those of you, who want to learn the truth, go to the source. Dave opened a new temple on Linden Blvd, opposite McDonald's, by Supthin. Here is something for you to read and maybe next time do your research before you respond.

This is message is for Caribcook and Lisagee. The head pujarie of the Shree Maha Kali Temple in Inwood Street will use his Voodoo Spells and breakup marriages of many couples. The young women would then go back begging say "Uncle Lewis, please help bring my husband back". The young women claimed that Lewis Pancham told them that he will live 100 years and that Mother Kali told him to sleep with these young girls and have babies to run his Church. Unfortunately, these babies never make the world. Instead, these girls got a disease there is no cure. They will then complain to Dave Sukhu in who will also do the same to these girls. So please you two people do not recommend people to either Dave Sukhu or Lewis Pancham as the saying goes "like father like son". And if you examine the people who go to Dave Sukhu Church, they are all sleeping with one another wife or husband. This is not a good example for innocent people. The Hindui Organizations need to pull those garments out of their bodies they do not deserve it. They are a disgrace to the public and the Hindui Organization.

Originally Posted by **lisagee**
Can you assist with providing information about Sangani Baba? I have a loved one who is being effected [sic] by Sangani. Someone has offered or prayed to Sangani Baba, and in turn, an innocent person is now suffering for many years. What can be done to permanently remove the doings of Sangani

202

Originally Posted by **Guest**
*HELLO......I HAVE BEEN A PUJARIN AT A TEMPLE IN
TRINIDAD AND I FEEL YOUR BEAT BRO. I LEFT THE
TEMPLE BECAUSE OF ALL THE THINGS GOING ON. I
HAVE BEEN TO AMY OTHER TEMPLES AND MANY
YOUNG PUJARINS ARE RUNNING THESE TEMPLES.
THESE ARE SADA TEMPLES. I DO NOT AND I
REPEAT I DO NOT BELEIEVE IN OFFERING BLOOD
OR RUM OR EVEN CIGARS. WITH RESPECT TO
WHATS GOING ON IN YOUR LIFE PERTAINING TO
OTHER PUJARIS AND/OR OTHER TEMPLES I AM
VERY SORRY THAT U HAVE TO GO THROUGH
THOSE THINGS. I MAY NOT KNOW U BUT I DO
UNDERSTAND WHAT IS GOING ON HERE. MY GURU
DOES MANIFEST BHAIRO BABA AND HAVE GIVEN
ME JUSTICE FORGIVE ME EH BUT SOMETIMES I
DOES FEEL IT ENT BHAIRO. U KNOW. [sic]
SOMETIMES I DOES [sic] GET THAT FEELING THAT
IS WHY I LEAVE. I KINDA WANT TO GO BACK BUT
HOW CAN I BE SURE IF IT IS THE POWER TALKING
IN MANIFESTATION. WHAT SIGNS CAN I LOOK FOR?
CAN U GIVE SOME ADVICE BRO.*

sitaram, this is for bhairo child,
*I attend a temple in Trinidad as well. I visited many others
though, except for those that engage in ritual practices of
sacrificing animals. My temple buddies forbid me to go to
such temples (for example, Pasea,...... no offense) since
we perform puja differently. I really need to understand
this form of worship that my buddies refrain from. I once
posed a question to bhairo in manifestation, and I asked
him about offering blood. He questioned me and asked
me if I will give him that and I told him no. He asked why
and I said, "well that is not good for u baba". He then
replied......"exactly if u give me something that is not
good for me, then I will give u something that is not good*

for you." I really I'm confused by this reply. What does he mean? Does he mean that when u offer blood you will get things that are not good for you? Does he mean that blood worship adds to negative karma? Can you enlighten me?

.

Hey guys !!!
Stop going to any Pujaris in the temple. Most of them are the real begger in the context of knowledge; who only know how to empty your pocket. And, what we're gonna do knowing the Gods and goddesses ??? Until and unless you don't find any capable Guru you'd never be on the right path which may lead you to the divinity. Simply acquiring knowledge about deities and other stuffs will made us only a Pujari. Are we daring enough?

Dear INNOCENT,
Well, though I am not with all the knowledge you long to know   I'm   trying...
In human civilization there are full of good and bad. If someone tries doing something in a nice way...many other may try doing it other way. Just take the rules in any country...isn't the rule broken ???
The rules have been made to walk us on the right path but there are lotta people who go against. Such thing applies to the Tantra and the Pujas too.
Truly the old scriptures don't tell about animal sacrificing...Later, people to make fun and pleasure started doing so and became a ritual even in the Puja. Well there are Two main types of Tantra Sadhans..1) Dakshin Marg 2) Bama Marg
Bama Marga applies all the sacrifices etc.
Tell you the truth about Nara Bali (human sacrifice) in Dakshin Kali Temple in Nepal (the Kali ma here is

worshiped by the Tantics from round the globe)....only few decades back, they used to do the Nara Bali but Dr. Narayan Dutt Shrimali during his 18 and half years of sadhana period in Nepal make them to put it off. Dr. Shrimali is the only authentic person in all the ancient knowledge from the Rishis. Though his departure has created blankness, still a person away from crowd, appointed by him as his heir is in the way providing the path.

Well, if I am to suggest you, you can go to any temples...just make sure not to get involved to any thing wrong goes there. And if you are with GURU, then you don't need to go to any temples. You will find the God waiting for you with the grace of Guru.

But Guru, where to find ????????????????

Hey innocent and unknowing,

Lemme tell you something my bhairo baba loves to talk in proverbs and riddles. Maybe you did or are doing something he does not like. If you cant figure it out aski him. I personally dont do sacrifice cuz I am Brahmin but blood sacrifice does not affect me. Bhairo baba always says do as I say not as I do, he loves women but he will punish you for womanising, he loves alcohol but does not like his devotees to drink except rum that is parsad. He is temper itself but he does not his devotees to be hasty. Do you see where I am goin with this? And as for my temple, tell you friends to mellow because Pasea temple is the first Kali temple and the most powerful it is the root of all the other Kali tempes in Trinidad. You seem to frown upon the offering of blood yet you have a pic of narsimha. Interesting. Hope bhairo and maa kali guide you. Take care.

Jai Shree Maha Shakti Kala Bhairava

You and your baba are foolish. He cannot even comply with the Vedas Himself and asks his devotess not to do this and that.
Very tamsic. Rum? Women? Sacrifice? Haha Your guru will become a Brahmrakshas. So will you as his followers after death. Kali will most defo not agree with such worship nor accept it. By the way NArsimah Bhagvan ripped up Danav Raaj to rid evil. Also what God does, we cannot do. For if it was the case then Shiv drank Halahal Poison. Will you drink it?

Hey Bhairo Child
It's wrong. Totally wrong. Your baba, I dunno about him but could be a kinda fake. Well, can he manifest the Bhairava to you??? Ask him. The world is filled with so many Babas, Gurus and Bhagavans who love making the crowd go crazy behind them but talking about knowledge, they are not more than the Beggars. Yes, I agree that Bhairava Pujaris do the things as you told, eat meat, drink alchohol, go to women...etc...But we gotta fathom their depth, but how??? We can't getto know anyones' reality untill and unless we don't rise up to Sadhanas. You, Mr. Bhairava Child, You...can be more powerful and more knowledgeable than the Baba of yours but you gotta dare to indulge yourself in sadhanas.
Regards

I don't know why you guys associate this "kal bhairo" with Madurai Veeran! I am a true Tamilian from Tamil Nadu, and I know about this stuff. You ask any Tamilian who kal bhairo is; he will look at you puzzled! I ran across a Guyanese "madrasi" temple website, and they call sangili karuppan as master of the sea...LOL! Sangili Karuppan and Madurai Veeran were people who lived during Pandyan times; they just became martyrs who eventually got formed into subdeities. They were real people, Sangili was a forest bandit who was enemies w/ king Madurai veeran, and a lot of these sub-deities were people who became martyrs. You watch, given due time....forest brigand Veerappan who was shot and killed last year will become a sub-deity...lol! He and Sangili Karuppan lived the same life, next thing you know, you will see a tall colorful statue of a man w/ a rifle, smeared w/ Vibhoothi, Kumkumam, and Santhanam...LOLLLLLL

Innocent,
A martyr is basically someone who had lead such a life to where the people loved him so much, that his death basically sets an example for future followers. There is no such thing as "Sanganee Baba", that is actually Sangili Karuppan, or the "dark one w/ the chain", who was a Robin Hood type figure who feuded w/ local king Madurai Veeran. You have to understand, these "sub-deities" were once people who got absorbed into local folklore and eventually became deities, and you can ONLY see them in front of Tamil Nadu villages as guardians who are believed to protect the villages. Remember, they were once alive.
Oh my goodness. I have only one question, do you go to temple to gossip or to pray? There are so many things going on in the world around us and you will concentrate on other people stories, about who says what and where and how?
Shame on you all! *Just go to temple and pray. If other peoples business bothers you so much, you can pray at home at your own altar and achieve enlightenment. What's so hard about that? Now everyone is making up nasty stories about other people and spreading gossip about pujaries! I repeat,* ***shame on you all!***

Hey Bhairo child,
How are u?
Well, I pray a lot and do a lot of devotion. The devtas are merciful to my family. I really don't want them to suffer and I fear for the land that I dwell, but maybe my grandparents did what they did for a reason.
I will not be at any haste to make any serious decision pertaining to the land but I will continue my own devotion.
I perform temple duties at the Mandir, but I don't do much devotion there. I prefer to do my own thing home.
I do my best to rely on the guidance of the devtas and devis. All I need is faith, trust and belief in them. And most importantly I need to love them.
So I do my best to be a great devotee and child to them.
Thanks for being concern
Sitarama......

HEY EVERYONE!
Now and then, I do visit many other temples in the country, I like the atmosphere very much, for gracing my presence at any temple, makes me happy and excited. 🎎
I know that there will be people with negative characteristics in all temples. (That of which will tell u alone that mother disowns no one, despite their ignorance and wrong doings).
However, it must be remembered, that any where u go u will always meet all sorts of people! The greatest test for all of us is to learn how to live with these people AND ACCOMODATE EACH OTHER'S DIFFERENCES. ☺

Life is all about socialization. And socialization involves learning how to practice good ethics and teach the younger generation the value of sharing, respect, caring, appreciation, love, discipline and tolerance etc

208

Many of our religious leaders are so caught up in ego and riches. Temples and other religious shrines seem not to be a place of worship anymore but a growing business. The religious leaders are so concerned about the structure and status of temples, churches, mosques and are hardly concerned about the cognitive and spiritual development of those that they are leading.

We need to grasp reality and set an example for our future. If our religious leaders are failing to lead us towards the right path of self actualization and living a decent life on earth, then we need to take control of our lives and be passionate for one another.

<u>We need to do something positive now.</u>
All of us have different forms of knowledge.
All of us are gifted.
All of us are unique.
And all of us have strengths.
We therefore need to pull our knowledge, strengths, and giftedness together.
We must refrain from dwelling on one another's weaknesses and mistakes.
We must create our own destiny.
We have to make a change.
JAI MAHA DURGA!
JAI MAHA KALI!

Has anyone heard about these so-called Gods? How was Kal Bhairo born or any of the above names?
Someone told me that she went to a kali temple and was told to worship the above to giving alcohol and cigarette - I don't feel right about this - please reply if you know anything - I want to help my friend.
Regards

It is DIFFICULT to stop these sacrifices ESPECIALLY if they have been in your family lineage. Just like you, I don't feel it is right to give animal sacrifices. If it's the first time your friend is performing these sacrifices, I think you might help by telling her about the consequences of killing animals. This might well deter her.

If it's in the family lineage, hmmm believe me it IS complicated to stop and the resulting consequences might be painful. It is definitely not an easy decision to take.

Our Hindu religion is divided into 3 different sectors: Sanatan, Aryasamaj and Madras. Many Hindus follow the Sanatan culture.

It is essential that first one understands that this world is made up of ying and yang, [good and bad, I can also describe it in a quote, "for every action, there is a reaction"]. I will explain only what I know personally from the madras culture but for further knowledge about this topic, you may visit a very educated pujari (known as a pundit in the Sanatan culture) at 107-34 Inwood Street, Queens, NY.

Let's start with Kal Bhairo also known as Madurai Veeran. He is another form of Lord Siva, he is the one who punished Brahma because he lied and he did so by taking off one of Brahma's head with his pinkie finger nail. Lord Brahma was also cursed and no humans are to ever worship him because of what he has done. Kal Bhairo is always on the right side of Kali ma, he is there as a guardian, he was given permission to be the guardian when he asked her for that. Kali ma, another form of Mother Durga, is the universal mother in the Madras culture. When she came to destroy the demon Raktabija, she came in fury. One drop of Raktabija's that fell on earth, there would be 1000 of him formed. Kali ma takes

64 different forms, for every demon she killed, she took their name. To help in this war, she created creatures that are like dogs to drink the blood before the demon multiplies again. After the war, when everything was over, the gods gave Kali ma a Kaliyug [like an era] to rule. But the creatures she created, they will still be alive, she could not uncreate them, so it was said that the devotee of kali ma can offer her an animal sacrifice and doing so, the animal will be blessed and reborn as a human. This will feed the creatures for they cannot be undone. They were created to drink blood. Note: during the ritual, if the animal does not bow its head for the sacrifice, then there will be no sacrifice. Katari ma also known as Parmeshwari ma is the last form of Kali ma and she is the one who will take this sacrifice. Kal Bhairo also takes this sacrifice, when doing his puja, they can ask what they want, god doesn't make people bad, people do that all on their own. If you ask for something that you're not supposed to then it is your own fault. You're dealing with your own karma. Kal Bhairo is not Sangani. Sangani also known as Dee Baba is the landmaster. Badra Kali [another form of kali] gave him a balidan. He rules everything that concerns a business or schools, etc. Note: in the previous messages, someone stated that these deotas go where the the vegetarian [sweet] gods won't go, that is true. These Deotas can go anywhere that is dirty whereas the [sweet] gods will not go. This culture [not religion, religion is man-made] is very strict. When worshipping them, you must keep fast for 72 hours, no meat should be eaten, women should be clean, and couples should not be intimate with each other during the fast. It is true that you can get what you ask for when you ask these deotas, but mind you, it is your own karma. A good devotee will ask for health, strength and knowledge. Please note that in this culture, if you do ask for something that your not supposed to or you wish to harm others, you will suffer the consequences. You will be taught your lesson the hard way. These deotas also accept rum and cigarettes, and they accept it as prasad. In their form, they drink and they smoke. While in another form, they cannot. If they could do all this in one form then there would not be so many different forms of gods. The Pujari at the above mentioned temple has performed many miracles with the blessings of Kali ma. For people who are near death, for those who the doctor gave up on, for the sickly, he has helped them recover. It is true unfortunately, that this tradition passes on for generation BUT only if the fore parents makes promises on behalf of their kids. Like I stated before, people make mistakes and do wrong things, god doesn't make them do it. If I make a promise to god that if they give me a child, that my child and my child's future generation will forever worship that god, I just made a mistake and put my future generation in an obligation without ever thinking about the consequences. Why not instead ask that I will be grateful for a child and will offer prasad and/ or pujas? If your fore parents happen to do this then there are ways to prevent it from falling on future generations. These gods and devtas are here to help us, they are here to keep the balance in life, and you can't have everything in life. But you can achieve great things if you dedicate and pray. You must choose the right path and if you cannot or do not know the right path, then ask the divine kali ma to show you the right path. There are people out there that are in pain and each day is like a needle that hurts them, they have diseases and no hope for the future. I pray that they do find the goddess kali ma for there is a cure for everything, and I witnessed many miracles in this culture. One must not promise something that they can not keep. I am not sure who you are addressing your question to. If a person started this type of worshipping and would like to stop, there is a way I believe that it will stop from falling on future generations. I am not sure if your friend will be able to come out of it because if they promised to continue it then they will be breaking a promise. Your friend should go to temple and speak to the pujari or speak to the devatas.

There is a ritual to end the Madras worshipping and it involves going to Ganga ma. The pujari will have to look that up and speak to him before doing something like this, if its done wrong, then it will still go on. The pujari will have to explain what must be done.

Hasn't Lord Krishna condemned these types of worship as tamasic? I am just asking, so please don't be offended. Isn't it clearly mentioned that Lord Krishna is the only person to be worshipped, and other devatas can only be worshipped as parivaras?

You guys got it wrong.
That individual riding a white horse w/ red eyes and a big mustache that stands in front of every Tamil Nadu village is Ayyanaar, NOT MADURAI VEERAN. And associating Madurai Veeran w/ Kal Bhairo is wrong. Basically Veeran is a martyr, like Sangili Karuppan. Sangili Karuppan was basically a Robin-Hood type individual, who is supposed to be another form of Karuppusamy. Sangili (means chain in Tamil), and this form of Karuppusamy is seen w/ a big mustache, bound in chains, and w/ his hand raised w/ a machete. Sangili Karuppan or Karuppusamy stands next to Ayyanaar or Muniswaran. Muniswaran also has a more earthly form known as Mun

Originally Posted by madras
Kal Bhairo is a god also known as Madurai Veeran. She gives rum and cigarette because either mother kali or her brothers or sisters told them to give it.
(email for any other questions)or shezz sck

No.
Muniandy, Ayyanaar, Karuppusamy, Muniappan, and these "kaavals" (guardian sub-deities) like smoking cigars, drinking liquor, and eating meat. That is why sometimes the pujari when in a trance, smokes cigars.
Trust me I KNOW, I am a Tamilian (Madrasi) representing Theni District, Tamil Nadu, I've seen all this. And Madurai Veeran hails from Madurai District in Tamil Nadu, he was a king/warrior during the Pandya Dynasty times. Madurai Veeran is also depicted w/ two wives: Ponni and Velaiyamma.
You guys got the names wrong. "Sangili" means chain in Tamil. "Karuppan" means dark man, "Karuppu" means black. "Veeran" means brave heart.
Some of you need to learn Tamil.

Originally Posted by Guest
Dont Go to the Jamaica Kali Mandir or Shree Maha Kali Mandir... Ur Gonna Get Corrupted. **People fail to realize that the more places you go to in search for help is the reason why you are punishing the way that you are. Puja and devotion to any Ma and/or any Baba must first start from home. If you keep wandering in search for help, you will never attain that help unless you are willing to help yourself. Helping yourself includes maintaining your fast and observance of that time you have selected to perform your puja. It**

involves so much more than just that..... I agree with this guest... especially since I myself have went there and ended up worse than when I went. Now I can say I helped myself b/c I did. I started doing my own stuff that I learned at home and I can say I am better off

Katari ma also known as Parmeshwari ma is the last form of Mother Kali. She is both good and bad in different ways. In the madras culture, she is worshiped and offered persaud. Persaud can be Sweet and it can also be rum and cigarettes. She also accepts animal sacrifices. [Please see thread for Kal Bhairo aka Madurai Veeran] One can describe her as a two side blade. In the madras culture, she is called to enter a devotee's body to help people who are sick, in pain, who would like to speak to her or just see if they are going in the right path, for any reasons, she will come to listen and take care of you.

Please Note: She is not to be take lightly! She is a devi who can go anywhere, even the dirtiest places where other gods can't. If you have witnessed her in someone, it usual means that someone has sent Katari to harm this person or this tradition of Katari's worshipping has been in that family and that the family has promised continuance of her worshipping by their children and so on.

As an example: This is what happens sometimes which shows how evil PEOPLE are. They go and ask Katari ma to harm another person because they don't like that person and for that, they will offer persaud, rum and cigarette, mala, flowers, etc. Now she will do that because she has just been fed persaud but NOT without consequences. Just because you have fed her does not mean you will not suffer the consequences of wanting to harm others. Not only have you sinned but she will come back to teach you a lesson! As for the other person who the harm is being done to, the person will suffer but if the *person is good, lives a righteous life, prays and is spiritually elevated, then the harm will be VERY minimal. If the person is also bad, and leads a terrible life, and harms and abuses people, then this is the way karma catches up to them. [Two side blade] Everything happens for a reason, and sometimes us humans do not understand, not that we don't have the capabilities.*

Katari harming an innocent boy

I need urgent help. One of my cousins aged 16 is being possessed by Katari it seems his family has some south Indian enemies and they did this act. When he is possessed he speaks differently, his skin color goes dark and he picks a knife to kill people, he is controlled by nearly 3 or 4 muscular persons. I am a devi upasak and I don't know how to please Katari to ask her to go back to who sent her. When the boy is possessed he says he wants to kill himself since he has been asked to do just that. If anyone can help will be highly blessed in saving this boy.

If this is the last form of kali aka Parmeshwari correct Param Eshwari (param -before; Eshwari - consort of Eshwarar: Lord Shiva) how can she be last of kali. according to what I have learnt Maa Kali has ten main forms known as Mahavidyas: they are 1) Kalika, 2) Tara, 3) Shodasi, 4) Bhuvanesvari, 5) Bhairavi, 6) Chinnamasta, 7) Tripur-sundari, 8) Bhagalamukhi, 9) Dhumavati and 10) Matangi. Which one is Kateri? or Parmeshwari? NONE. In Shakti worship or according to you MADRAS CULTURE Katari is closely identified with the sixth form of Durga Maa that is to say Kaatyaayanee (nurse) to fix problems of women i.e. menses, cycles and other impure things that would not probably be seen by

other devtas. It seems to me your roots like me are that of the Caribbean worship however humble to say a lot of what we have learnt is wrong. Parameshwari worship is of tribal India worship where instead of giving Devi Durga goats and fowls they give wild boars (to get one in the Caribbean is hard so they now give pigs) but still what is wrong with that) they is no written way to puja her for her rituals are handed down from generation to generation she is not double sided her way is just very strict. Please correct me if I am wrong but this is what I have come to learn for I have read many of texts and I am yet to come across Madrasi culture. Do they only worship kali in Tamil Nadu? Don't get me wrong I worship the divine devi but she does not belong to Madrasi culture alone and if you were a true madrasi you would know that. Don't get me wrong and I am sorry if you are offended but my aim is not to ridicule or brag of knowledge for I am still learning but what I have read from many of the texts you have posted I think you need to double check or reinvestigate your knowledge source.
pujarie. five.o

A Hindu priest sexually assaulted two underage sisters - conning one of them into having sex with him during a bogus cleansing ritual that involved spreading oil over her naked body, prosecutors said yesterday.
Ramlal Ramadhar, 59, was charged with statutory rape for the attacks, which allegedly occurred in 2002 and 2003 but came to light after one of the girls, now 19, confided to a college counselor.
"Under the guise of being their religious leader," Ramadhar allegedly took "advantage of the youngsters and their trust in him by robbing them of their innocence," Queens District Attorney Richard Brown said.

"Fortunately, one of the sisters found the courage to come forward."

Ramadhar, whom authorities say was a police officer in his native Trinidad, allegedly promised to help the then 16-year-old get rid of "evil spirits."

He allegedly lured her to an apartment in December 2002 and asked that she take her clothes off and lay atop a white sheet with her arms outstretched. Then he began to chant, put coins on her and rubbed oil from head to toe before sexually assaulting her, according to a criminal complaint.

In February 2003, Ramadhar allegedly lured her to an Econo Lodge on Rockaway Blvd. where he repeated the ritual and the assault, the complaint says. "Now I have to do this to complete the ritual and I am sorry but I have to do this," he allegedly said before raping her.

Ramadhar told cops he knew his actions were wrong but his wife, Stella Ramadhar, called the alleged sex attacks a "big misunderstanding."

Ramadhar faces up to four years in prison for third-degree rape. He was arraigned Thursday and ordered held on $50,000 bail by Queens Criminal Court Judge Alex Zigman.

Chapter 26
The Power of Geographic Location

This article was previously published in "*New Age Astrology*", by
Joseph F. Goodavage

Perhaps these assignations, which were known even in remote ancient times, are not just coincidence, but actual conformance to cosmic law. There are other correlations to half the number of Zodiacal Signs, which seem to relate to each hemisphere of the Earth. People who have been on both the Northern and Southern Hemispheres know that the water runs down a drain in counter-clockwise direction south of the equator and clockwise in the Northern Hemisphere. Hurricanes, tornadoes and other low-pressure storm centers in the Northern Hemisphere swirl in the counter-clockwise motion, but in the Southern Hemisphere this is reversed. Even smoke spirals upward in the opposite direction on each half of the Earth.

If seen from "above," (North) the planets of the solar system appear to rotate counter-clockwise motion. From the southern side of the solar system ("below"), they would be seen to rotate in the opposite direction.

No civilization of any kind has ever originated in the Southern Hemisphere; people from the Northern Hemisphere founded every modern nation existing south

219

of the equator today. This dominance of the north over the south manifests itself even among nations, states, and cities. Wherever a war or conflict has arisen, either civil or international, the northern nation-or northern part of that nation-emerges victorious or dominant. Ireland is one example where during the 1800s the north and south grew further apart due to economic differences. In the north the standard of living rose as industry and manufacturing flourished, while in the south the unequal distribution of land and resources—Anglican Protestants owned most of the land—resulted in a low standard of living for the large Catholic population. A second clear example is the United States; both before and after their American Civil War, the North dominated the South in this country, and it still does. Although Washington, D.C. is the nation's Capital, New York is the financial center of this country (New York being farther north than Washington).

The United States traditionally dominates Mexico, while Mexico, in turn, dominates its neighbors to the south, except for those in the Southern Hemisphere where the situation seems to be reversed. For this reason, the European nation of South Africa will never be dominated or conquered by any other African nation. Canada, on the other hand, has not yet fully developed its potential. Yet this northern nation has always come out ahead of its dealings with the United States, a much more powerful and industrially developed land.

Canada therefore, is the land of the future, as are other nations in the northernmost climate.

Civilization moves westward on the terrestrial sphere, and dominance moves northward. If the borders of two nations occupy the same general latitudes, then the nations whose capital city is farther north will always be somewhat better off than its neighbor (or rival). Look at China's dominance over India and her rivalry with Russia.

A lot more than severe weather conditions led to the defeat of both France's and Germany's great armies in their invasions of Russia. And why is it that the mighty Soviet Union could not defeat the little Finland in the late 1930's?

And so is man, who is believed until recently that he alone possessed the ability to think and reason. How many of our decisions are stimulated by "instinct" ad exogenous forces-and how many by what we like to call free choice?

What if all the foregoing coincidences are not coincidences? Humanity has always assumed that it enjoys complete Free Will. But, no proof plus no evidence equals case closed.

Yet, if we do possess free choice, did we "choose" to evolove from blobs of intimate matter? No, we did not choose the gift of life. We didn't choose our sex, our family, our race, or our evolution. Perhaps nothing is a matter of choice after all.

Teilhard de Chardlin, in 'The Future of Man,' tells us; "...if as history suggests, there is really a quality of the inevitable in the forward March of the Universe-if, in truth, the world cannot turn back-then it must mean that the individual acts are bound to follow, in the majority and freely, the sole direction capable of satisfying all their aspirations towards every imaginable form of higher consciousness. Having been initially the fundamental choice of the individual, the Grand Option that which decides in favor of a convergent Universe is destined sooner or later to become the common choice of the mass of Mankind. Thus, a particular and generalized state of consciousness is presaged for our species in the future: A 'conspiracy' in terms of perspective and intention."

In such a case, we have little (if any) free will, and science's blindness to "coincidences" that are not coincidence is preordained. The power that different locations exert over us and how they help us create our experiences are also somehow preordained.

Chapter 27
How to Find Your Birth Code Number

Your Vedic Birthcode or ISHTA DEVTA

J ust like your fingerprints, everyone has a birthday code that can never be duplicated with the same name. This forms a unique code since no person born on the same day will have the same name; if they do, they will have similar experiences in life.

People with similar birthdates can experience the same events in their lives, and more so when their birthdates and names are similar. A person's birth date marks the beginning of their lifeline, and so it is regarded highly as a coordinate point that can determine the direction and the path that the lifeline of the person will take. The name of a person determines the characteristics of the person's lifeline as they proceed from birth towards death. This chapter is restricted to information about the birthday code.

The foundation of your life is embedded in the Birth Code itself called the ISHTA DEVTA. This code is used as a base number to determine how every other DEITY affects your life in terms of achievements, objectives, beliefs, emotions and more. It will explain your relationships with others, your marriage, love life, your likes and dislikes. It will determine the kind of career you follow, the type of car you should buy for success, the type of colors suited best for you, the type of jewelry you should use for success and more. The Birth Code will advise you when to travel safely, when you should have children, when you should buy a house for success, what address is lucky for you and where you should buy it...and more

To find your birthday code or ISHTA DEVTA, the following table has been provided. Each birth date from January 1 to December 31 is included in the table. Against each month and day of birth, you will find the Vedic Code that matches that day of birth. This number or code will be referred to as your Birth Code or Karmic Lord or Your Angel Guide.

Against each birthday, a code is given between 1 and 9. That code from your birthday is going to be used frequently in this chapter and throughout this book whenever a reference to your Birth Code is made to you, the reader.

TABLE 2.1 - VEDIC BIRTH CODES									
	YOUR DAY OF BIRTH								
YOUR MONTH OF BIRTH	1	2	3	4	5	6	7	8	9
	10	11	12	13	14	15	16	17	18
	19	20	21	22	23	24	25	26	27
	28	29	30	31					
JANUARY	2	3	4	5	6	7	8	9	1
FEBRUARY	3	4	5	6	7	8	9	1	2
MARCH	4	5	6	7	8	9	1	2	3

APRIL	5	6	7	8	9	1	2	3	4
MAY	6	7	8	9	1	2	3	4	5
JUNE	7	8	9	1	2	3	4	5	6
JULY	8	9	1	2	3	4	5	6	7
AUGUST	9	1	2	3	4	5	6	7	8
SEPTEMBER	1	2	3	4	5	6	7	8	9
OCTOBER	2	3	4	5	6	7	8	9	1
NOVEMBER	3	4	5	6	7	8	9	1	2
DECEMBER	4	5	6	7	8	9	1	2	3

Table 2.2 contains key names of Hindu and Christian Gods, which we will refer to as key name codes in this book. This will add more substance to the numeric codes so as to give more life and better meaning to the Vedic Codes mentioned throughout this book.

TABLE 2.2 – BIRTH CODE KEY NAME CODES		
VEDIC CODES No	NAME CODES HINDU	NAME CODES CHRISTIAN
1	BRAMHA	JESUS
2	DURGA	MARY
3	VISHNU	MOSES
4	GANESH	ABRAHAM
5	NARAYAN	EVE
6	KALI	SAUL
7	SHIVA	SOLOMON
8	LAXMI	DAVID
9	INDRA	ELIJAH

In the following chapter, a brief explanation of your life is written to give you an idea of the importance of the day you began your life. This marks also the beginning point of your lifeline. During the nine months when your mother carried you in her womb, these karmic effects – together with your genetic codes – were transferred as part of your life.

Chapter 28
Applying Your Birthcode to Your Life

Your Vedic Birthcode or ISHTA DEVTA

fter finding your BIRTHCODE in the previous chapter you may now apply it to your life and read the details given for your Birthcode in the following paragraphs. There are NINE Vedic code interpretations in this chapter and one of them will apply to you. Please bear it in mind that all of the information provided may not have happened in your life yet, as most of this info covers your whole life. If you are yet unmarried then you will not have experienced some of the qualities until you grow older. However this book is yours to keep and you can always refer to it back later to see if the information became correct.

Find out which of the following Birth codes apply to your life and read the interpretation that follows.

You Life Based On Vedic Birth Code #1
* You are independent, lonely sometimes and like to be in charge.
* You will achieve high status in career and position in life.

* You are very spiritual in your thinking and you think constantly.
* You are very bossy and commanding in your actions toward others.
* You were very lonely as a child and independent.
* You always feel that others leave you alone a great deal.
* In marriage you are cautioned not to be too dominant or your independence may result in your partner leaving you for another.
* You worry a great deal and this may result in mental nervousness.

As the first number, **one** represents the origin, the solitary eminence of the Sun, and the creator. It is a powerful and creative number, associated with strong masculinity, and people bearing it may become leaders. It refers very much to the self, so people who have it will be individual, with a tendency to be inventive, determined, and possessed of a pioneering spirit. Along with such power must go responsibility, and unless the person is careful, there is a risk of falling into selfishness, egotism, and severe bossiness. If their schemes fail, they may become aggressive or introverted; even if their schemes succeed, they may become overbearing and ruthless.

Karmic Characteristics Based On Vedic Code #1
At the time of birth one of your parents was promoted to a leadership position. As a child you were left alone a great deal and may have experienced loneliness being away from your parents. You are a very independent person who does not like to follow others' advice unless it is beneficial to you. Most of the time you like to do your own thing. You may be very dominating and moody. You are unable to follow orders easily and may lead most of

your life as a single person. You enjoy being alone sometimes and will specifically take time to contemplate on your opportunities and your emotions. You strive very hard to achieve a high position in career opportunities. You are willing to study a great deal and may become very dominating in your home. You are required to avoid letting this dominant characteristic affect your relationship as this could result in your being divorced or separated from your lover. If you are unable to submit yourself willingly to be loved by others your love life may be one of emptiness. Avoid taking people for granted and expecting people to follow your commands. This is a mistake and may create much unhappiness in your life. If you were born at an inauspicious time without proper consultations with priests you may experience much loneliness in life and rejection by all.

Your Life Based On Vedic Birth Code #2
* You like to shop a great deal and specifically look for bargains.
* You are a great cook and will make a great chef at any restaurant.
* Any dishes prepared by you will be tasty to others.
* You are advised to always serve food to reap good karmas.
* Anyone who visits your home and are fed will bless you with prosperity.
* You do not like to deal with work that involves too many calculations.
* You have a kind heart and are very helpful to others...sometimes too much.
* Others may take advantage of your kindness.
* You are a very religious person.
* You have a great voice and may become a famous singer.
* Marriage may become difficult as a result of illicit affairs.

* You can receive a great deal of love...but cannot give it.
* You are not romantic but like to be romanced by your beloved.

Just as one is associated with maleness, **two** is associated with femininity, being gentle, intuitive, harmonious, and romantic. It is symbolized by the Moon and suggests a mental creativity and an ability to mix well with other people, but an inability to be forceful, to make decisions, or to carry tasks through to their necessary conclusions; more mental power than physical.

Karmic Characteristics Based On Vedic Code #2

You are a kind and generous individual and very true in your feelings for others. You like to assist those that are distressed or those who need help genuinely. You have very few enemies and you are loved by many. Normally according to previous karmas you should be happily married, have a romantic lifestyle and be a dedicated homemaker. These individuals must be properly matched to those individuals born under BIRTH CODE 5, 8 and 1. You are a very cooperative person and will work easily with others. If you are a female you are extremely romantic in love life and very emotional when it comes to being deceived by others. You are very self-sacrificing and can be an ideal spouse. You love the world and would like to give to the world a lot of yourself. In career you may become very popular and may be well known by your community. You are a good cook and will enjoy others in this way. You are advised not to let your ego dominate your personality as this may create great conflicts in your life. Always try to be humble and spiritual. Usually if you are spiritual, all your wishes are granted in life. You do not wish to be extremely rich but you do require a comfortable lifestyle. Hindus who are suffering marriage problems should be attending meditation classes, learn how to be humble and pay respects to elders and priests in your community. For prosperity in life you should always offer something to drink or eat to any person visiting your home. Christians should humble themselves and be more charitable to the church and the community to ward off any negative influences.

Your Life Based On Vedic Birth Code #3

* You are usually very skinny, small in stature and a thin waist.
* You are very argumentative and usually think you are always right.
* You may experience loss of children or abortions in your life.
* You will experience also problems with regard to the uterus.
* You may also experience cramps or lower back pain.
* You are childish in your ways...people think you are immature.
* You hesitate to accept responsibility.
* You may have many children.
* You may be involved in publishing, writing or selling of books.
* Your career may involve some form of communication.

Threes are creative and disciplined people, associated with the planet Jupiter. Growth, success, luck, happiness, and fertility are suggested, though on the negative side the person may also be gossipy, moody, overcritical, sometimes rather shy or pessimistic or unimaginative, and prone to leaving jobs half done. You will get on especially well with other Threes.

231

Karmic Characteristics Based On Vedic Code #3

Usually you are a very jovial and happy person. In most cases your ego will not allow others to upset you or prevent you from achieving your desires or your satisfaction to be right always. You are very youthful looking and even in old age will look ten years younger than you really are. You may have a petite body and may enjoy such hobbies as dancing, music, and swimming. You express yourself very clearly to others and may be asked to give speeches to groups of people. You love children and would very much like to have them around you. Children enjoy your company because you are very playful. Other adults may find you immature at times and in love relationships your partner may think you are very childish in your ways. If you are negative you may be denied the opportunity of having children. If such is the case an astrologer may be very helpful to you. You like to read a great deal and can be a good communicator. You may spend a great deal of your time on the phone. A career associated with electronic communication may be very beneficial to you. Those who are educated may find themselves wanting to publish or write books as you make an excellent author. If you are not religious your negativity may present you with many difficulties in life which may create great losses through younger people. Also you may experience the sickness of children around you. Christians are advised to meditate on Jesus Christ as a teacher and on the words 'The Lord is My Shepherd and I am the Sheep.'

Your Life Based On Vedic Birth Code #4

* You are very hardworking and conscientious.
* You have a high temper and may experience many stressful moments.
* You are very determined in your attitude and will not admit defeat easily.

* If you want something, you are determined to have it at any cost.
* Your health may be affected by too much work.
* You will do very well in life if you own a home.
* Real estate investments are very lucky for you.

There is completeness in **four**, because mathematically it is a square. It is associated with the earth and its four seasons, and people under its influence tend to be very down-to-earth, systematic, practical, and stable, upholding law and order, using logic and reason in their actions. Yet there is also an earthbound and unimaginative side to these people, who may be over-fussy about small details, lazy, weak, and prone to worrying too much. Occasionally, a Four will have a stubborn, rebellious streak. Friendship is difficult

Karmic Characteristics Based On Vedic Code #4
You are an extremely hard working person and sometimes people refer to you as a workaholic. You are very slow and methodical in your actions. It is very hard for someone to get you to change your mind once you have made a decision. And even if you do agree to comply you may experience difficulty adapting to the change or anything new in life. You are very dutiful in your home and may be found to be constantly doing something around the house. You make an excellent carpenter and may be very successful in the field of construction. As a contractor you may become very wealthy in life. You are a collector of antiques or articles of memory. You may be the owner of many homes or none if you are negative. You may also be a landlord and if you are negative may experience many troubles and court problems with tenants. You may acquire properties through inheritance from your parents or a dead relative. If you are employed in a business of your own you may

be working more hours than you really get compensated for. If you are in a regular job you may be asked to put in a lot of overtime. If you are negative your most major problems in life may be related to your career. Laziness may definitely bring you down to poverty and ruin. You are advised to avoid placing yourself under too much pressure or tension as this may surely create high blood pressure problems. Avoid overwork and lifting of heavy equipment. If you are not an attorney you may experience delays and problems through attorneys. You may experience also rheumatic pains in your joints. If you are a positive person you may settle down into a very comfortable and large home, well decorated and taken care of by your spouse. Christians are advised to study the experiences of Abraham in the Old Testament.

Your Life Based On Vedic Birth Code #5
* You change your mind a great deal and very quickly.
* You love to travel and will experience many changes of residences.
* It is very hard for others to access your thinking.
* You have great intuitive powers and will usually know things ahead of time.
* You can read others personality very easily.
* You can feel the energy of others and may know their thoughts about you.
* Usually you are too helpful to others to the detriment of yourself...your give of yourself too much.
* You do many things to help others without asking for compensation.
* Your connection with the universe is very profound and your mission in life seems to be to help others.
* You give great counseling and advice to friends and family.
* You are not very lucky with relative and family members.

* You make friends easily...friends help you the most in life.
* The more good actions in life, the more beneficial it will be for you.
* You have the ability to develop psychic powers and may heal others by touching.
* You may experience problems with the government, IRS or immigration
* At some point in your life you will be influenced greatly by a spiritual leader.

Five represents the senses. There is activity, change, a hatred of routine, a need for novelty, and a reputation for unpredictability. Such people are energetic, adaptable, resourceful, intelligent, and quick to learn. They may be too demanding of others, too impulsive, prone to spreading themselves too thin through too many projects at once. They make friends very easily, but are difficult to live with.

Karmic Characteristics Based On Vedic Code #5
Sex, romance, lust, beauty and physical satisfaction are some of the qualities in your life. You are very much attracted to the opposite sex and you, yourself, may be quite a handsome person. You may be easily tempted into having illicit affairs if your willpower is weak. On the other hand individuals like you can become perfect husbands or wives. If you find the right spouse you will be extremely faithful. The right spouse in this case means that he or she must be an extremely willing and skilled lover and he or she should be romantic. If these qualities are present in your marriage everything else falls into place. You will enjoy traveling and may visit many places in your life. You can bring change to a lot of peoples' lives and are sometimes great advisers to all others except yourself. Wherever you are present some

change may occur. It is also possible that with proper knowledge and guidance you may bring about enormous changes to world philosophy and thinking. You are a great writer and can tell convincing short stories that may change people's beliefs. It is also possible that you may change your residence many times in your life and may live mostly away from your birthplace. Your greatest downfall can be lust or sexual indulgences. If you are negative you may want to make love to every member of the opposite sex you come into contact with. Your taste for music can be of a wide variety and you may be concerned mostly with satisfying your bodily needs rather than your mental needs. If you are positive, you may become an extremely skilled businessman or politician and may achieve very wealthy and successful positions in life. At some point in your life you may be accused falsely by others and may be stuck with many debts and loans that you may not be able to repay. You are the carrier of good news or bad news and may even like to gossip or involve yourself in informative conversations. To enjoy this karma you must learn to be sincere in all your actions. Be religious and be respectful to elders and keep an open mind

Your Life Based On Vedic Birth Code #6

* You like to be in charge and have a very strong ego.
* You may experience a career with many responsibilities, which you may handle well.
* If you fail to handle your responsibilities in life you will experience misery.
* You may experience a lower or upper back pain...if not headaches or migraines.
* A bad diet may affect your blood pressure and health.
* If you are not working for the government, you may be constantly harassed by government problems.

236

* If you are having a difficult time repaying your debts, you could lose your home through foreclosure.
* You may be a very responsible person and may have a business of your own.
* You do not accept astrology or occult studies very easily.
* You feel very frustrated, especially when you cannot have things your way.
* Your key to happiness is acceptance and spirituality.
* You should avoid the color red.... it creates pain.

Six is the number of the emotions. Mathematically, it is a "perfect number," because it is the sum of its factors, 1, 2, and 3. People under its sway tend to be reliable and well-rounded. There is a love of home, of peace and beauty, and harmony. Sixes tend to be artistic, and good with children and animals. They may also be too sympathetic, too self-sacrificing, too stubborn, too concerned with duty, perhaps too interfering. But they are among the most popular of people, making good friends and partners.

Karmic Characteristics Based On Vedic Code #6
Responsibility, high tempers and power are some of the qualities in your life. It is possible that as a young person growing up you possessed a very strong personality and a high temper. You may have many quarrels with relative and friends because of jealousy or a battle for power. You like to be in charge and are not willing to take orders from others very easily. You prefer to be a supervisor or boss instead of an employee. Your ego is very high and this may present many difficulties in your life where you may be unable to admit when you are wrong even when you know you are. If you are negative it is quite possible that you may be suffering from a serious pain in your lower back for which doctors are unable to find a cure. It

is recommended that you see the Hindu Priest or Astrologer for proper advice on how to get rid of this back pain, which can become very irritating sometimes. In addition to this affliction you may also suffer migraine headaches, which may be as a result of your inability to control your anger within. If positive and religious you can be an excellent marriage partner provided you assume proper responsibility for your family and relationships. You are accident prone and must be careful when handling machinery or vehicles. Employment with the government or the military forces may be very beneficial to you and you are advised to seek such opportunities. On the other hand, you enjoy power and ruler ship over your life and your environment. As a leader or supervisor you perform excellently and earn respect from others. If you allow your ego to make you a non-believer in religion or god you may suffer prolonged diseases such as high blood pressure, heart problems or cancer. These diseases may develop as a result of constant meat eating, drinking alcohol or taking unnecessary drugs. It is advisable that you should be a vegetarian if possible and maintain a meditation schedule. For other non-believers it is possible that you may experience many difficulties with the courts, attorneys and mortgage companies. You must learn to maintain your responsibility with regard to loans or any monies borrowed. Married individuals may experience many separations between themselves and their spouse. This may occur as a result of unexpected responsibilities which may create misunderstandings. People who are usually divorced as a result of this may find themselves to be very unhappy after the divorce, your wealth and prosperity lies in staying married. Christians are advised to read the book of Proverbs and follow the advice given there for worship of the Lord.

Your Life Based On Vedic Birth Code #7

* Your mind is running at a thousand miles an hour.
* You are constantly thinking and analyzing everything.
* Sometimes you keep most of your thoughts to yourself.
* You do not tell your plans very easily to others.
* You feel you are right in everything 99% of the time.
* Sometimes you think everyone is against you.
* You are a very beautiful woman, or handsome in the case of males.
* You attract the opposite sex very easily.
* Your need for love and romance is very high.
* You experience many difficulties in your marriage.
* A sure key to happiness for you is meditation and music.
* You are very kind hearted and are sometimes deceived easily by your lovers.
* You should avoid the color black...wear light colors.

Seven is the most significant and magical of the numbers. It has long been held sacred, as is shown by the extraordinary frequency of seven in mythology, the Bible, and classifications of all kinds: there are seven notes in the musical scale, seven phases of the Moon, seven seas, seven heavenly bodies in the old Ptolemaic system, seven wonders of the world, seven hills of Rome, seven virtues, seven deadly sins, seven days of creation, seven plagues of Egypt, seven sentences in the Lord's Prayer, seven trumpets in the Apocalypse, and many more. The seventh son of a seventh son is believed to possess great magical powers. People who are Sevens are sometimes great thinkers and may have an occult or psychic side. They may be researchers, investigators, or inventors. They have an affinity with the sea and often travel widely. But they must use their powers wisely, avoiding pride and cynicism, and accepting that their talents will never make them materially rich.

Karmic Characteristics Based On Vedic Code #7
Number sevens have a secretive and sometimes very private personality. You hardly speak what you are thinking but your mind is running at 100 miles per hour. However, when you do speak your words are like fire ready to destroy the person you are directing it at. People around you see you as an egg shell ready to break with the slightest intimidation so your partner or lover feels like he or she is always walking on eggshells because he or she never knows when you are going to find something wrong with him or her. Your criticism of others can be very high and may prevent others from getting very close to you. You tend to hold back a lot of your personal feelings about others. Even your beloved one will ask you when you are going to say "I love you." It is very important that you do not analyze others too much for there are no such persons who are perfect in everything. The first lesson you must learn in life is that no one can be perfect. Once you have learnt this your love life and your marriage life will be much happier. You possess a very high temper and may sometimes speak very harshly to others. If this is a quality that is carried into your marriage it may surely end in divorce. Out of all others in this astrological analysis you possess the highest ego there is. You will never admit when you are wrong. You will never admit when you feel weak inside and you will always put up an outward appearance much different from the one that is inner. Your true feelings never seem to come out, even though your true feelings given to the other person will solve all the problems. If you are an extremely negative individual you may be addicted to drugs, alcohol or smoking. You may also be constantly complaining over petty or unnecessary matters. A small matter may worry you a great deal. You are constantly studying or reading if you are not sleeping or relaxing

watching TV. You are very slow in your movements and may experience many delays in your life as a result of this. You may get married very late in life. If you do get married early there may be a possibility of separation. Late marriages are usually more successful. Your interests may lie in the field of medicine and if you study medical sciences you will be successful in a career associated with it. If you are a positive individual you may become a priest, a yogi or saint. If you are religious you may experience inner encounters with God and other divine manifestations of the universal deities. If you happen to find yourself a GURU you may experience a divine connection through that personality. If this path is followed most of your wishes will be fulfilled in life and your desires may become a reality. You may encounter many religious individuals in your life. You are advised to pay much attention to what they say for their advice may be very beneficial to you. Respect must be given to all holy people or elders in the family. Christians are advised to say the Lord's Prayer 11 times everyday.

Your Life Based On Vedic Birth Code #8

* You love money and you constantly think about it.
* You may have a business of your own at some point in life.
* Money flows through your hands very easily.
* If you are spiritual and conservative, the money will stay.
* You love expensive things and may love to shop a great deal.
* Your favorite color may be pink if you are a female.
* You have a strong ego.
* Investments in the stock market may prove to be profitable.
* You love jewelry and may own of lot of them.

241

* You must avoid wearing anything black; this will kill your prosperity in life.
* Silver and pearls are very lucky for you and will make you prosperous.

Eight people will achieve success but not necessarily happiness. They may possess the drive and ability to lead, and thus receive material wealth and recognition, but they can often drive themselves too hard, repressing their feelings, suffering tension, and missing out on satisfying relationships.

Karmic Characteristics Based On Vedic Code #8

All of your actions and your thoughts are related to money. You may become a wealthy businessperson or a bankrupt millionaire. You like to buy expensive and extravagant items. Your taste is very luxurious and your thinking is very materialistic. You worry a great deal about money and may be a big spender or a big saver according to your karma in this life. You may experience sudden prosperity in life and then all of a sudden find yourself in poverty again for this is a very karmic influence that you are born under. This life that you lead presently may account for all the good or bad actions you have performed in previous lives. This is called the judgment life for you. As a businessperson you may own a very large and profitable company. As an employee you may be earning a very high salary. If you are negative you may be unable to save any money in the bank. You may also experience a great deal of financial problems and may lose money through the opposite sex. Your spending may be more than your income. Other negativities are revolution, rupture, excess materialism, deceit and trickery with regard to money, etc. On the other hand if you are a positive and a very spiritual person you could become very powerful and financially

242

very wealthy in life. Your understanding of material aspects will be excellent throughout your life and you will be a very successful money earner. You are an excellent negotiator in business transactions and may achieve most of your wealth after your marriage. You possess a special ability to analyze financial trends and gambling secrets that few people may know about. If you are careful about your health and the kind of food you eat you may live a very long life, possibly up 108 years. You may become very wealthy through investments in real estate or stock markets. Your sexual vitality is very high and this may present some interesting romantic adventures in your life. You seek occupations that are very political and powerful such as City Manager, Corporate Director, etc. This power or money could well go the other way as much as it promises it is destructive. This karma is called the judgment of life where all actions from past lives are in this life are accounted for. Christians are advised to follow the parables outlined in the New Testament in the teachings of Christ and look upon him as the true TEACHER of mankind.

Your Life Based On Vedic Birth Code #9
* You may have a high temper and a suspicious mind.
* You may experience the death of very close family member.
* Be careful of accidents and traffic violations.
* Alcohol is very damaging to your life...avoid it.
* You think very deeply about life and may be extremely religious.
* If you are positive you may become famous.
* You make a great politician or spiritual guru.
* You will live a long life and may work in a hospital.
* Working for the government will be very beneficial for you.

* You seem to be always struggling to fulfill your desires in life.
* You spend more than you earn and will have financial problems.
* You are very honest and may lose in partnership because of this.
* Negative husbands may abuse their wives physically and mentally.
* You have a loud voice and love to shout at other sometimes.
* The key to your happiness...attend churches and donate yourself to charitable organization.

One symbolizes the beginning and **Nine** embraces all the previous numbers and symbolizes finality and completeness. In numerological terms, it reproduces itself, as the digits of all multiples of 9 add up to 9; for example, 4 x 9 = 36, and then 3 + 6 = 9. It is a sacred and mystical number, with many Biblical and legendary references: nine orders of angels, a nine days' wonder, nine points of the law, nine months of pregnancy, nine lives of a cat, and so on. Nines are determined fighters; they tend to be compassionate, determined, seekers after perfection; but also self-regarding, impulsive, possessive, and moody. Their friendships tend to be with Threes and Sixes. Sometimes you doubt the existence of God and sometimes you believe in God. You are a child of the Sea and must pray to the Ocean for the fulfillment of your desires.

Karmic Characteristics Based On Vedic Code #9
Your temper, your passions and your inner self are constantly erupting like a volcano. If you are positive you may experience a very highly spiritual or psychic connection with the universe. You could become very famous in life and will make an excellent Priest or

Brahmin. A positive involvement with the government may put you in the position of a police officer, congressman or even president of a country. A negative involvement with the government may bring you into association with criminals, accusation of a crime or in conflict with the courts, the IRS or lawyers. You are very high natured and usually need the companion of the opposite sex constantly. After marriage your frustrations can easily result in aggressiveness if you are denied sexual attention from your lover. Even though you are aware that you are wrong in many things you may deny that such things are happening to you and this usually result in negative attractions to life. If you are negative you may become an alcoholic or a drug addict.

This type of life may surely bring you into contact with the courts and the prisons. Your harshness to others and your temper must be controlled otherwise you may experience divorces, violent encounters with your spouse or lover and possible exposure to distress from criminals. On the other hand if you are positive you may experience many unique religious psychic and astrological experiences. You could become very famous or very notorious. It is possible that you may experience misfortune and accidents in the middle part of your life. If you are negative and insult or criticize religious groups or individuals you may receive a curse from God. This may come in the form of cancer, aids, tuberculosis or any other incurable diseases. Your karma in this life is to read, learn, meditate, teach and learn the wisdom of life. Some of you may become hermits, yogis and gurus prepared to save the world from sin and destruction. Your knowledge is very high and encompassing. You could develop a great love for others without boundaries. You usually experience the death of many friends and family. Your home may also be located close to a cemetery or a large body of water. You may also experience natural disasters such as hurricanes and earthquakes, etc. Your life may change every nine years and depending upon whether it's positive or negative the change may follow accordingly. You have the ability to request from god directly all the things you desire in life. However this can only be done if you maintain positive relationship with the government, peaceful love life with your spouse, and respectful humility with elders and priests. Even if you are a judge and you have violated the divine principles of life you may be struck down. The only way to achieve success in your life is to meditate, seek out a TEACHER and maintain a strict meatless meal. You must always be ready to follow the philosophy of truth and be willing to teach or give without selfishness. Christians are advised to fast and maintain a regular attendance to church services and charitable work.

Chapter 29
The Vedic Building Code

The General Effect of Location on its Inhabitants

A dd up the digits of the building or home number to get a single digit as the Vedic Building Code. For example, if your house address is 3149 Macabee Drive, add the 3+1+4+9 and then reduce the results (17) to a single digit to get the Vedic Building Code, i.e. 1+7=8. The #8 is the Vedic Building Code for this address. The name of the street is not important. If the address were 3993, the Vedic Building Code would be #6. Now add up your address number on your home (or apartment) and then read the interpretation of your house code in the next page

This prediction will give you an idea of what kind of karmic connection you have to your home. How it is that your home helps you or hurts you to achieve what you desire in life.

TABLE 12.1- VEDIC HOME CODES									
BUILDING CODE	YOUR VEDIC BIRTH CODE								
	1	2	3	4	5	6	7	8	9
BldgCd#1	2	3	4	5	6	7	8	9	1
BldgCd#2	3	4	5	6	7	8	9	1	2
BldgCd#3	4	5	6	7	8	9	1	2	3
BldgCd#4	5	6	7	8	9	1	2	3	4
BldgCd#5	6	7	8	9	1	2	3	4	5
BldgCd#6	7	8	9	1	2	3	4	5	6
BldgCd#7	8	9	1	2	3	4	5	6	7
BldgCd#8	9	1	2	3	4	5	6	7	8
BldgCd#9	1	2	3	4	5	6	7	8	9

Vedic Building Code #1
This home is usually a very large home or in the extreme very small. People who live in this home are achievers and individualistic personalities who are constantly seeking to lead and dominate. This indicates that new ideas are created or new projects are being thought of constantly in this home.

People who are negative in this type of home are usually lonely and tend to seek solitary moments when they are troubled. To avoid any and all troubles, they should welcome all visitors in this home as special guests and always give them something to drink or something to eat. Divine pictures must be placed in the eastern corner of the house.

Vedic Building Code #2

A loving couple sometimes resides in this home. Individuals living here are very cooperative and helpful to each other and to visitors. True love between the residents of this home exists and children are also well behaved in the home. Usually this home is a medium-sized home and is well decorated by the elder females in the house. Food is cooked always in this home and the inhabitants love to shop and decorate.

To obtain maximum benefits in this location one should be very cooperative, generous and kind to all. A picture of mother or grandmothers should be maintained in the northern corner of this house and, for Christians, a picture of the Virgin Mary should be maintained in the same location.

Vedic Building Code #3

A home with this number consists of all comforts, lots of food and a lot to drink. Some of these homes are extremely large also. A large television or movie rack is definitely a part of this home. The occupants of this home are very youthful looking and there are usually many children living in this home. The absence of children in this home will indicate that unhappiness exists here. A library is also present and people in this home are supposed to read a lot of books.

In this home also many people find it very comfortable to pursue educational studies and the children who live here will definitely attend some college or university. Little angels or child angels govern this house. Pictures of child angels should be kept in the eastern corner of the house. A sacred heart picture of Christ should be maintained in the same corner for getting rid of negative forces in this home.

Vedic Building Code #4

This is an extremely large home. Usually these buildings are divided into several units. Sometimes part of it is rented. It is a home that requires constant maintenance and work. People living in these homes are always trying to build their lives upward, and the women of the home are constantly complaining that their domestic work is never finished. There is always a presence of religious statues and pictures in this home. The individuals living in this home work very hard for very low income. However, their life takes an upward trend very slowly and surely. A picture of Buddha or Christ in a meditative posture should be maintained to avoid quarrels in the home between couples.

Vedic Building Code #5

Sex, romance and love are very prevalent in this home. The negative qualities to look out for here are deceit, fraud, and false hopes. Women in this home are usually very attractive in appearance. People in this home who are spiritual are also constantly traveling. Almost everyone in this home owns a car and in some cases one person may own two cars. The couple who lives here is very loving and the women are extremely beautiful looking. The men in this home are usually not fat. This home can also be a very lucky one for conducting business or professional services. There are also very high negative forces that can affect the individual in this home if they are not spiritual. Usually these homes have many cars or are surrounded by cars. People living in this home should avoid having illicit affairs or lustful thinking. A picture of Solomon or the angel Gabriel should be maintained in the eastern corner.

250

Vedic Building Code #6

Disagreements, quarrels, tension and responsibilities are the effects felt in this home. People living here who are lazy or irresponsible will suffer extremely hard emotional feelings in this home. Negative people will end up quarrelling with each other. Husband and wife will sleep separately from each other. Financial problems could become a reality if red meat is maintained as a regular part of the diet. Health can also be affected and if the payments for mortgage are not maintained, the residents of this home could end up in foreclosure. To avoid all these negatives constant meditation should be maintained. A special room should be dedicated to the Lord, as this house is extremely large. Tempers should be controlled. Duty should be the priority of all the residents in this home and a picture of John the Baptist should be maintained in a Christian home.

Vedic Building Code #7

This is a very large home also. A religious person or persons live in this home. The residents here are very slow in their actions and very laid back in their lifestyle. If a negatively rich individual owns this home, drugs, alcohol, and other addictions become prevalent here. Many of the activities in this home can be very secretive and the residents are constantly thinking or worrying about something. A positive effect on the house is that the residents here sleep very well and usually the beds are very large. Religious persons living here are usually very peaceful and are protected by divine forces. People in these homes should avoid criticizing and gossiping about others. Also, a picture of the cross without Christ should be maintained in the eastern corner of the home. A picture of Christ on the cross should be maintained in north side of this home.

Vedic Building Code #8

This is an extravagant, luxurious and large home. This can be an apartment building, a duplex or a home with several floors. The individuals in this home are extremely rich. Their income is high. Their furniture is expensive and their bills are high. Money comes very easily to the residents of this home and if negative, expenses will come instead. If the residents of this home are negative or have been cruel to others, eventually they are struck with serious sickness or diseases as a result of karma. For good luck the individuals should avoid excessive gambling or drinking or waste. For religious individuals, a picture of the brilliant Sun should be maintained in the eastern corner of the house. A picture of full moon should be maintained in the same position. People in the house are involved in some kind of business or investment.

Vedic Building Code #9

This is usually a very large home, which is very expensive and which requires a lot of maintenance. If a negative person lives in this house, he or she will most likely suffer from an incurable disease. It is important that anyone living in this house should follow all religious rules of living and they should at all cost avoid eating red meat, drinking alcohol or taking drugs. It is also very important that an altar of God be maintained in this home so as to avoid all problems. People in these homes tend to become famous or well known in their community. Childbirth could be difficult during the months of pregnancy. Most of the individuals living in this home seek knowledge and other interests related to religion, astrology and philosophy. It is important that a picture or statue of all the angels and deities be maintained in this home in the eastern corner and Christians should have a shrine dedicated to the saints of the Old Testaments.

An Ideal Home for an Ideal Couple

Who is a gentleman? Any educated person may be a gentleman. But without having a legitimate wife, even an educated man cannot be gentleman. And after marriage, life cannot run without money. But no one gets money without efforts. Hence, marriage and taking up some economic occupation are necessary to be a civilized man. A civilized man must also make his residence at an excellent inhabitation, which is managed well. There must be water near the dwelling and the general environment must be as clean and pure as possible. There must be two portions in a gentleman's house one for storing necessary provisions and the other for sleeping. His bedroom must have a comfortable bedstead with soft cushions and white sheets. All the cosmetics must be handy in the bedroom. Apart from musical instruments, music system posters of natural scenes and love scenes of couples must decorate the bedroom. The house must also have a swing, a lawn and a kitchen garden. The woman must use the inner portion of the house. It should have a bedstead with soft cushion. There must also be a smaller but comfortable bed nearby for lovemaking. The owner of the house must enjoy physical intimacy with his wife on this smaller bed. Light snacks and drinks must also be handy in this room. After a hard day's work, the evening of a gentleman must start with music. Guests may visit him at his time or the gentleman may visit someone else as a guest.

Chapter 30
The Vedic Home Code

How Your Home Affects Your Life

The house or apartment where you live will affect each person differently according to his or her Vedic Birth Code. Add the Vedic Building Code to your Vedic Birth Code and you will obtain the Vedic Home Code. For example, if your Vedic Birth Code is #5 (see Chapter 27) and your Vedic Building Code above is #6 then the Vedic Home Code is #2, i.e. (6+5=11 which is 1+1=2). Now we will provide a description on how your life will be affected by the location or the place where you live. This will be revealed by the Vedic Home Code. The following table will help you quickly to obtain your Vedic Home Code.

Match your Vedic Birth Code on the top row to your Building or House Code in the left column then cross them to find your Vedic Home Code #. For example if your Vedic Birth Code is #2 and your House Location Code is #5, the Vedic Home Code is #7. Now check on the next pages for the forecast about how the house affects you under Vedic Home Code #7.

TABLE 13.1- VEDIC HOME CODES									
BUILDING CODE:	YOUR VEDIC BIRTH CODE								
	1	*2*	*3*	*4*	*5*	*6*	*7*	*8*	*9*
BldgCd#1	2	3	4	5	6	7	8	9	1
BldgCd#2	3	4	5	6	7	8	9	1	2
BldgCd#3	4	5	6	7	8	9	1	2	3
BldgCd#4	5	6	7	8	9	1	2	3	4
BldgCd#5	6	7	8	9	1	2	3	4	5
BldgCd#6	7	8	9	1	2	3	4	5	6
BldgCd#7	8	9	1	2	3	4	5	6	7
BldgCd#8	9	1	2	3	4	5	6	7	8
BldgCd#9	1	2	3	4	5	6	7	8	9

Vedic Home Code #1 - Life in This Home

- You will feel independent, lonely sometimes and be bossy at home.
- You will achieve high status in career and position in life.
- You should be very spiritual in your thinking or you will worry a lot.
- You love to advise others; people will listen to your advice.
- You will have a lonely child or you will feel pressured.
- You always feel that others leave you alone a great deal.

- Marriage partners are cautioned not to be too dominant.
- You may become too independent for your partner's feelings.
- You may worry a great deal; this may result in mental nervousness.

Vedic Home Code #2 – Life in This Home

- You like to shop a great deal and look for bargains.
- You cook tasty foods and food will always be in this house.
- You may have a job that involves cooking while living here.
- Make sure you serve all those who come here to reap good karma.
- Anyone who visits you and is fed will bless you with prosperity.
- You hate when your peace and quiet is disturbed in this house.
- People see you as kindhearted and too helpful to others.
- Others in the home will take advantage of your kindness.
- You will be involved in religious activities while living here.
- You will be involved in singing or may become a famous singer.
- Your partner in marriage makes a lot of demands for attention.
- You hate when anyone shouts at you here; it makes you angry.
- You will receive a lot of romance; too much for you sometimes.

256

Vedic Home Code #3 – Life in This Home

- Here you are usually skinny, small in stature and have a thin waist.
- You are argumentative and usually think you are always right.
- You may experience loss of children or have abortions in your life.
- Women here experience problems with regard to their uterus.
- They may also experience cramps, lower back pain or bleeding.
- You are childish in your ways; people think you are immature.
- You hesitate to accept responsibility but are forced to do it.
- You interact with the children a great deal.
- You may be involved in publishing, writing or selling books.
- Your career may involve some form of telephone communication.
- You have many telephone lines or sets in this home.
- There will be many computers or television sets in the home.
- You will be involved with videos, television and music publishing.
- You may lose weight while living here; you will look 10 years younger.
- You may have dental or plastic surgery done while living here.
- You will feel very comfortable and lazy while living here.

Vedic Home Code #4 – Life in This Home

- You will be very hardworking and conscientious while living here.
- You may have a high temper because of many stressful moments.
- You will be determined in your attitude and will not admit defeat easily.
- If you want something done, you'll pressure others to do it immediately.
- Too much work and overtime will affect your health.
- It may take you a long time to buy a home, as you save money slowly.
- Your income and expenses will most of the time be equal; try hard to save.
- You are always busy doing something in this home; rest a little.
- Your mortgage may be high and your bills may be too stressful.
- Back pain and stomach problems will affect you from working.
- See the doctor regularly make sure your follow a spiritual life.

Vedic Home Code #5 – Life in This Home

- You will change your mind a great deal and quickly in this home.
- You love to travel and will travel to many places in the world.
- Because your thinking is fickle it's hard for others to know your thinking.
- You have intuitive powers and usually know things ahead of time.

- You will be able to tell if others are telling false things to you.
- You may be able know what others think about you by watching them.
- You will be helpful to others by self-sacrifice, forgiving enemies easily.
- You will help others without asking for compensation or money.
- You will have a psychic and profound connection with the universe.
- You will counsel and advise friends and family in their business.
- You are not very lucky with relatives; family members have no appreciation.
- You will make friends easily; friends will help you the most in life.
- The more good actions in life, the more beneficial it will be for you.
- Being a vegetarian while living here will give you no health problems.
- You may experience problems with the government, IRS or immigration.
- While living here you will encounter many great spiritual personalities.
- You will own more than one vehicle while living here.
- Your job may involve traveling or driving long distances or using public transportation.
- You will receive many long distance telephone calls or contacts from overseas.

Vedic Home Code #6 - Life in This Home
- In this home you like to be in charge; you have a very strong ego.

- Your job will thrust many responsibilities upon you.
- If you fail to handle responsibilities while here, you will experience misery.
- You may experience a lower or upper back pain, headaches or migraines.
- Eating red meat in this home may lead to high blood pressure problems.
- If not working for the government, you may have government problems.
- Credit card problems, high mortgages and loans affect you here.
- Make sure you pay all bills by cash while living here; avoid credit.
- You may be able to have a business while living here; avoid loans.
- You refuse to accept astrology, the occult or God very easily. Pray.
- You feel very frustrated when you cannot have things your way.
- You will experience inner fears and may think there is no help from God.
- Avoid the color red or black as it brings surgery and health problems.
- You may experience police or court problems while living in this house.
- You could have many traffic tickets also while living here.
- Your marriage will experience family problems while living here.
- There will be fears of divorce or separation while living in this house.
- You could experience robbery or burglary while living here.

Vedic Home Code #7 - Life in This Home

- Your mind is running a thousand miles an hour while living here.
- Your mind constantly thinks and analyzes everything.
- You keep most of your thoughts to yourself; you hardly ever talk.
- You will not tell your plans to other members of the household.
- You feel you are right most of the time; you have a strong ego.
- You will experience jealousy; you may think everyone is against you.
- You appear very beautiful or handsome in the case of males.
- You appear very sexy and attract the opposite sex very easily.
- You have strong urges for love, sex and romance; you are very passionate.
- If your spouse is negative you will ignore him or her a great deal.
- A sure key to happiness for you is meditation, chanting and music.
- You will make a good radio announcer, singer or religious leader.
- You may become too kind hearted and will feel deceived by your lovers.
- You should avoid the colors black and red; wear light colors.
- You will become critical of others and gossip while living here.
- You may have a fear of spirits while living here in this home. Pray.
- You will meet many religious priests, psychics and astrologers while here

Vedic Home Code #8 – Life in This Home

- You love money and constantly think or quarrel about it.
- You will have a business of your own at some point in this home.
- Money flows through your hands very easily; try to save some.
- If you are spiritual and conservative, the money will stay with you.
- You may purchase expensive items and will be attracted to luxury items.
- You will suffer from constipation problems and shortage of money.
- You may become involved in fashions, modeling or designing.
- You may have a strong ego and will feel that you are above others.
- Investments in the stock market may prove to be profitable.
- You will have money and will have people working for you always.
- You love jewelry and may own of lot of it. Silver and pearls are good.
- Avoid wearing anything black; this will kill your prosperity in life.
- You will be attracted to movies, yoga, stock market, etc.

Vedic Hope Code #9 – Life According to Indra

- You may have a high temper or a suspicious mind while living here.
- You will experience the death of older family members.

- Be careful of accidents and traffic violations while living here.
- Alcohol will be very damaging to your life; avoid it in this home.
- You may think very deeply about life and may become religious.
- If you are positive person you could become popular or famous.
- You may become involved in politics or become a leader.
- You will become confused and will sometimes have many doubts.
- Working for the government will be very beneficial for you.
- You will struggle to fulfill your desires while living in this home.
- You will spend more than you earn and bring financial problems.
- You will be very fickle and impulsive in your actions in these houses.
- Negative husbands may abuse their wives physically and mentally.
- You will have a loud voice and will shout at others sometimes here.
- The key to your happiness – donate yourself to work for charity.
- You may spend your money without keeping some for the bills.

I hope each person, who has read the above, will use this information to help them buy the proper home by code so that happiness for the family can be experienced.

There are many times when a person has moved into a home with a Vedic Building Code #9 and has fallen ill immediately or a relative dies after the move. If you form a Vedic Home Code of #6 or #9 with a building address, then it is advisable that you do not move in the home until you have consulted with a Vedic Code advisor.

Chapter 31
Panchaka or Untimely Death

Do People Die When God Chooses Their Time or Do We Create Our Death?

If a Man Drinks Alcohol Gets Drunk, Walks Across the Road and Gets Hit By a Car And Dies, Who Created His Death ....God Or Himself ......His Karma?

The Ancient Hindus were aware that there are times when the five energies or elements of life may be affecting the spheres and dimensions negatively. When *Agni* or the fire element is too strong it has destructive qualities; all connections between humans in the atmosphere are affected also, then ANY DEATH occurring at that time will affect the other four elements in the atmosphere negatively as well.

All family members are connected by *Karma* and *Soul*. Each child prepares the way for the next child. For example you will find that all children born under the *Ishta Devata Vishnu* will surely be followed by a brother or sister. This is a fact also observed in a person's *Birth*

265

Chart. A competent astrologer can find all the brothers and sister's (even those that were aborted) in a person's Patra or chart.

This connection between family members can also be proven when *one* of the main family members such as a father, mother or last child has a *negative* period under *Shanee* or Saturn, and all the rest of the family is affected. A famous example of this is O.J. Simpson when he was on trial for his wife's murder. The whole family, as well as others, was affected by this because of his strong soul connections to the family members.

All souls are connected to five members of a family, representing the five elements in nature, as well as the five senses in a human being. Every time a person dies an untimely death, he or she dies in *Panchaka*. Most of the deaths as a result of: *Accidents, Suicides, Murders,* etc. usually occur during *Panchaka*. Whenever a person dies during this time, he or she will affect *FIVE* members of this family. In some cases, weakness will be felt by these family members after 6 to 8 months and sometimes each year thereafter for four years a person will die related to the family.

Most of the bad influences of *Panchaka* can be avoided if *Pitri Pooja* is done regularly by all male members of the family, every year during *Pitri Paksh*. However, because many people are not performing this Pooja (Puja) to the forefathers and Pitris many Panchaka deaths occur. A Hindu Priest or Astrologer should be contacted immediately when a person dies so that he can perform a special ritual that will prevent the effects of a Panchaka death. Doing the Ritual will stop all further deaths for five years in the family.

266

Panchaka – Unlucky Death Days
Danger to the Family Members

What is Panchaka?

Panchaka occurs when the moon's longitude exist between 296 degrees and 360 degrees in sidereal calculation. Out of the total of the twenty-seven (27) star constellations, Panchaka occurs mostly in the last five (5) constellations. Thus there are 5 days (or sometimes 7 days) in every month that Panchaka will occur.

Panchaka is made up of the following 5 energies:

1. The 5 elements in the universe (water, fire, air, earth, ether)
2. The ruling star constellation
3. The lunar day or moon phase
4. The ruling Zodiac sign constellation
5. The Yog. This can be understood as the influence that is exerted on the planets as a result of the confluence between the sun and moon on that particular day. E.g.: On Siddha Yog, the influence on the planets is good and thus any Puja can be performed. Whereas on Dhriste Yog, the influence can cause bad eye on a person.

Why is Panchaka Important?

During Panchaka, the elements in the universe become unbalanced and this causes an imbalance within the family structure. If a death occurs during this period and the proper ritual is not performed, the dead person will carry another five (5) family members with him within a two-year period.

267

Can the Effects of Panchaka be prevented?
The 3-Step Cure

Step 1

To prevent the additional deaths in the family, the Pundit must first ensure that the death occurred in the Panchaka period. Very often this is easy to determine when there are only five (5) Panchaka days in a month. However, if there are seven (7) Panchaka days in a particular month, an inexperienced Pundit without the correct knowledge may easily miss the last two days and conclude that the death did not occur within the Panchaka period. This error will result in additional suffering within the family of the deceased person because other family members will begin to die.

Step 2

Perform a (Panchaka) Pitri Puja. Prior to the worship of Laxmi during the Puja, five (5) dolls made of Kush grass and white cotton are imbibed with life (Prana Pratistha). The five (5) dolls are then laid out in the coffin of the deceased person. They are taken with the deceased person to the burial ground or cremation site. This indicates to the deceased that he already has five (5) lives to carry with him.

If this is not done the following can happen:
- In a family of more than 9 children there is a 95% chance that the 1st, 6th, or 9th child will die immediately.
- In a family of 6 children, there is a 95% chance that the 1st or the 6th child is likely to die immediately.

- In a family of 5 children the 1st or 4th child is likely to die immediately.
- In a family of 4 children, the 1st or 2nd child is likely to die immediately.
- In a family of 3 children the 3rd child is likely to die immediately.

Step 3

What if the Funeral is over and the 5 Dolls are not placed in the coffin?
The family can still be rescued from disaster if the proper Pitri Puja was not done on the day of the funeral. Get a knowledgeable Pundit to perform a full Pitri Puja and imbibe five (5) dolls made of Kush grass and white cotton with life (Prana Pratistha). After the Puja, take the dolls to the sea and bury them in the mud or sand of the seashore. This will satisfy the deceased person that he has taken 5 lives with him.

Other Data Still in Research Phase

Even when death occurs outside of the Panchaka period, it has been noted that:
- Persons born on the 9th day of the 6th month (June 9) will take others with them when they die.
- Persons born on the 6th day of the 9th month (September 6) will take others with them when they die.
- Persons born on the 9th day of the 9th month (September 9) will take others with them when they die.
- Persons born on the 18th day of the 9th month (September 18) will take others with them when they die.

269

- Persons born on the 27th day of the 9th month (September 27) will take others with them when they die.

PLEASE NOTE:

When a chicken or any animal is killed at a Temple as a sacrifice…it is considered to be an untimely death. The Soul of that animal will try to take another life within that year in the family of the sacrifice.

Chapter 32
Rescuing Ancestors from Hell

T his is a chapter about life. Granted, it has a title that implies death. But both life and death are man-made concepts emerging out of the constructs of human language and human beliefs. In the chapter, you will come across language that includes *Soul, Karma, Reincarnation, Ghosts, Hell, Heaven* and other such words that you may either want to know more about, or to discount immediately. That is a choice you as a reader must make. It is your concept of *Free Will*. The origin of this information begins with an innocent enough question from a young university student to his Spiritual teacher – a student who seems perturbed by the apparent conflict between Karma and Free Will.

"Guru-Ji, I am confused. On one hand you tell me that the actions of my ancestors affect my life and on the other hand you tell me that I can exercise Free Will to change my life?"

"Both are relevant, my young friend. Tell me. Why are you here? Why do you come to see me?"

"Because, I am sad, no matter how hard I struggle, nothing seems to work for me. I come upon roadblock after roadblock. Sometimes success seems so close and at the last moment, the earth seems to shift from under my feet and I fall again."

"So you are seeking Happiness?"

"I guess so."

"Isn't the sole quest of humans the achievement of *Happiness*? We must remember that out of this quest for happiness comes *desire*; and when Desire is thwarted, *anger* results. From Anger springs irrational *Thoughts, Words* and *Actions*; then from this irrationality, our daily *anxieties* originate; our Anxieties lead to *unhappiness* and cycle self perpetrates.

"Sounds as if you just described the cyclical process of reincarnation Guru-Ji?"

"Sort of, the happiness cycle is but one example of the cyclical nature of life. As a more natural example, think of a tree. It begins from a small seed that grows and blossoms into a huge trunk, deep anchoring roots and a myriad of strong branches covered in lush green leaves. It bears large quantities of fruit that spreads and propagates to locations both near and far away from the site of the original tree. Then the tree grows old, withers and dies. It becomes again a part of the earth."

"But the tree lives on because its species is propagated thousands of times over."

"You've got it my young friend. Lineage and ancestry are very relevant to our quality of life on the face of this planet. A healthy fruit bearing tree will propagate healthy trees that bear sweet fruits and a diseased tree will bear fruits filled with rot and worm holes. If your ancestors were the Rockefeller family, for instance, you would have been a rich and famous man. On the other hand, if your ancestors were from a notorious family, you will be suffering from their sins."

"But I am my own individual. Why should I have to suffer for the actions committed by someone else?"

"You are an individual indeed – an individual soul that is housed in this material body of flesh and bones. Your soul, called the Jivatman in Hinduism, is a minuscule part of the Cosmic Soul or Paramatman. Remember that the universe is a connected web of life. Through the universal mother, the cosmic egg or Hiranyagarbah, like the single fruit bearing tree, yields billions of souls which are born and reborn again and again. Only when right actions subjugate wrong actions does the soul or Jivatman once again be permitted to merge with the Paramatman or Absolute. If on the other hand, wrong actions exceed right one, the soul will have to endure birth after birth. With every birth in human form, the soul gets a renewed opportunity to walk the path of truth, because it is only in this human form that the soul has the power of discrimination between right and wrong."

"So you are saying that I am not really this 'me' that I think I am; but rather I may very well be a reincarnated soul of myself when I existed as one of my ancestors?"

"That is likely."

"And that is why I have to bear the sins or actions of some past life?"

"You are beginning to make sense of all this, my young professor. When a person dies, his thoughts, his desires and sometimes his very image remains in 'limbo land' – a dimension existing parallel to ours but one which we are not able to perceive with our 5 senses. They continue to exist in this way until another opportunity arises for that soul to take birth in a different womb."

"So this is how ghosts or spirits come into being? And that is why we only feel them as cold spots or see them as fleeting images or shadows?"

"Yes. But remember that not all dead ancestors remain as ghosts."

"I understand Guru-Ji. For those who lived a life of truth and whose actions were for good and righteousness, their souls get an opportunity to reemerge with the Cosmic Soul or Paramatman. Those whose actions were not for good; those who committed wrong against others etc. linger in the 'nether land' or the dimension of the ghosts."

"As they lived their lives in the human form, they continue to be that way in the ghost form. This is why people say that ghosts are miserable beings. If they were accustomed to steal, hurt and make other people's lives miserable, that is exactly what they will continue to do in death. So when one lives in a house which is haunted by spirits you will find that a lot of things will go wrong in that person's life because of the unseen influences of those spirits."

"Is there a way to help these spirits, Guru-Ji? The scriptures refer to the sufferings of the souls in Hell. I believe in Hinduism you refer to it as Patal?"

"Allow me to refer you to *Garuda Purana Part I Chapter 225*. Read this chapter when you get a chance, my young friend. Verses 3- 6 reads:

> '*After casting off the outer garment (i.e.: the gross body) the man takes another body (the subtle one). In 12 days, he is led by the attendants of Yama (God of Death). The water libations with gingelly seeds offered by the kinsmen in the world as well as the ball of rice (pinda) offered by them is partaken of, by him in the region of Yama. From there, the meritorious man goes to Heaven and the sinner goes to Hell. After experiencing the benefits of heaven or torture of Hell, the individual (soul) enters the womb of women.*'

You must remember, however, that a life coming back from heaven will be born into a righteous family of a righteous womb and one coming back from Hell will be born of a sinful womb. Thus the law of Karma is fulfilled. Now let us go on to see if we can answer your question about whether we can help to rescue some of these sinful souls lost in the depths of Patal. More importantly, why must we try and rescue these souls? Is there any benefit to us in this generation if we do rescue some of them?"

"Well for one, we will stop their suffering. Sometimes you can hear these ghosts making weird wailing sounds as if they are in great pain or misery. We will also break the cycle of re-birth through sinful wombs. Sometimes a child born in poverty or with disease may not have a good enough opportunity to change his or her fate."

"You are almost too noble in thought my young philosopher. You are correct though. But there is a more down-to-earth reason as well. If you throw a rope to a drowning man and help him back to shore, will he not be eternally grateful to you? In the same way, by rescuing the souls of your ancestors from the suffering of their various Hells, will they not be grateful to you? For one thing they will stop being miserable and stop influencing your life in negative ways. Secondly, now that they have been rescued, will they not now shower thanks and blessings upon you? So now your life becomes easier and you have ended the cycle of sinful birth. Plus, you have now acquired knowledge to guide you in your actions in this life to avoid falling into the same pitfalls over and over again."

"Okay, Guru-Ji. I now understand the *need* to rescue the souls of my dead ancestors. But *how* do I go about this? *What* do I need to do?"

"You do show the impetuous impatience of youth."

"Oh no! Now you will teach me *Patience!*"

"You are catching on really quickly. However let us leave that for another lesson and proceed with the "Search and Rescue Mission" for your ancestors. The Vedic name for the process is Sraddha. This process is accomplished by the performance of a Pitri Puja or as you may wish to name it an "Ancestral Search and Rescue Puja."

"You do have a sense of humor Guru-Ji. I always thought of Vedic priests as silent, serious types."

"I guess we are in some ways. It is good that you mention Vedic priests – someone who has authentic knowledge of the Vedas, because the Pitri Puja is not to be toyed with. Although it is not very difficult to perform, someone who lacks the proper knowledge can cause mistakes that can lead to disastrous consequences. I will therefore provide you only with a 9-step outline. The overall purpose of the Pitri Puja as we said before is to rescue the lost souls to bring peace, happiness and prosperity to the lineage and to the land."

Step 1
Ritual to Mother Earth for permission to rescue lost souls.

Step 2
Ritual to go down to the lower regions (Hell; Patal) of the Universe to rescue all lost and displaced souls.

Step 3
Ritual to the Lord of Obstacles to remove all blockages from the search and rescue mission.

Step 4
Ritual to the Female Energy of the universe asking for permission for lost souls to be re-born in higher wombs.

Step 5
Ritual to transport the lost souls through the ethereal sphere into the higher regions of the Universe.

Step 6
Ritual to allow the souls receive new light from the 7 moons.

Step 7
Ritual to provide balance to the lost souls by taking them through the Solar System.

Step 8
Ritual to take the lost souls to a heavenly abode where they are able to receive love, knowledge, spirituality and ultimately achieve freedom from all sins. This ultimate achievement is called moksha or final liberation.

Step 9
Ritual for the re-formation of the Earth by burning all the negative influences.

"You are right Guru-Ji. Going down into the dark depths of Hell does seem like a dangerous expedition."

"But one that is well worth it my young scientist. The persons who are desirous of rescuing the souls of their ancestors must prepare a short family tree with all the names. At the appropriate time during the ritual, the performer will then call on their ancestral fathers and mothers as we enter the lower regions of the Universe. All the ancestors who have committed sins, either knowingly or unknowingly, all who have taken lives and all others who are considered lost souls will be called upon to present themselves at the location of the ceremony. Once there, they will be taken upwards through the ethereal sphere and in so doing, we will be able to correct some of the mistakes they have made in the past. We do it to avoid the continued suffering which can go on for many generations. We must be able to rescue the souls of the ancestors who committed these great sins so that the family line can be successful on earth. In turn when the lost souls are rescued, then the future generations will be blessed with wealth, happiness and prosperity."

Chapter 33
How to Rescue Ghosts or Earthbound Spirits

The Following Is an Explanation in the Ancient Puranas

I shall tell you how the ghosts become free and also how the person knows that he is tormented by a ghost.

He (The ghost-afflicted man) shall explain the signs and symptoms to the astrologer. If he dreams of a holy plant like a Campaka or of a mango tree laden with fruits or if he dreams of a Brahmin or of a bull or himself in a place of pilgrimage or of the death of a kinsman and if in dream he takes this as truth, this is all due to pretadosa. Mysterious events do often occur if the ghost has bad intentions.

If a person desires to visit a holy place and his heart is set upon it, but somehow there is a break in carrying out his desire that is due to the bad intention of a ghost.

The evil intentions of the ghost come in the way of holy man whose pious activities are disturbed at each step or take an evil course or if a person falls victim of eradication and turns cruel, O lord of birds, that is due to the bad intentions of a ghost.

If a person performs holy rites for the redemption of a ghost, he will find his actions fruitful. The ghost shall be satiated permanently.

If one's father or mother dies either due to accident or due to a foul play, one shall have to adjourn religious rites, pilgrimages, nuptial rites and the annual Sraddha.

How do these ghosts come into being? How are they redeemed from pretahood? What are their features? What is their diet, O lord? How are the ghosts propitiated? O lord of deities, where do they stay? Please favor me, O lord, with an answer to these queries.

It is the men of sinful actions actuated by their previous misdeeds who become ghosts after death. Please listen to me, I shall tell you in detail.

One who discards the family customs, takes to other customs, is without knowledge and good character, definitely becomes a ghost.

He who desecrates well, tanks, lakes, parks, temples, water sheds, groves of trees, almshouses etc., and misdirects any one in religious rites for monetary gain is a sinner. After death he becomes a ghost and remains as such till the final deluge.

Out greed of people upset the boundaries of villages and destroy pasture lands, tanks, parks, underground drainage, etc., they become ghosts.

Sinful persons meet with death at the hands of Candalas, infuriated Brahmins, serpents, animals with curved teeth or in watery graves or struck by lightning.

Those who meet with foul death such as committing suicide by hanging from a tree, by poison or weapon, those who die of cholera, those who are burnt to death alive, those who die of foul and loath some diseases or at the hands of robbers, those who are not cremated duly after death, those who do not follow sacred rites and conduct, those who do not perform Vrsotsarga and monthly Pinda rites, those who allow sure as to bring sacrificial grass, twigs and other articles of home, those who fall from mountains and die, those who die when walls collapse, those who are defiled by women in their menses, those who die in the firmament and those who are forgetful of Vishnu, those who continue to associate with persons defiled due to births or death, those who die of dog biting or meet with death in a foul manner, become ghosts and roam over the earth.

One who discards one's mother, sister, wife, daughter or daughter-in-law without seeing any fault in them, obtains ghost hood surely.

One who deceives his own brother, kills a Brahmana or a cow, drinks liquor, defiles the preceptor's bed, steals gold and silk garments, becomes a ghost, O bird.

One who usurps a deposit, deceives a friend, enjoys other man's wife, kills other's faith, is cruel, definitely becomes a ghost.

Rituals to Appease the Lost Souls and Earth Bound Spirits
Making the Land Calm Down So That It Can Bless Its People

Pitri Puja is known as the prayer to Rescue the lost souls to bring peace prosperity and wealth to the land and the Present and Future Children... If a grandfather becomes an outcast or vagabond or squanders away his ancestors' wealth, this denies the future children of their inheritance, joy and wealth that they were supposed to enjoy, due to the sin committed by that ancestor or grandparent. Thus, the future children and grandchildren will suffer.

Think of it this way: If you were the son of Rockefeller, you would have owned a bank; if you were the son of Kennedy, you would have a plane; if you were a child of a movie star, you would be a star too To avoid the continued suffering which can go on for generation, we must be able to rescue the souls of the ancestors who committed these great sins, so that the family line can be successful on earth. In turn when the lost souls are rescued then the future children will be blessed by the rescued souls with wealth and prosperity.

The following are the steps to do this ritual:

Step 1
Ritual to Mother Earth for permission to rescue lost souls

Step 2
Ritual to go down to the lower regions of the Universe to rescue all lost and displaced souls

Step 3
Ritual to the Lord of Obstacles to remove blockages to the rebirth of lost souls.

Step 4
Ritual to the Female Energy on earth asking for permission for lost souls to be reborn again

Step 5
Ritual to take the lost souls through the atmosphere into the higher regions of the Universe

Step 6
Ritual to pass the souls through the 7 moon so as to provide new light to the lost souls

Step 7
Ritual to provide planetary characteristics and balance to the lost souls by passing them through the Solar System

Step 8
Ritual to take the lost souls to heavenly abode so that they can receive love, knowledge, spirituality and (moksha) freedom from all sins

Step 9
Ritual to finalize the reformation of the Earth and Universe by burning the negative influences and forces affecting earth

Chapter 34
How to Distinguish Spirits

The Following Is an Explanation in the
Ancient Puranas

There are many other spiritual entities called grahas or spirits that can possess a person. All (except the navagrahas) are said to have been born of the anger of Lord Shiva or Rudra. Most grahas are generally malefic in nature but there are a few that may be good. These spirits also can be divided into two, viz., **passive** and **active** and these can be distinguished from the natures and dispositions of the planets.

Some "devtas" attack persons to murder them; some do it to get oblations and some do it for enjoying with their victims. The first do not leave their victims without killing them; the second leave the victims after getting their dues; and the third also do not leave their victims but they can be pacified.

The signs or symptoms, by which the people affected by these Devtas can be distinguished, are detailed in other treatises. By examining them, the names of the Devtas also can be known.

The Different Kinds of Graha

1:     **Deva Graha**
   a) Bathe early
   b) Anoints his body with scented perfumes
   c) Is calm
   d) Spends his time mostly in places of worship
   e) Talks, eats and estimates little
   f) Is not easily angered
   g) Likes flowers and perfumes
   h) Is strong in mind
   i) Is gentle in looks

2:     **Asura Graha**
   a) Decries Devas
   b) Praises Asuras
   c) Hates Brahmins
   d) Is cruel hearted
   e) Looks slantingly
   f) Is fearless and haughty
   g) Laughs patronizingly
   h) Exhibits signs of wonder at everything
   i) Displays dummy shows
   j) Eats much
   k) Shakes his body

3:     **Naga Graha**
   a) Is an addict of sweet
   b) Drinks and curds (dugbha)
   c) Bites his lips often
   d) Looks around with his red shot eyes
   e) Is very irritable
   f) Frequents hilly places

g) His body shivers

h) He squashes (or bites) his teeth

i) Is fond of flowers

4: **Yaksha Graha**

a) Makes one brave

b) Charitable

c) Gives power of quick comprehension

d) Seeks pleasure always

5: **Gandharva Graha**

a) Makes one talk little

b) Fond of perfumes and flowers

c) Skilled in music and dance

d) Sitting on mounds of sand

e) Produces melodious sounds with his facial movements

f) Is fond of drinking milk

g) Laughs and plays much

6: **Rakshasa Graha**

a) Is running to and fro'

b) Eats his own flesh

c) Drinks blood and liquor

d) Lives in a lonely place

e) His body is of copper color

f) Has no sense of shame

g) Is quickly angered

h) Is unclean

i) Wanders in the nights

j) Is hefty

7: **Heydra Graha**

a) Is smiling

b) Has downward gaze

c) Keeps his fingers folded

d) Rest his head on his knee cap when sitting
e) Is fierce-looking

8: **Kasmala Graha**
   a) Smears his body with dirt
   b) Is unclean
   c) Sleeps on ashes
   d) Laughs and weeps alternately for no reason
   e) Proves ungrateful to women
   f) Terrifies animals
   g) Always eats
   h) Is quarrelsome
   i) Sensual
   j) Misappropriates other's wealth
   k) Irritable
   l) Talks very little

9: **Nistheja Graha**
   a) His body is lusterless
   b) He is always tired and worn out
   c) Looks askance at all people
   d) Reserved
   e) Mocks at physicians

10: **Bhasmaka Graha**
   a) Talks irrelevantly
   b) Hates others
   c) Has a cold and dark body
   d) He will have angular looks
   e) Is not satisfied with any amount of food
   f) Is clean

11: **Pitru Graha**
   a) Performs *pinda kriyas*
   b) Is fond of flesh
   c) Is fond of sugar

    d) Is fond of gingelly seeds

    e) Is clean

    f) Is unruffled

12: **Krisa Graha**

    a) Prefers solitude

    b) Is lean

    c) Runs to and fro'

    d) Produces wailing sounds

    e) Does not reply even when questioned

    f) Is not satisfied with any amount of food

13: **Vinayaka Graha**

    a) Often removes the dust of his legs

    b) Produces sound now and then

    c) Vomits always

    d) Bites his teeth making katakata sounds (half-guttural and half-dental)

14: **Pralapa Graha**

    a) Injures his own body

    b) Is lean

    c) Dances round

    d) Has no thoughts about anything

    e) Sometimes laughs

    f) Talks much without any purpose

15: **Pisacha Graha**

    a) Exhibits harsh and hard voice

    b) Talks senselessly

    c) Likes dirty and worn-out things

    d) His body is foul smelling

16: **Anthyaja Graha**

    a) Talks ill of others

    b) His eyes are red and moving

c) He is niggardly
d) Smears his body with dirt
e) Refuse
f) Eats much
g) Shakes his legs for no reason
h) Has plaintive speech

17: **Yonija Graha**
a) Eats much
b) Is able to read others' minds
c) Likes flesh
d) Eyes are swimming round
e) Behaves shamelessly
f) Smells like that of a goat
g) Cannot move most of the limbs in his body

18: **Bhutha Graha**
a) Can be recognized in a person who beats all who approach him
b) Climbs trees
c) Talks incoherently
d) Apes all
e) His nature is never changing

19: **Apasmara Graha**
a) Falls unconscious with shooting eye-balls after spitting large quantities of phlegm   and is motionless
b) His body is yellow in color
c) Bites his teeth
d) After sometimes recover consciousness

20: **Brahmana Graha**
a) Shows desire to get garlands of white flowers and dress
b) Chants Vedas

    c) Spreading Kusa grass

    d) Observes all the religious ceremonies of a Brahmin

    e) Worships God

21: Brahma Rakshasa Graha

    a) Eats meat

    b) Wears black

    c) Observes all the religious ceremonies of a Brahmin

    d) Worships God and the Devil

22: Kshatriya Graha

    a) Likes red flowers and red dress

    b) Runs to and fro'

    c) Dances round and round

    d) Laughs aloud

    e) Writes on palm leaves and paper

    f) Is able to stand excess of cold and heat

    g) Acts and roars like Kshatriya

23: Vaisya Graha

    a) Yawns, laughs and cries aloud

    b) Complains always

    c) Imitates a merchant

    d) Initiates selling and buying

    e) Dances round and round

    f) Talks rubbish

    g) Is quickly angered

    h) Is immodest in his actions

24: Sudra Graha

    a) Consumes his own urine and stools

    b) Talks indistinctly

    c) Rubs his private parts

    d) Cries and laughs for no reason

e) Laughs at Brahmins
f) Pretends love for women
g) His limbs shiver and shake

25: **Neecha Graha**
  a) Has several signs mentioned before in a mixed form

26: **Chandala Graha**
  a) Has several signs mentioned before in a mixed form

27: **Vyanthara Graha**
  a) Has several signs mentioned before in a mixed form

28: **Soumya Graha**
  a) Utters the words "give me something, I shall go"
  b) Sings slowly
  c) Laughs gently

29: **Aagneya Graha**
  a) Says "I will not go"
  b) He beats his own body
  c) Utters harsh words

30: **Hanthukama Grahas**
  a) Will not leave the body and hence no treatment is necessary

31: **Hanthu Kama**
  a) Will try to jump down from trees, hillocks
  b) Plunge into deep waters
  c) Fall in the blazing fire
  d) He will wring his hair

e) Smile

f) Dance round the physician talking and crying

32: **Bali Kama Graha**

a) As 31:

b) He looks around and pretends fear

c) Has stomach pains

d) Excessive feeling of heat

e) High fever

f) Hunger

g) Thirst and severe headache

h) Often says "give me what you owe me"

i) Retires if given the Bali

33: **Rati Kama Graha**

a) As 31:

b) Always afraid of something

c) Plays on the bodies of women

d) Talks of winning words

e) Troubles non

f) Counts love after bathing

g) Putting on flowers and ornaments

h) If his request is ignored, he lies down as if polluted

i) Does not leave the man though his troubles can be minimized by periodical Balis and Pujas.

34: **Hanthu Karma Graha**

a) Is murderous

Appendix 1
Tracking a Devotee's Life on a Negative Year

The following is an example of how a devotee spent his day while he was under the influence of a negative year of Vedic Code #9, even though the month in that year was a good one. I am presenting this chapter for the sake of all my devotees who would like to have a better understanding of the Vedic code. Instead of fighting their karma and asking questions like "Why am I going through this bad experience?" they will realize that it is not a random experience, but one created a while ago by their own past actions. A devotee must realize that whenever he is experiencing anger or suffering, quarrels, that it is a result of karma and God. They are placed in that position because they themselves have done negative actions in the past and God is bringing them closer to understanding the lessons of life. For example, if two lovers quarrel, it is because each one of them is expecting the other to bow to him/her without question; that expectation overshadows their doubt about whether God wants them to do what they are supposed to do presently, or whether they understand that this task has been given to them for purposes that will fulfill their happiness later. Quarreling will only postpone their later happiness and rewards of their karma. A person experiencing difficulty to accept their duties and tasks is like a person struggling against the direction of the wind. Such a person must realize that bowing to the universe and to the Lord of Time will create good karma for the future.

Today's Date	02/11/2002	Home Vedic Code	8
His Vedic Code	5	Office Bldg Code	5
Wife's Code	2	His Office Bldg C	7

SCENARIO

- Repairs are being done to the house bldg Code # 5
- Wife lives at House Bldg # 8
- Subjects is expecting 2 visitors – One visitor is a Vedic Birth Code #2, the other a Vedic Code #3
- Subject is expecting another visitor whose base is # 4
- Subject has to go to court to avoid a lawsuit payment on a violation and Association disagreement & violation

ANALYSIS

- The two visitors add up to Vedic Code #5, and when added to the year 2002(4) is equal to #9
- The House Bldg Code being repaired is a #5 and when added to 2002 = 9
- The Subject is a Birth Code #5 and when added to the year 2002 = 9

294

- The Subject's wife is a B.C #2 and when added to the year 2002 = 6
- The Subject & his wife are a marriage Code of 7 so when added to Day Code #2 (February 11= 1+1=2) = 9
- The Subject's office is a Bldg Code #7 and when added to the Day Code for February 11 is = 9
- The Subject is a Vedic B.C. #5 and when added to the Day Code(2) & Month Code(2) i.e. 5+2 +2 = 9
- The Subject's wife is a Vedic Code #2 and when added to the day Code & month Code (2 + 2 +2) = 6
- The Subject is a Vedic Code #5, the home is a Bldg Code # 8, and the Day Code is #2, all added up = 6
- The Subject Vedic Code(5) when added to the additional arriving visitor (4) are 5+4 which adds up to 9

WHAT HAPPENED?

Subject got up early that morning and prayed but forgot to remind his wife to cook the cabbage before going to court. This would have made him win the case, but he lost the case.

Before leaving home, subject had very little to eat and hurried out of the house. He had to write a check for $3,000.00 for bills for the home Association on the Bldg Code #8 house He also had to give $3,000 to the Contractor, Jagat (Birth Code#6) for finishing the repairs on the Bldg Code #5 house.

When he left the home, Subject forgot some items, so he turned back his car and went back home for the items, which proved to be unimportant later, a typical behavioral effect when affected by 9 days

When Subject went to pick up the two visitors from the office, they were not ready so he was delayed. The car suddenly would not start and the starter was considered the problem. After replacing the problem it was found that the battery was the problem and so on. This is a typical effect of the #9 on the day.

On his way to the house, subject got caught up in traffic, the expressway was closed. He was delayed getting to the house bldg Code # 5.

On arrival at the house Bldg code # 5, the contractor could not keep his word to work that day; he showed signs of unwillingness to work, and did not want to cooperate with the two new helpers... Subject had to pay him anyway.

Subject then rushed to the courthouse only to find out that the Judge was going to be late (a typical #9 effect). When the Judge did arrive, Subject lost the case and had to pay to the Plaintiffs $3,186.00

After leaving court, Subject's parking fees were higher than usual, because he spent too much time in court but he did not complain.

Subject arrived at the house Bldg Code # 5 to find that the two contractors were idle, since the original contractor went away with his car. Subject decided to take the two of them to Home Depot himself. After shopping for more than an hour and coming to the register, Subject found out that his wife never paid the Home Depot bill, so he had a lot of delays to carry the contractors back to the Building to start commencing the work (keep in mind the two contractors are together Vedic Code # 4 and the House #5 which is equal to #9.

By this time, Subject was hungry, so he was anxious to go home to eat but then he remembered that he had to pick up the new visitor from the airport, so he stopped at a McDonald's to get a sandwich, the lady there was protesting to give him veggie-sandwich, but gave it to him anyway. The Subject called his wife about airport schedule and she did not know what the arrival schedule was, so Subject could not go to the airport.

On arrival at home, Subject being hungry, ate his food quickly, but while eating he decided to ease his mind by discussing some of the experiences of the day with his wife. All of a sudden, the wife jumped up, raised her voice and used some rude language, saying that she does not want to hear about his problems and that she was not interested in carrying his burdens. She accused him of not being a good businessman, etc. Subject knew she was not knowledgeable about business herself, and realized that she would be any thing but positive to deal with today. Subject decided to leave the home #8 for the office #7.

On arrival at the office, subject was looking forward to rest, but found out that the bed was missing out of the sofa; the room was in a mess, the bathroom toilet bowl was overflowing, all the rooms were in a mess...Hence sleeping would now become impossible.

He tried to sleep, but was disturbed a few times, he tried to fix the toilet bowl, but it got worse and needed more fixing afterward.

After talking to the contractor again, he got more disappointing news: they were not going to complete the work until later.

The new visitor called from the airport saying he was detained by immigration authorities for two hours. On arrival he had a cold.

Subject along with the new visitor will now go and pickup the other two visitors. He arrived late after some traffic problems and was delayed considerably by the other visitors; he had a late dinner that night, and finally went to bed past midnight.

CONCLUSION

As you can see the day, the house and the office, the two contractors and the subject, and the house with the two contractors were all a total sum of 9.

As you can see, interpreting the codes of your year, your month, and your day could be very helpful if you knew it ahead of time. Later, the house was sold without the construction being completed and the new owners who bought it at a good time built a multi-million dollar Condo Resort there.

Appendix 2
Vocabulary

Ascending Node Of Moon:	Rahu
Asura:	Demonic Spirit
Bhuta:	Spirit From A Person Who Died A Violent Or Sudden Death Without Proper Funeral Ceremonies
Bhuvar:	Atmosphere Above the Earth
Brahma:	Creation
Budh:	Mercury
Buthas:	Ghosts As A Result Of Untimely Death
Chakras:	Body
Chandra:	Moon
Churning:	Time Moves Forward
Daiva:	Divine Spirits
Descending Node Of Moon:	Ketu
Durga:	Female
Ganas	Spiritual Servants
Ganesh:	Fruit Or Child
Ganga:	Water
Gayatri:	Realization

Gopis:	Incarnation of All Previous Sages that Wanted to Love the Lord
Guru:	Jupiter
Guru:	Teacher
Hanuman:	Wind - Ether
Indra:	Uranus
Kal Bhairo:	Ghost Of Sacrificed Animals Possessing A Human
Kal Bhairo:	The Devil Posing As God
Kali:	Controller Of Time
Kateri or Katari:	A Female Demon Who Feeds On Blood Of Animals
Krishna:	Incarnation of the Universe in the Form of Love
Kundalini:	Foundation
Laxmi:	Light
Laxminarayan:	Energy
Lingam:	Marriage
Mangal:	Mars
Naraka:	28 Hells Below The 7 Lower Regions
Nav Grahas:	Planets
Panda - Vedwa Brahmin:	A Priest Who Does Funeral Ceremonies
Patala:	7 Lower Regions Below The Earth
Pisacha:	Demon Created By A Man Who Was A Liar A Drunkard ,Adulterer, Criminal Or Insane

Preta:	Person Who Died A Departed Spirit Headed for Pitriloka
Preta:	Spirit Of A Deformed Or Cripled Person, Or Person Who Died Prematurely
Prethas:	Lingering Souls Of Sacrificed Animals
Puja Diagram:	Action To Change The Universe
Puja:	Ritual to the Universe to Create a Change in one's life.
Rakshas:	Man With Evil Thoughts
Rama:	God In Form Of Man
Ramayan Katha:	The Story of the Lord, Incarnation to Destroy the Demons that Inhabited the Earth
Rawana:	Negative Man Or Demon
Rudra:	Pluto
Saraswaty:	Knowledge
Seeta:	God In Form Of Woman
Shanee:	Saturn
Sheshnaag:	Desire
Shiva:	Male
Shukra:	Venus
Surya:	Sun
Varuna:	Neptune
Vishnu:	Space
Yamraj:	God Of Death

The Author – Swami Ram Charran

Swami Ram Charran is the spiritual head of the Jyotish Ashram and Hindu Learning Center. His lineage is traced back to a small village in the Indian state of Uttar Pradesh prior to the period of indenture-ship and transmigration to the colony of British Guiana. He was born and raised in a Brahman family in the County of Berbice and even in his early years, he always expressed an interest in a deeper understanding of the mysteries of the universe. As a child, he listened to teachings of the two famous Hindu epics, the Ramayana and the Bhagavad Gita and tried to read any literature about Vedic philosophy on which he could lay his hands. In his early twenties, he emigrated to the United States of America and commenced studies in the Science of Physics at the City College of New York State University. Through the works of scientists such as Fritjof Capra and writings such as The Dancing Wu Li Masters, Ram began to make the link between the Physical Sciences and the Vedic Scriptures. He began to see the relationship between the dancing atomic particles and the dancing Nata Raja. He began to see the relationship between the seven visible colors in sunlight that was discovered by Sir Isaac Newton and the illustration of the seven horses that drew the chariot of

302

the Sun God Surya Devta, a picture which is thousands of years old. He also saw the relationship between the planets and the Nav-Grahas of the Vedic Scriptures.

Intrigued with this connection between what was written in the Vedic Scriptures thousands of years ago and the confirmation of what modern scientists are now finding, Ram left the prestigious learning environment of the world renowned university and joined the simple life of the yogis amidst natural settings at the Siddha Meditation Ashram in the Catskill Mountains. There he pursued a rigorous discipline of learning, devotional service and spiritual development.

1. Healing

Swami-ji has healed thousands of suffering people from the effects of the dark forces and negative energies. His research into the world of paranormal activities led him to an understanding of how negative energies; ghosts, spirits and other paranormal influences affect peoples' lives in very adverse ways.

2. Prediction

Through a combined understanding of the 108 elements in the universe, the multiple aspects of the Hindu Gods and the nine (9) digits in our mathematical system, Swami-ji developed a computer program that enables him to predict a person's past, present and future with almost 100% accuracy.

3. Jyotish

In 1990, Swami-ji published the first English Panchang called the Hindu Patra. Through this work, which Swami-ji keeps current from year to year, he has simplified the Jyotish Yoga for the pundits in the West. His Vedic Astrology handbooks are distributed through subscription, in North and South America, the Caribbean, Europe and India.

4. Puja

Through his in-depth Vedic learning, Swami-ji has brought back the ancient Puja rituals into focus to help people change their lives. He follows the 16 upacaras that are outlined in the sacred scriptures as he shows how the ancient Puja ritual affirms our scientific understanding of the planetary system in the universe. Through the use of the scientific puja process, people are able to change their karmas and very quickly resolve life to enjoy a better future.

5. Vedic Teaching

Swami-ji has dedicated his life to healing, to learning and to teaching. He travels frequently to different parts of the world to heal the suffering and has established the Hindu Learning Center of the Jyotish Ashram to teach the sacred Vedic philosophy and its relationship to the world of modern science.

People will generally turn to God and seek out the spiritual path under the following circumstances:

- When they desire something specific
- When they have the quest for knowledge
- When they are suffering

If you feel that you are suffering and that your life is not progressing as it should; if you feel that your health is deteriorating for unexplainable reasons; if you feel that your prosperity is being drained away; if you encounter repeated problems with your job or business; if you suffer from frequent family quarrels and tension, then you may be suffering from the blockages caused by the build-up of negative energies. Swami-ji understands the orchestrations of the universe. Swami-ji will be able to help you.

Swamiji conducts seminars at various locations in North America, Europe and the West Indies. Some of the topics covered are:

- Meditation, Chanting Yoga
- Kundalini, development of Chakra Yoga
- Vedic Astrology, Jyotish Yoga
- Vedic (Puja) Rituals Yoga
- Planetary Calming Yoga
- Gyana Yoga (Universal Secrets)

100 YRS VEDIC ASTROLOGICAL CALENDARS FOR ALL BIRTHDATES

* LOOK AT YOUR LIFE FOR 100 YEARS OR LOOK AT THE CHARTS OF PEOPLE WHO WERE BORN SINCE 1930 TO 2030.... GREAT FOR ASTROLOGERS and PUNDITS!!!

CHECK OUT WWW.VEDICPATRA.COM – Available only at www.swamiram.com stores

Saving the Generation Line so that there is continuity not extinction

* Pitri Puja is the key to long life and rebirth

Understanding the process of life and death through the science of re - incarnation is important to keeping the generation line going. When there is extinction of familes, loss of sons and loss of generation, then Pitri Puja is necessary to save the generation from extinction. Darwin was half correct...we do evolute thru the species (as stated in the Garuda Puran) but only thru the process of reincarnation via the soul. Pitri puja is necessary in all families regularly....every year

Ritual to remove Obstacles

* Ganesh puja to remove obstacles from your life

We all have inner and outer obstacles. Most of the time we create our own obstacles which when added to our inherited ones make it more difficult for us to live happily. With the wisdom and enormous intelligence provided when we worship Lord Ganesh we can remove these obstacles to progress in our life. When prayed to lord Ganesh removes the blockages to wealth, business and career progress in our life as well.

Correcting your life karmas for happiness in love and marriage

* A ritual to the lord of time- Lord Shiva – to correct your love , marriage and family life so that you can have success and prosperity with all

The right time or wrong time of performing anything will detrmine its success or failure. The great lord of time known as the Mahakal or Mahadeo determines this timimg in our life. The time to be born, time to marry, time to get children, the male sexual energy, the blessing of woman to get married are all determined by his blessing. Our kundalini, chakras and our length of life is decided according to our connection with the Lord shiva rituals

REBIRTH YOUR LIFE THROUGH THE UNIVERSAL MOTHER

* At the time of birth your own mother's karma may have been negative so a Durga Puja corrrects these karmas and brings your life back to normal with success and prosperity for your whole family.....

Each one of us carry the spiritual genetics of our mother and father. When the Mother has created us with certain negative karmas, we suffer a great deal in life, which we inherited from the generation. Performing Durga puja removes all of these sins from our life by rebirthing us through the universal mother called Nav-Durga or 9 forms or qualites of the mother...As a result of this our life will take on a new path and we will live happily and prosperous

UNDER WHAT STAR WERE YOU BORN?

* 27 CONSTELLATIONS IN THE UNIVERSE ....YOUR SOUL CAME FROM ONE OF THOSE TO EARTH...FIND OUT WHICH ONE IT IS..ITS CALLED YOR NAKSHATRA?

Everyone has a personal star constellation that matches the day of birth. The star system you come from is known in Vedic astrology as your Nakshatra or karmic path based on your Past life. When you take birth the soul journeys from one of these star systems to take birth on Earth. For 100 years of birth dates this book can provide detail forecast on your life path and karmas you will face in this life

An overview of your life
* THE RASI MALA OR HINDU BIRTH SIGN

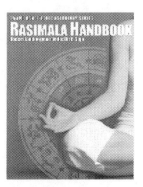

The unique vedic astrological handbook for the layman. No knowledge of astrology is needed. This Hindu zodiac Moon sign handbook is refered to as the RASIMALA in Vedic astrology. The forecast of a person's whole life is based on the Moon's position every 3 days as it moves from sign to sign. You will never regret getting this book as it tells all you want to know about anyone in your life as wellas yourself.

VEDIC ASTROLOGY HANDBOOK
THE PATRA

* Avoid all dangers, sickness and disappointments in life!
* Know when things are going to happen before time so that you can avoid the bad ones!
* Find out about your children, your family members, your in-laws, your job, your love life, your business your money, your health and more..
* Find out how all these will affect you this year.....

* Get Swami Ram's book : THE VEDIC PATRA...a vedic astrological handbook that is essential to all who love true astrology...predictions are 95% accurate!

Available at
www.swamiram.com

www.authorhouse.co
m ,
www.amazon.com ,
Barnes & Noble,
Chapters and London
Book stores.